GAME DEVELOPMENT ESSENTIALS:

GAME STORY & CHARACTER DEVELOPMENT

Marianne Krawczyk
Jeannie Novak

GAME DEVELOPMENT ESSENTIALS:

GAME STORY & CHARACTER DEVELOPMENT

Marianne Krawczyk
Jeannie Novak

DELMAR
CENGAGE Learning™

Australia • Brazil • Japan • Korea • Mexico • Singapore • Spain • United Kingdom • United States

DELMAR
CENGAGE Learning™

Game Development Essentials: Game Story and Character Development
Marianne Krawczyk
Jeannie Novak

Vice President, Technology and Trades SBU: **Dave Garza**

Editorial Director: **Sandy Clark**

Senior Acquisitions Editor: **James Gish**

Project Manager: **Sharon Chambliss**

Channel Manager: **William Lawrensen**

Marketing Coordinator: **Mark Pierro**

Production Director: **Mary Ellen Black**

Senior Production Manager: **Larry Main**

Senior Production Editor: **Thomas Stover**

Art & Design Specialist: **Nicole Stagg**

Cover Design: **Chris Navetta**

For product information and technology assistance, contact us at
Professional & Career Group Customer Support, 1-800-648-7450

For permission to use material from this text or product, submit all requests online at **www.cengage.com/permissions**
Further permissions questions can be emailed to
permissionrequest@cengage.com

Library of Congress Control Number: 2007922480

ISBN-13: 978-1-4018-7885-6

ISBN-10: 1-4018-7885-7

Delmar Cengage Learning
5 Maxwell Drive
Clifton Park, NY 12065-2919
USA

Cengage Learning products are represented in Canada by Nelson Education, Ltd.

For your lifelong learning solutions, visit **delmar.cengage.com**

Visit our corporate website at **www.cengage.com**

Printed in Canada
2 3 4 5 12 11 10 09

CONTENTS

Introduction

Game Story & Character Development

playing the story

Since the game industry can sometimes treat story in games as an afterthought, we decided to write a book that addresses creating solid story and character as part of the game development process. "Gamestory" is in its infancy, and there are several different schools of thought regarding how features of both storytelling and games intersect. Our collective experience comes from both traditional and game-specific storytelling. Since elements from traditional storytelling can and should be used in games, it's important to reflect on storytelling traditions and game design techniques alike.

In this book, we clarify the marked differences between traditional and game storytelling. In games, the player experiences what the main character experiences during the course of the story. The challenge for the game developer becomes how to guide players through the game space while allowing them to have their own personal story experience and even story "co-authorship." The answer might lie in what we call "storyplay"—the melding of both storytelling and gameplay, which gives players control over both *what* the story is about and *how* that story is experienced.

This book was written in order to help students, game designers, and professional writers learn how to combine the elements of storytelling and gameplay into a new form ("storyplay") and help create more compelling and dramatic game experiences. Until recently, game designers were often responsible for developing story and writing dialogue—yet many did not have storytelling and character development skills. Although writing professionals from other industries (such as film and television) are now starting to migrate to the game industry, most of them don't have a strong background in gameplay and non-linear storytelling. This book helps to provide students, game designers and writers alike with the necessary skills to create dramatic tension and intricate storylines that allow for player choice and co-authorship.

We hope that, in reading this book, you will start thinking about how game and story elements intersect by breaking their components down into small parts. This will allow you to examine how story technique is used in games and how gameplay elements cross into story territory. You will find that this cross-pollination can create an unforgettable game experience.

Marianne Krawczyk
Sherman Oaks, CA

Jeannie Novak
Santa Monica, CA

About the *Game Development Essentials* Series

The *Game Development Essentials* series was created to fulfill a need: to provide students and creative professionals alike with a complete education in all aspects of the game industry. As more schools continue to launch game programs, the books in this series will become even more essential to game education and careers. Not limited to the education market, this series is also appropriate for the trade market and for those who have a general interest in the game industry. Books in the series contain several unique features. All are in full-color and contain hundreds of images—including original illustrations, diagrams, game screenshots, and photos of industry professionals. They also contain a great deal of profiles, tips and case studies from professionals in the industry who are actively developing games. Starting with an overview of all aspects of the industry—*Game Development Essentials: An Introduction*—additional books in this series focus on topics as varied as interface design, project management, artificial intelligence, gameplay, level design, audio, player communities, online games, mobile games, and game development history.

Jeannie Novak
Lead Author & Series Editor

About *Game Story & Character Development*

Game Story & Character Development provides an overview of storytelling and character development—including the history of storytelling, genre-specific storytelling, and traditional storytelling elements, game-specific storytelling elements, character archetypes, game-specific character development, character dialogue, and the intersection of story and gameplay.

This book contains the following unique features:

- Key chapter questions that are clearly stated at the beginning of each chapter
- Coverage that surveys the topics of planning, production, prototyping, playtesting, marketing and management of player communities
- Thought-provoking review and study questions appearing at the end of each chapter that are suitable for students and professionals alike to help promote critical thinking and problem-solving skills
- A wealth of case studies, quotations from leading industry professionals, and profiles of game developers that feature concise tips and problem-solving exercises

- An abundance of full-color images throughout that help illustrate the concepts and techniques discussed in the book
- A companion CD that contains documentation, concept art, movies, dialogue excerpts, storyboard samples, and software demos

There are several general themes associated with this book that are emphasized throughout, including:

- Differences between games and other entertainment media (such as film)
- Usability and player control as primary aspects of game development
- Gameplay as the intersection of story and game elements, and "storyplay" as a new form of storytelling

Who Should Read This Book?

This book is not limited to the education market. If you found this book on a shelf at the bookstore and picked it up out of curiosity, this book is for you!

The audience for this book includes students, industry professionals, and the general interest consumer market. The style is informal and accessible, with a concentration on theory and practice—geared toward students, writers, and game designers.

Readers that might benefit from this book include:

- Professional writers and producers in film and television who are interested in migrating to the game industry
- Game designers who are interested in honing their storytelling and character development skills
- College students in game development, interactive design, entertainment studies, communication, writing, and emerging technologies programs
- Art, design, writing and programming students who are taking introductory game development courses
- Professional students in college-level programs who are taking game development overview courses
- First-year game development students at universities

How is This Book Organized?

This book consists of three parts—focusing on story, character and gameplay.

- Part I—Story (Ch 1-4): This part focuses on the history of storytelling, genre-specific story elements, traditional storytelling devices, and game-specific storytelling.

- Part II—Character (Ch 5-7): This part focuses on traditional character archetypes, game-specific character development, and dialogue construction.
- Part III—Gameplay (Ch 8-9): This part focuses on the integration of story and gameplay, the concept of "storyplay," and game design documentation (GDD) elements.

How to Use This Text

The sections that follow describe text elements found throughout the book and how they are intended to be used.

key chapter questions

Key chapter questions are learning objectives in the form of overview questions that start off each chapter. Readers should be able to answer the questions upon understanding the chapter material.

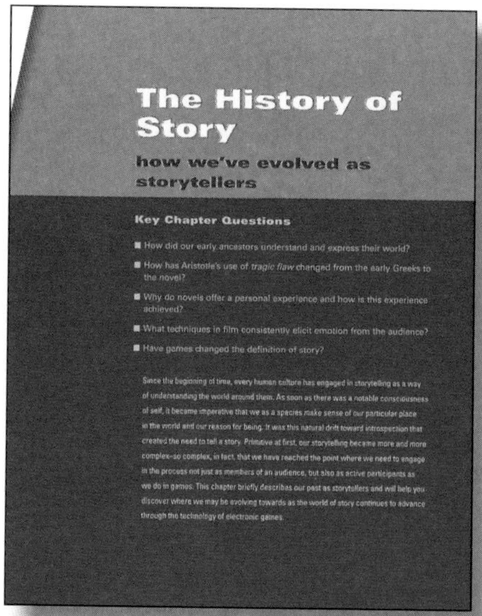

The History of Story

how we've evolved as storytellers

Key Chapter Questions

- How did our early ancestors understand and express their world?
- How has Aristotle's use of *tragic flaw* changed from the early Greeks to the novel?
- Why do novels offer a personal experience and how is this experience achieved?
- What techniques in film consistently elicit emotion from the audience?
- Have games changed the definition of story?

Since the beginning of time, every human culture has engaged in storytelling as a way of understanding the world around them. As soon as there was a notable consciousness of self, it became imperative that we as a species make sense of our particular place in the world and our reason for being. It was this natural drift toward introspection that created the need to tell a story. Primitive at first, our storytelling became more and more complex—so complex, in fact, that we have reached the point where we need to engage in the process not just as members of an audience, but also as active participants as we do in games. This chapter briefly describes our past as storytellers and will help you discover where we may be evolving towards as the world of story continues to advance through the technology of electronic games.

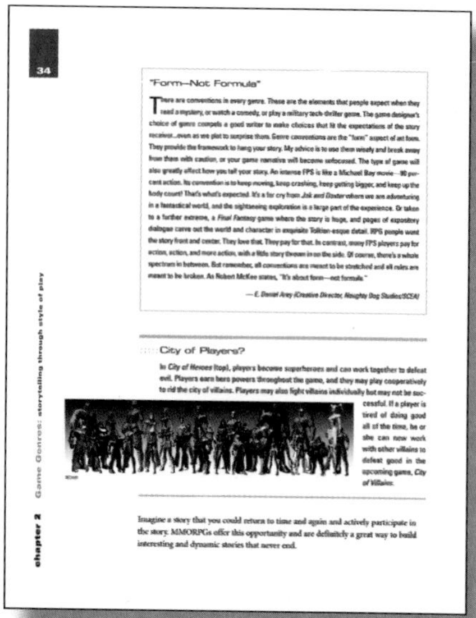

34

"Form—Not Formula"

There are conventions in every genre. These are the elements that people expect when they read a mystery, or watch a comedy, or play a military tech-thriller game. The game designer's choice of genre compels a good writer to make choices that fit the expectations of the story receiver...even as we plot to surprise them. Genre conventions are the "form" aspect of art form. They provide the framework to hang your story. My advice is to use them wisely and break away from them with caution, or your game narrative will become unfocused. The type of game will also greatly affect how you tell your story. An intense FPS is like a Michael Bay movie—90 percent action. Its convention is to keep moving, keep crashing, keep getting bigger, and keep up the body count! That's what's expected. It's a far cry from *Jak and Daxter* where we are adventuring in a fantastical world, and the sightseeing exploration is a large part of the experience. Or taken to a further extreme, a *Final Fantasy* game where the story is huge, and pages of expository dialogue carve out the world and character in exquisite Tolkien-esque detail. RPG people want the story front and center. They love that. They pay for that. In contrast, many FPS players pay for action, action, and more action, with a little story thrown in on the side. Of course, there's a whole spectrum in between. But remember, all conventions are meant to be stretched and all rules are meant to be broken. As Robert McKee states, "It's about form—not formula."

— E. Daniel Arey (Creative Director, Naughty Dog Studios/SCEA)

City of Players?

In *City of Heroes* (top), players become superheroes and can work together to defeat evil. Players earn hero powers throughout the game, and they may play cooperatively to rid the city of villains. Players may also fight villains individually but may not be successful. If a player is tired of doing good all of the time, he or she can now work with other villains to defeat good in the upcoming game, *City of Villains*.

Imagine a story that you could return to time and again and actively participate in the story. MMORPGs offer this opportunity and are definitely a great way to build interesting and dynamic stories that never end.

chapter 2 Game Genres: storytelling through style of play

tips

Tips provide advice and inspiration from industry professionals and educators, as well as practical techniques and tips of the trade.

sidebars

Sidebars offer in-depth information from the author on specific topics—accompanied by associated images.

quotes

Quotes contain short, insightful thoughts from players, students, and industry observers.

profiles

Profiles provide bios, photos and in-depth commentary from industry professionals and educators.

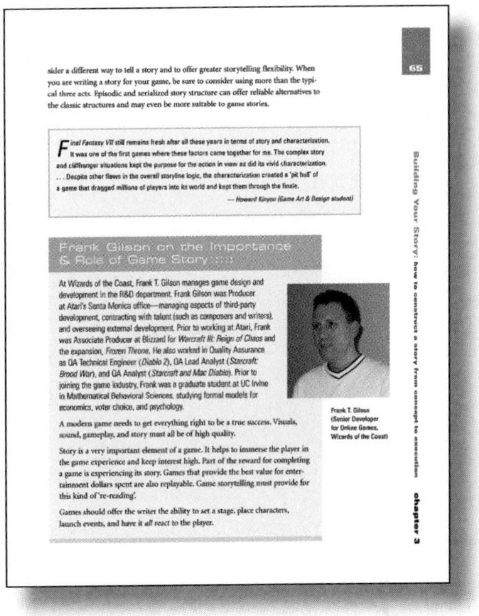

65

sider a different way to tell a story and to offer greater storytelling flexibility. When you are writing a story for your game, be sure to consider using more than the typical three acts. Episodic and serialized story structure can offer reliable alternatives to the classic structures and may even be more suitable to game stories.

Final Fantasy VII still remains fresh after all these years in terms of story and characterization. It was one of the first games where these factors came together for me. The complex story and cliffhanger situations kept the purpose for the action in view as did its vivid characterization. . . . Despite other flaws in the overall storyline logic, the characterization created a 'pit bull' of a game that dragged millions of players into its world and kept them through the finale.

— *Howard Kinyon (Game Art & Design student)*

Frank Gilson on the Importance & Role of Game Story::::

At Wizards of the Coast, Frank T. Gilson manages game design and development in the R&D department. Frank Gilson was Producer at Atari's Santa Monica office—managing aspects of third-party development, contracting with talent (such as composers and writers), and overseeing external development. Prior to working at Atari, Frank was Associate Producer at Blizzard for *Warcraft III: Reign of Chaos* and the expansion, *Frozen Throne*. He also worked in Quality Assurance as QA Technical Engineer (*Diablo 2*), QA Lead Analyst (*Starcraft: Brood War*), and QA Analyst (*Starcraft and Mac Diablo*). Prior to joining the game industry, Frank was a graduate student at UC Irvine in Mathematical Behavioral Sciences, studying formal models for economics, voter choice, and psychology.

Frank T. Gilson (Senior Developer for Online Games, Wizards of the Coast)

A modern game needs to get everything right to be a true success. Visuals, sound, gameplay, and story must all be of high quality.

Story is a very important element of a game. It helps to immerse the player in the game experience and keep interest high. Part of the reward for completing a game is experiencing its story. Games that provide the best value for entertainment dollars spent are also replayable. Game storytelling must provide for this kind of 're-reading'.

Games should offer the writer the ability to set a stage, place characters, launch events, and have it *all* react to the player.

Building Your Story: how to construct a story from concept to execution   chapter 3

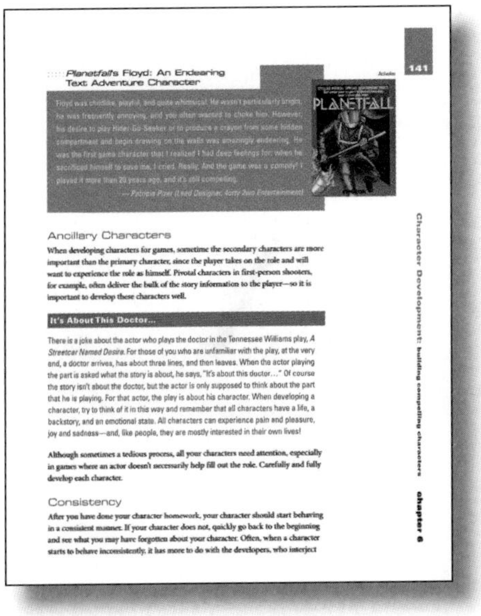

141

::::*Planetfall's* Floyd: An Endearing Text Adventure Character

Floyd was childlike, playful, and quite whimsical. He wasn't particularly bright; he was frequently annoying, and you often wanted to choke him. However, his desire to play Hider-Go-Seeker or to produce a crayon from some hidden compartment and begin drawing on the walls was amazingly endearing. He was the first game character that I realized I had deep feelings for: when he sacrificed himself to save me, I cried. Really. And the game was a comedy! I played it more than 20 years ago, and it's still compelling.

— *Patricia Pizer (Lead Designer, Korry Zero Entertainment)*

Ancillary Characters

When developing characters for games, sometime the secondary characters are more important than the primary character, since the player takes on the role and will want to experience the role as himself. Pivotal characters in first-person shooters, for example, often deliver the bulk of the story information to the player—so it is important to develop these characters well.

It's About This Doctor...

There is a joke about the actor who plays the doctor in the Tennessee Williams play, *A Streetcar Named Desire*. For those of you who are unfamiliar with the play, at the very end, a doctor arrives, has about three lines, and then leaves. When the actor playing the part is asked what the story is about, he says, "It's about this doctor…" Of course the story isn't about the doctor, but the actor is only supposed to think about the part that he is playing. For that actor, the play is about his character. When developing a character, try to think of it in this way and remember that all characters have a life, a backstory, and an emotional state. All characters can experience pain and pleasure, joy and sadness—and, like people, they are mostly interested in their own lives!

Although sometimes a tedious process, all your characters need attention, especially in games where an actor doesn't necessarily help fill out the role. Carefully and fully develop each character.

Consistency

After you have done your character homework, your character should start behaving in a consistent manner. If your character does not, quickly go back to the beginning and see what you may have forgotten about your character. Often, when a character starts to behave inconsistently, it has more to do with the developers, who interject

Character Development: building compelling characters   chapter 6

case studies

Case studies contain anecdotes from industry professionals (accompanied by game screenshots) on their experiences developing specific game titles.

notes

Notes contain thought-provoking ideas provided by the author that are intended to help the readers think critically about the book's topics.

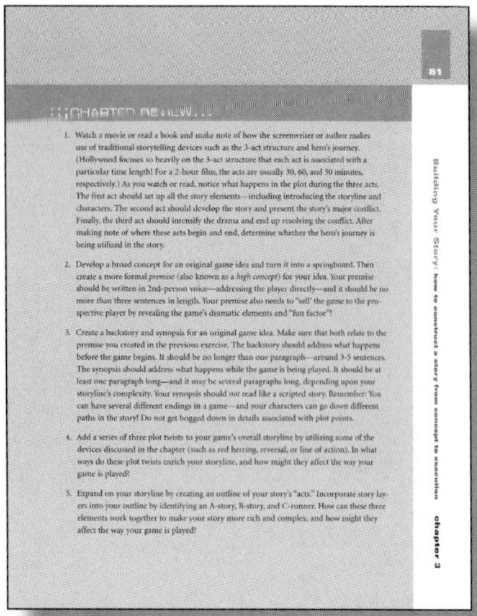
81

:::CHAPTER REVIEW:::

1. Watch a movie or read a book and make note of how the screenwriter or author makes use of traditional storytelling devices such as the 3-act structure and hero's journey. (Hollywood focuses so heavily on the 3-act structure that each act is associated with a particular time length! For a 2-hour film, the acts are usually 30, 60, and 30 minutes, respectively.) As you watch or read, notice what happens in the plot during the three acts. The first act should set up all the story elements—including introducing the storyline and characters. The second act should develop the story and present the story's major conflict. Finally, the third act should intensify the drama and end up resolving the conflict. After making note of where these acts begin and end, determine whether the hero's journey is being utilized in the story.
2. Develop a broad concept for an original game idea and turn it into a springboard. Then create a more formal *premise* (also known as a *high concept*) for your idea. Your premise should be written in 2nd-person voice—addressing the player directly—and it should be no more than three sentences in length. Your premise also needs to "sell" the game to the prospective player by revealing the game's dramatic elements and "fun factor"!
3. Create a backstory and synopsis for an original game idea. Make sure that both relate to the premise you created in the previous exercise. The backstory should address what happens before the game begins. It should be no longer than one paragraph—around 3-5 sentences. The synopsis should address what happens while the game is being played. It should be at least one paragraph long—and it may be several paragraphs long, depending upon your storyline's complexity. Your synopsis should *not* read like a scripted story. Remember: You can have several different endings in a game—and your characters can go down different paths in the story! Do not get bogged down in details associated with plot points.
4. Add a series of three plot twists to your game's overall storyline by utilizing some of the devices discussed in the chapter (such as red herring, reversal, or line of action). In what ways do these plot twists enrich your storyline, and how might they affect the way your game is played?
5. Expand on your storyline by creating an outline of your story's "acts." Incorporate story layers into your outline by identifying an A-story, B-story, and C-runner. How can these three elements work together to make your story more rich and complex, and how might they affect the way your game is played?

Building Your Story: how to construct a story from concept to execution chapter 3

chapter review

A *chapter review* section at the end of each chapter contains a combination of questions and exercises, which allow readers to apply what they've learned.

About the Companion CD

The companion CD contains the following media:

- Torque game engine (GarageGames)
- *Tabula Rasa* concept art (NCsoft)
- *Path of Neo* concept art and movies (Shiny Entertainment)
- *God of War* storyboard (Sony Computer Entertainment of America)
- *Area 51* dialogue (Midway)
- *Orbz* game demo (21-6 Productions/GarageGames)
- *Marble Blast* game demo (GarageGames)
- *Think Tanks* game demo (BraveTree Productions/GarageGames)
- Game design document template (Chris Taylor/Gas-Powered Games)
- *Sub Hunter* game design document (Michael Black/Torn Space)
- Sample concept art (Capcom)
- Sample concept art (Valve)

About the Instructor's Guide

The instructor's guide (available on CD format) was developed to assist instructors in planning and implementing their instructional programs. It includes sample syllabi, test questions, assignments, projects, PowerPoint files, and other valuable instructional resources.

Order Number: 1-4018-7886-5

About the Authors

Writing professionally for the past several years, Marianne Krawczyk got her break when her first feature, *Popular Myth*, was quickly optioned. Moving onto the hit Saturday morning show, *Sweet Valley High*, Marianne learned the ins and outs of the writers' room. Marianne focused even more of her attention on writing for children and was hired to write and develop the animated project *Swamp & Tad* for Wild Brain Studios. Later that same year, Marianne wrote *Caffeine* for Studios USA/Universal Television, a pilot based on the comic book series of the same name, and in January 2005 a story for the upcoming animated series *Bratz*. Marianne has successfully transitioned into the world of video games, understanding the delicate relationship between story and gameplay. She wrote the story for Sony's highly acclaimed *God of War*—an epic journey though the turbulent world of Gods and men. She was also hired to rewrite the dialogue for Midway's *Area 51*—a military sci-fi first-person shooter. A highly sought-after game writer, Marianne is currently working on several other non-disclosed video game projects.

Luis Levy

Jeannie Novak is the founder of Indiespace (http://indiespace.com)—one of the first companies to promote and distribute interactive entertainment online—where she consults with creative professionals in the music, film and television industries to help them migrate to the game industry. In addition to being lead author and series editor of the *Game Development Essentials* series, Jeannie is the co-author of three pioneering books on the interactive entertainment industry—including *Creating Internet Entertainment*. Jeannie is a game instructor and course development expert at the Art Institute Online, UCLA Extension, Art Center College of Design, Academy of Entertainment and Technology at Santa Monica College, DeVry University, Miami International University, and Westwood College. Jeannie has developed or participated in game workshops and panels at Macworld, Digital Hollywood, and iHollywood Forum. She is a member of the International Game Developers Association (IGDA) and has served on selection committees for the Academy of Interactive Arts & Sciences (AIAS). Jeannie was chosen as one of the 100 most influential people in high-technology by *MicroTimes* magazine—and she has been profiled by CNN, *Billboard Magazine*, Sundance Channel, *Daily Variety*, and the *Los Angeles Times*. She received an M.A. in Communication Management from the University of Southern California (USC), where she focused on games in online distance learning. She received a B.A. in Mass Communication from the University of California, Los Angeles (UCLA)—graduating summa cum laude and Phi Beta Kappa. When she isn't writing and teaching, Jeannie spends most of her time recording, performing and composing music. More information on the author can be found at http://jeannie.com.

Acknowledgements

We would like to thank the following people for their hard work and dedication to this project:

Jim Gish (Acquisitions Editor, Delmar Cengage), for making this series happen.

Sharon Chambliss (Developmental Editor, Delmar Cengage), for easing the pressure while always maintaining a professional demeanor.

Tom Stover (Production Editor, Delmar Cengage), for his constant positive attitude and responsiveness during crunch time.

Niamh Matthews (Editorial Assistant, Delmar Cengage), for her ongoing assistance throughout the series.

John Shanley (Creative Director, Phoenix Creative Graphics), for his focus and commitment to making the books in this series look superb.

Oscar Trapp (Production Manager, Phoenix Creative Graphics), for his diligence and attention to detail during the layout and compositing phase.

Rachel Pearce Anderson (RPA Editorial Services), for her thorough and thoughtful copyediting.

Ben Bourbon for his clever and inspired illustrations.

Per Olin for his organized and aesthetically-pleasing diagrams.

Guzel Gjenasaj, Leslie Waller, Graham Anderson, and Ralph Lagnado for helping to research, find, track, and clear the many images in this book.

David Koontz (Publisher, Chilton), for introducing Jeannie Novak to Jim Gish.

A big thanks also goes out to all the many people who contributed their thoughts and ideas to this book:

Aaron Marks (On Your Mark Music)

Adam Garner

Allen Varney

Amy Albertson (Ubisoft)

Andrew Helm (CMD Group)

Bill Brown (Bill Brown Music, Inc.)

Brian Dalton

Charlie Yee

Chris Avellone (Obsidian Entertainment)

Chris Taylor (Gas-Powered Games)

Dan Arey (Naughty Dog)

David Brin

David Freeman (The Freeman Group)

David Jaffe (Sony)

David Perry (Shiny Entertainment)

Deb Mars (Sony)

Deon Vozov (Essential Soundworks)

Don Daglow (Stormfront Studios)

Fletcher Beasley (Beat Revolution Music + Sound)

Frank Gilson (Wizards of the Coast)

Gordon Walton

Hope Levy

Howard Kinyon

Isabel Davila

Janet Wilcox

Jeffery Davis (Loyola Marymount University)

Joe Wright (Sony)

Justin Contreras

Kevin Saunders (Obsidian Entertainment)

Kofi Jamal

Lucien Soulban (Ubisoft)

Mark Soderwall

Mark Terrano (Microsoft)

Matt Case (CMD Group)

Mike Daley (Blindlight)

Patricia Pizer (4orty 2wo Entertainment)

Richard Dansky (Red Storm Entertainment/Ubisoft)

Rita Mines (Sony)

Shannon Studstill (Sony)

Sheldon Brown (University of California, San Diego)

Sheldon Pacotti (Secret Level)

Starr Long (NCsoft)

Stevan Hird (Midway)

Steve Caterson (Sony)

Steven Duncan (Loyola Marymount University)

Dr. Susan Scheibler (Loyola Marymount University)

Warren Spector (Junction Point Studios)

Whitney Wade (Sony)

Thanks to the following people for their tremendous help with referrals and in securing permissions, images, and demos:

Brian Hupp (Electronic Arts)

Catherine Crowther & Cathy Campos (Lionhead)

Cecelia Hernandez (Atari)

Chris Brandkamp & Ryan Miller (Cyan)

Chris Brooks

Chris Glover (Eidos)

Christina Cavallero (Sony)

ClipArt.com

Daniel James (Three Rings Design)

Dave Timoney (Gas-Powered Games)

David Perry & Andrew Green (Shiny)

David Swofford (NCsoft)

Denise Lopez (Blizzard)

Dennis Shirk (Firaxis)

Doug Lombardi (Valve)

Estella Lemus (Capcom)

Janet Braulio (Nintendo)

Jarik Sikat (KOEI)

Jay Moore (GarageGames)

Liz Buckley (Majesco)

Luis Levy

Melody Pfeiffer (Tecmo)

Michael Paeck (JoWooD Productions)

Mike Mantarro, Megan Korns & Kehau Rodenhurst (Activision)

Norbert Aujoulat (CNP – Ministere de la Culture)

Rod Rigole, Lori Inman & Kevin Crook (Vivendi Universal Games)

Sven Liebich (Phenomic)

Teresa Cotesta (BioWare)

Theresa Jones (Monolith)

Winsome Young & Helene Juguet (Ubisoft)

Zach Wood (Midway)

We would also like to thank the following reviewers for their valuable suggestions and technical expertise:

Brian Windsor, The Ohio State University

Steven Herrnstadt, Iowa State University

Chris Klug, Carnegie Mellon University

Questions & Feedback

We welcome your questions and feedback. If you have suggestions that you think others would benefit from, please let us know and we will try to include them in the next edition.

You may contact the publisher at:

Delmar Learning
Executive Woods
5 Maxwell Drive
Clifton Park, NY 12065
800-998-7498

Or the series editor at:

Jeannie Novak
Founder & CEO
INDIESPACE
PO Box 5458
Santa Monica, CA 90409
310-399-4349
jeannie@indiespace.com

DEDICATIONS

For my parents, Ed and Laura, who gave me everything—and for Whitney, who graces me with kindness everyday. Thank you.

— Marianne

For Luis, who has many amazing stories to tell. Thank you for your creative inspiration.

— Jeannie

Part I: Story

CHAPTER 1

The History of Story

how we've evolved as storytellers

Key Chapter Questions

- How did our early ancestors understand and express their world?
- How has Aristotle's use of *tragic flaw* changed from the early Greeks to the novel?
- Why do novels offer a personal experience and how is this experience achieved?
- What techniques in film consistently elicit emotion from the audience?
- Have games changed the definition of story?

Since the beginning of time, every human culture has engaged in storytelling as a way of understanding the world around them. As soon as there was a notable consciousness of self, it became imperative that we as a species make sense of our particular place in the world and our reason for being. It was this natural drift toward introspection that created the need to tell a story. Primitive at first, our storytelling became more and more complex–so complex, in fact, that we have reached the point where we need to engage in the process not just as members of an audience, but also as active participants as we do in games. This chapter briefly describes our past as storytellers and will help you discover where we may be evolving towards as the world of story continues to advance through the technology of electronic games.

Cave Paintings

You wouldn't think that we, as a sophisticated 21st century society, have much in common with the people of the Paleolithic era. *They* were nomadic people; *we* are settled. *They* hunted and gathered; *we* have food delivered to us. *They* lived short, brutal lives; *we* have an expanding life expectancy. In fact, outside the bottom-rung basics of food and shelter, what could we possibly have in common with a people that lived approximately 30,000 to 10,000 B.C.? After all, with automobiles, microwaves, and digital video recorders, we theoretically have a great deal of extra time to engage in self-actualization. We dress up in tuxedoes. We discuss the "human" condition. We create art! Those poor, naked nomads were eking it out in caves. Simply put, there is nothing we can possibly have in common with those humble beginnings of humanity. Or is there?

Ben Bourbon

While life may have been difficult, with the elements always against them, somehow these people had the time to create art and tell stories. Upon first discovery, cave art was thought to be purely decorative with no complex meaning. Then, as patterns began to emerge, so did many theories: fertility, magic, ritual, symbolism.... Many speculate—but, without a time machine, we'll never know for sure what the images meant. There are even those who believe these colorful pictures flickering in the firelight were the earliest form of entertainment. Add some hand shadow characters and there you have it: the first interactive storytelling experience.

Regardless of historical fact, let's assume for a moment that–whether reality or fantasy, ritual or symbol–these paintings communicated events. From this we can further assume that through each "event" there is an associated human experience—in short, a story... a story in pictures. Ask any film aficionado the definition of the modern day movie, and they'll tell you: a story told in pictures.

This might seem to be a rather simplistic view—but, while these images were primitive, they were not simple. The paintings found at Lascaux, France, for example, display all the elements necessary in storytelling: theme, character, conflict, resolution, and message.

A clear story is depicted in *La Scene du Puits,* a rare cave painting from Lascaux: man against bison.

In the above cave painting, a man is prostrate and probably dead. A bison stands over him. From this we can conclude that the man has been killed by the bison. There are several story elements that have existed since cave paintings were used as storytelling vehicles—each of which is depicted in this particular example:

- Theme: Man against nature—survival.
- Characters: "Man" and "Bison"
- Conflict: Life or death. Both characters want the same thing (survival), but only one will achieve it.
- Resolution: The bison won.
- Message: Perhaps man should go vegetarian next time!

We shouldn't spend all our time in the dark, so let's step out of the cave and into the light—the light of language and, more specifically, spoken word.

Next we'll look into the oral traditions that not only kept our cultures alive but developed the way we tell stories.

Oral Traditions

Is it any wonder that the word "story" is part of the word "history"? Throughout human existence, stories have been orated for many reasons—but the foremost was to preserve a culture's historical record and to pass information from generation to generation. In doing so, there is an established sense of self and community. While text offers the benefits of publication and reaching a broader audience, one should

Ben Bourbon

never underestimate the power of the spoken word. In fact, most of the world's major religions began through verbal communication. Christianity, for example, started as small tales—told through several generations, sometimes at great peril to the teller. No matter your personal beliefs, there is no denying that from these stories our world has been inexorably altered. Pretty powerful stuff from a few simple spoken words!

Much of William Shakespeare's work explores the notion that words have "issue" —that, once released into the world, words will take on a life of their own regardless of the teller's original intent. This is kind of an Elizabethan version of the game, *Operator* (sometimes known as *Grapevine* or *Telephone*), where a few words or sentences are told through a line of several people. By the end of the line, the original sentiment is usually completely different than what the first person said.

This very idea can be seen in the beliefs of many traditional Native American communities. Certain tribes believe that the spoken word is the physical manifestation of creative thought. Positive words carry positive energy, and, conversely, negative words carry negative energy. Because of this view, many ceremonies and religious rituals are only known through the spoken word. Moreover, the moment is ephemeral, making the individuals privy to the experience bond to the extended family of clan, tribe, community, and culture.

Across the Atlantic, stories were being told in the form of folktales—which are defined by the passage from generation to generation by word of mouth. These folktales can be further broken down into various types of story.

Ben Bourbon

"The Fox and the Grapes" is a typical fable–using an animal to demostrate the idea that it is easy to despise what you cannot have.

Fable

A type of allegory, a *fable* is a short tale that is meant to convey a cautionary or moral truth. Usually animals with human attributes are the principal characters that illustrate the shortcomings of humanity. In the classic fable "The Fox and the Grapes," the Fox reaches for the Grapes, but cannot get them. As he walks away, he claims that the grapes are probably sour anyway and he never really wanted them in the first place. This demonstrates the idea that it is easy to despise what you know you cannot have.

Myth

When strictly defined, a *myth* is a religious-centered story that explores the origins of man at the creation of the world. Myths are considered true by both orator and audience, and the main character is usually a god who takes an alternate form. An example is the myth of *Hercules.* Before Hercules is born, his mortal father, Amphitryon, is called away to war. During his absence, the deceitful and randy Greek God Zeus disguises himself as Amphitryon in order to sleep with Hercules' mother, Alcmene. The result of their night together is Hercules—half mortal, half god.

Ben Bourbon

The story of Hercules' parents is a classic example of a myth.

Legend

A legend exemplifies the quality of human nature after the creation of man. Legends are also believed by orator

Ben Bourbon

"The Legend of Sleepy Hollow" is a spooky and fun legend that is retold and shared during Halloween.

and audience and deal with subjects such as the paranormal, as in "The Legend of Sleepy Hollow" and single heroes such as King Arthur. "The Legend of Sleepy Hollow" follows the misadventures of Ichabod Crane, his rival (Abraham Van Brunt), and the woman they both wish to marry (Katrina Van Tassel). Within the legend, Van Brunt tells Crane of the Hessian Soldier that was decapitated in battle. Every year the ghost, or Headless Horseman, roams the countryside in search of a new head. The hauntings coincidentally stop the night Ichabod Crane disappears forever.

Urban Legend

In contemporary society we have few legends left. The tabloids are too busy finding scandal for anyone to maintain hero status for long, let alone become a legend. However, our lack of heroes hasn't stopped us from telling stories. *Urban legends* fill the gap nicely by being reported as true events. The sheer number of urban legends in U.S. popular culture prompted the release of the film *Urban Legend* in 1998. Examples of popular urban legends include "The Hook" and "The Babysitter"; the films *I Know What You Did Last Summer* and *Don't Answer the Phone* were based on these legends, respectively.

Ben Bourbon

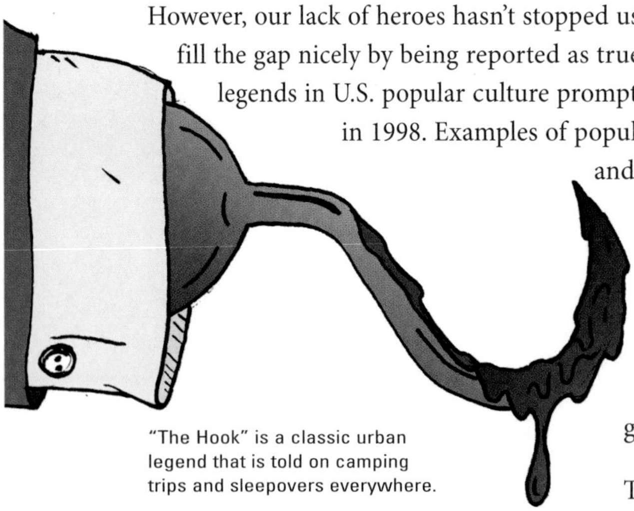

"The Hook" is a classic urban legend that is told on camping trips and sleepovers everywhere.

From European fairy tales to American tall tales, the list of folktales goes on and on.

Today we still find orally driven stories. Slam poetry and rap music speak of contemporary life and culture. Some tales are cautionary, and some are not—but it doesn't matter, since the tradition will continue as long as we have a voice to tell our stories.

Netlore: Hoaxes, Rumors, and Urban Legends

Stories travel fast these days! Now that a great deal of our communication takes place online, countless spammers have started hoaxes, rumors, and urban legends via email. Topics range from Microsoft or AOL cash giveaways, to phone scam or virus warnings, to fake boycotts or petitions. Sites such as http://truthorfiction.com and http://snopes.com track and debunk these hoaxes. Be sure to check these sites out before forwarding that seemingly important petition or warning to everyone in your address book! This just promotes the chain-letter effect, helping spammers get their message out to as many people as possible. For more information on netlore, see http://urbanlegends.about.com/library/blhoax.htm.

This section would not be complete without a nod to the artists who engaged in the tradition. The bards, troubadours, and minstrels of yesteryear are the writers, musicians, and poets of today. Unlike the bards of the past who were employed by the royal elite, modern-day storytellers are employed by the masses. They write songs, television programs, films, and games—often lending their work to the interpretation of other storytellers… such as directors, singers, artists, designers, and actors.

Ah, the Theater!

Historically, while most cultures had rituals that pantomimed important acts of worship, it wasn't until the Greeks that theater took its place among the pillars of storytelling. In fact, the word "theater" comes from the Greek word "theatron," meaning "seeing place."

Ben Bourbon

Originally, Greek plays were rituals performed at the festival of Dionysus until they eventually developed into the dramatic form. While there are many Greek playwrights who contributed (Sophocles, Aristophanes, Euripides), it wasn't until Aristotle that we started to see actual thought and structure emerge as a cohesive form.

Aristotle believed drama to be the most direct response to humanity's need to imitate experience. From this thought he was able to derive the basics of storytelling: a beginning, middle, and end. Pretty basic stuff, but prior to the Greeks no such formal structure existed. He also organized the need for plot, character, thought, diction, music, and spectacle. Needless to say, these are the core elements on which classic structure and contemporary storytelling are founded. If you analyze any current movie, TV show, or game, you'll find that it uses Aristotle's elements—even 2,500 years later!

Beyond the basics, Aristotle is responsible for the concept of the *tragic flaw*—a character flaw in a protagonist that causes his ultimate demise. Most would argue that King Oedipus was defeated by pride; Macbeth was brought down by ambition; and Othello was overcome by jealousy. Writers still ponder the tragic flaw as they look to develop character. There are countless Greek contributions to this single art form. In fact, the Greeks are responsible for all we know today in the world of theater: drama, comedy, and satire. The Romans, who aggregated elements of many cultures and released them into the mainstream, were quick to adapt the Greek form of theater—and, in the Roman practice of "if it ain't broke, don't fix it," much of Roman theater remained as the Greeks originally intended. It is worth mentioning the Romans because they were responsible for the exporting of all things Roman. Anything that was adopted as Roman, such as theater, was spread to the vast reaches of the empire—and, in essence, most of the civilized western world. Had it not been for the Romans and their extensive empire, many great works of literature, art, and drama would have been lost to history.

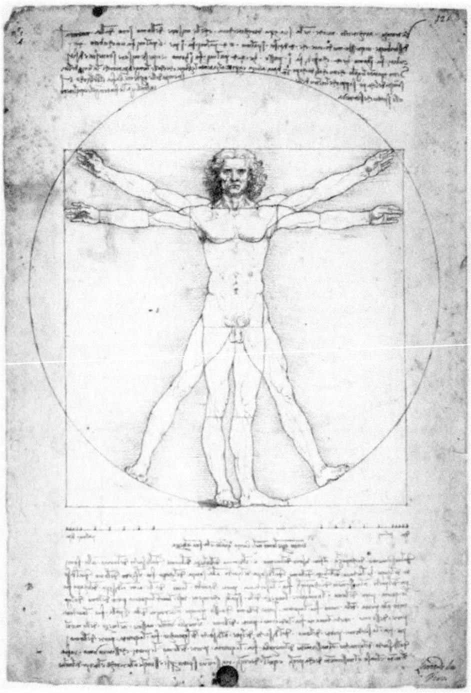

Leonardo Da Vinci's Vitruvian Man is a classic example of Renaissance art and thought.

Although the Renaissance had already begun, the destruction of Constantinople (now present-day Istanbul) in 1453 by the Turks ensured the return of Greco-Roman art and literature from the east back into the city of Rome. Secular humanistic and scientific reason began to outshine a darker view of humanity. Man once again became the central figure of beauty and divinity. It was a new dawn for civilization and the theater was no different.

Later, as the Renaissance drifted to Elizabethan England, playwrights such as Christopher Marlowe, Thomas Kyd, and William Shakespeare were heavily influenced by the classics of Greece and Rome. Today, Shakespeare is still thought to be the most profound thinker, the most performed dramatist, and the most accomplished writer of the English language. His uncanny understanding of human behavior and his ability to communicate those thoughts through his vivid characters, mastery of language, and theatrical technique created exceptionally compelling drama.

To this day we see elements of his stories throughout our popular entertainment. *The Lion King* is a retelling of *Hamlet*. *Titanic* is *Romeo and Juliet*. Season 2 of the HBO series, *The Sopranos,* is a lightly interpreted version of *Macbeth*. Why? Simply put, Shakespeare had the ability to touch on the universal—that simple truth in all of us that makes us human. His stories, as all good stories, are eternal.

Of course, theater didn't end with the Elizabethans. It continued throughout the centuries, each period taking on its own unique expression of drama: French Classicism, 18th century Neo-Classicism, and 19th century Romanticism. In the east, India, China, and Japan were developing dramatic forms that would later influence western theater. Variation began to appear—burlesque, vaudeville, musicals. Eventually the written play became a work of literature in its own right, separate from the live onstage performance.

Up until now, the storytelling experience had been shared. The act of reading made it solitary and indeed completely different.

The World of Text

With the invention of the Gutenberg printing press in the mid-15th century, written language became more accessible to the common people—and, in enlightened societies, most became literate. It is here, as the masses became educated, that the elements of storytelling through text take wing, most notably through the novel.

Ben Bourbon

As storytelling devices, novels have great flexibility. They have the room to be episodic in nature; they can cover vast landscapes of time and place; and they may develop the plot slowly with several subplots to help support the central theme. The novel gives us a way to tell a story through a single human experience. It is during this period that we begin to see the emergence of the character as an individual—warts and all. The use of a tragic flaw usually reflects a single Achilles heel (such as jealousy) that ends poorly for the hero. This flaw is a symbol of the tragedy—even though the character is much more complex than this symbol alone.

In a novel, we see the basic elements of plot, character, and conflict, but here is where the form departs from its predecessors. Characters in a novel often struggle with internal conflict consisting of guilt, pain, love, hate, birth, and death, all in complex human terms. It's probably the first time storytellers such as Fyodor Dostoyevsky, Leo Tolstoy, and Frantz Kafka explored the human condition without the constraints of moral dictum, an emblem, or a message. The novel allows the reader to go inside the inner workings of the character. The associated human experience becomes cerebral, and the manifestation of the experience can be profound.

Further, the author has the unique ability to speak directly to the reader. It is personal and private and, although many people may read the same book, there is no denying that the reading experience is solitary and as such may differ greatly from others' personal experiences. Attending a theater performance is distinct from reading a book in this way, since the live audience can have a "shared" experience.

Film: Back into the Cave

As we explored with the cave paintings, humans have been telling stories visually since the beginning of existence—but since those early endeavors we have developed a complexity and a technology for telling a story. Film may not be the first form of visual storytelling, but it is certainly the most sophisticated thus far.

Ben Bourbon

Beginning with the invention of film in the 1800s, the photograph was as effective at telling a story as those early paintings. One could infer the story's theme from the action in the still, but inference lent more to human imagination than actual storytelling.

The zoetrope was the first machine to offer a story of moving pictures.

In the early 19th century, scientists began to take note of a visual phenomenon. They found that displaying a rapid sequence of pictures gave the illusion of motion—the motion picture. As these experiments continued, a device called the Zoetrope—a mechanical toy consisting of a sequence of pictures on the inside surface of a slotted drum—produced the same effect when whirled. Soon afterward, Thomas Edison invented the Kinescope, an individual viewing device. Eventually projection followed and the first celluloid stories were born.

Birth of a Nation: Manipulating the Audience through Story

D.W. Griffith's controversial *Birth of a Nation* was among the most significant first achievements in film. The crosscutting techniques and story development demonstrated the new medium's ability to manipulate an audience emotionally.

In the early 20th century, as technology continued to develop, an entire film industry and associated culture began to emerge. Literally, stories told in pictures without the benefit of sound or dialogue became a national pastime in America. From comedy to satire to melodrama to tragedy, all the elements from the past were brought forth into this unique art form until there was a new rumbling on the horizon.

> The Warner Brothers are making a whole talking picture with this gadget, The Jazz Singer. They'll lose their shirts.
>
> — *Singing in the Rain (1952)*

Although the above quotation is from a fictional film, the idea in Hollywood at the time was ubiquitous. No one thought that "talkies" would ever amount to anything. They were wrong. Once the public had its first taste of Warner Bros.' *The Jazz Singer*, it was all over for silent films. Many musicians and actors alike found themselves out of work with the introduction of this new technology.

After 30 millennia of storytelling, it all came crashing together in the art of film—which incorporated visuals, like those cave paintings so may years ago; audio, like the first orally driven narratives; both dialogue and character, like the Greek dramas; and complex human stories, like the novel. All of the elements were there—and, furthermore, they could be saved seemingly for eternity.

Film Preservation: An Ongoing Effort

Unfortunately, film does not last for eternity—and there is now an active effort not only to restore the films of the past but to preserve them digitally. The archivists at many of the major studios work tirelessly to provide cultural memories for generations to come.

Ben Bourbon

The illusion of motion, the use of sound, and the technique of two or more separate shots interwoven into a scene (known as *crosscutting*) tell a story that is uniquely film. A film narrative is a series of sequential events tied together through causality. A cat, a telephone ringing, and a house burning down are separate events. When a phone rings and startles a cat, making it jump and knock down a candle, which ignites the drapes thus burning down the house, and the owner comes home and wonders why no one answered his phone call—and how did that fire get started? Now *that's* a story (or at least a first act).

Louis B. Mayer: Stories Become Big Business

Louis B. Mayer thought of himself as a salesman. When he discovered that people would pay money and essentially leave the venue without a single material item, he was intrigued. Mayer was only partially right. He did retain the product, but people didn't leave empty handed. They left having had an experience—something they would pay for again and again.

While film told larger than life stories, there was a need for stories reflective of everyday life. Fortunately technology and television answered the call.

Television

Television also combined all the elements of storytelling into one mechanism. Sprung from the oral traditions of radio broadcast and the visuals of film, this medium started a whole new revolution.

Ben Bourbon

The first television programs were broadcast live. Similar to a theatrical play, it gave us the sense that anything could happen. If something went wrong, the audience would see through the ruse. Today, we occasionally see programs broadcast live and these are usually considered special events. The Super Bowl debacle of 2004 is one example of how anything can and does happen on live TV.

As a storytelling form, television again takes us further along the road of story evolution. In terms of fiction, television offers the unique personal experience of having the characters of your favorite TV show come into your living room and tell you their stories week after week.

From the storyteller's perspective, TV offers many of the same benefits attributed to the novel. It can develop a story slowly, episodically. The slower pace of revealing a character is a more interesting development process and ultimately can make a more intriguing story. For the audience, the time spent each week with the characters offers the element of intimacy. The audience comes to understand the character probably better than they would their own friends and family because they get to see the character in moments alone—small, private moments that make us understand why the character behaves in a certain way. Due to this intimacy, there is sometimes an interesting effect known as *parasocial interaction*. This happens when the audience becomes so attached to a character that they actually believe that character is real.

::::: The "Lovable" Mobster?

The HBO cable series *The Sopranos* features, in most people's terms, a rather hateful character. Tony Soprano is a killer, a mobster, an adulterer, and a bigot. He is morally reprehensible—but he has all the problems of the Everyman, too: He has trouble with his aging mother. His teenage kids are giving him grief. His wife nags him. The people that work for him complain and bicker. We watch Tony because in many ways we can still relate to him. Perhaps he is morally questionable—but we forgive him because, in the end, he is like us.

Ben Bourbon

Another way television uses a narrative is with the "reality" television trend, which allows people from all walks of life to experience things that they ordinarily would not. Reality TV programs often use a "game show" format, and there is often a lucrative prize for the winner.

Many in Hollywood would argue that the popularity of reality TV shows has to do with the low price tag. While it's true that the shows are not expensive to make, they still must be viewed regularly to get high ratings. Perhaps the extreme situations and large cash prizes are a draw for viewers—but what really makes people watch these shows week after week? No longer are viewers watching fictional characters, they are watching actual people—just like themselves! Most who watch can't help but wonder what they might do in the given situation or how they would play the game. Viewers are taking on the roles of the "characters" in the shows. Perhaps the experience is vicarious, but this experience is edging ever-closer to interactive storytelling.

There is another step emerging in the world of story—a virtual place where character and audience collide, where the causality of the story is actually created by the audience. Some of the development of this new medium depends on technology—and some of it depends on the reaches of human imagination. But either way, games are the new front lines of story evolution. In the pages to come, we'll look at story and character in the traditional storytelling sense and see how they might be translated into the evolving world of games and the new frontiers of story.

:::CHAPTER REVIEW:::

1. How did cave paintings launch the storytelling tradition? A picture can paint "a thousand words"—and still images can convey powerful, emotional stories. Search for some modern paintings and photographs online. Research the artists/photographers and historical contexts. How do images convey stories? Choose one of the images you found and create a story that you feel might be depicted in the image.

2. Why do you think fables, myths, and legends have had so much impact on storytelling? Create an idea for a game that's based on a fable, myth, or legend (traditional or urban). What is the universal theme being conveyed by the story you created? Why would your idea make a compelling game?

3. In this chapter, you learned about the respective qualities associated with the theater, books, and film. How can these qualities influence a game's story and create a rich experience for players? Apply the spontaneity of theater, the literary components of books, and the visual aspects of film to your original game idea.

4. What is the difference between the structure of film and television stories? Choose a popular game and modify its storyline so that it contains an episodic structure. What elements of the game story will you need to change in order to accommodate this new structure—and how can you improve on the game story by making these changes?

CHAPTER 2

Game Genres

storytelling through style of play

Key Chapter Questions

- What are some common game genres?
- How do game genres differ from genres in other media?
- How do game genres further a story within a game?
- What are some conventional story elements in game genres?
- How can genres be combined to enhance a game?
- How do game genres reflect style of play?

The French word *genre* translates to style, type, or kind. In Hollywood, the use of the word *genre* means the very specific backdrop or subject matter. Often a film is classified as a genre such as horror, science fiction, comedy, romance, or action. These descriptions help both the filmmakers and the audience discern and define what the film is about—and, in the case of the audience, it allows room for choice. For example, when a couple goes on a date for the first time, they might want to see a romantic comedy. If it's Halloween weekend, teenagers might want to see a horror film.

In games, genre doesn't have to do with the content of the story as it does in film—but it refers to the *style* of the game. For example, a puzzle, strategy, or role-playing game could contain horror, romance, or comedic elements.

In the pages to come, we look at how the distinct styles associated with several game genres apply to games – and we'll discuss why most game genres are well-suited to certain storylines.

Action

We've already discussed the Paleolithic Era and our fur-clad ancestors, the cave men—who come to mind again when we think about the *action* genre. When the cave people were not painting the insides of mountains, they were most likely out trying to find something to eat—while not being eaten themselves! It is here that the physiological *fight or flight* response probably evolved. This innate reaction is our body's primitive, automatic response that prepares the body to fight or flee from a perceived attack. Adrenalin surges through our blood stream, our muscles tense, and we must either put up our dukes or bolt. It is this same basic survival instinct that is invoked when we play action games. The action genre, as you may assume, is all about action—but, more to the point, it is about how players react to the fast-paced engagement of the enemy.

Ben Bourbon

The real reason we developed opposable thumbs.

Is the Genre the Message?

Marshall McLuhan is known for coining the phrase, "The medium is the message" in his work *Understanding Media.* This phrase simply means that the technology that delivers the information has far more impact than the information itself. You will see that this notion also applies in game genres.

The only goal of these games is survival. Destroy your enemies and/or outrun your enemies. Either way, survive to the next level. These simple life and death stakes make the game focus on player reaction—*reflexive* time rather than *reflective* time. In essence, there is absolutely no time to think. It's all instinct and skill. Like our ancestors so long ago, our brains simply cannot process incoming information fast enough.

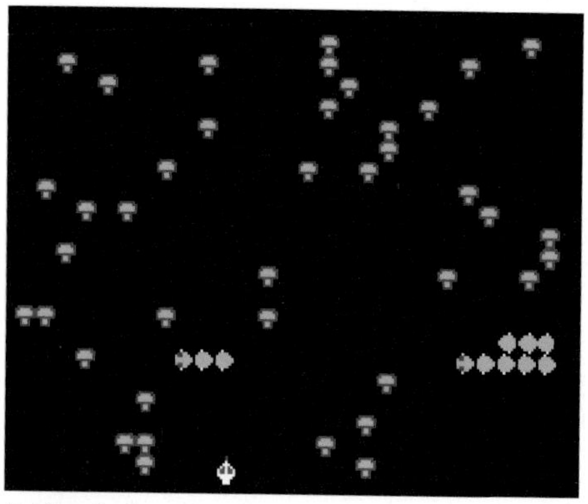

Atari Interactive, Inc.

In the classic arcade game *Centipede*, the player must rely on quick reflexes in order to survive.

Therefore, our bodies take over with the use of fast twitch muscles. (Hence the term "twitch" games!)

Just as there are subgenres in other media, games also have classified genres within genres.

Ben Bourbon

"Looks like Larry's playing that 'twitch' game again!"

Platformers

Platformers were the earliest types of action video games. Actions in the game usually include jumping and dodging obstacles. Sometimes collecting items is part of the game as well. First found in arcades in the form of *Donkey Kong* and *Frogger*, platformers are also popular in console games such as the *Sly Cooper* and *Ratchet and Clank* franchises.

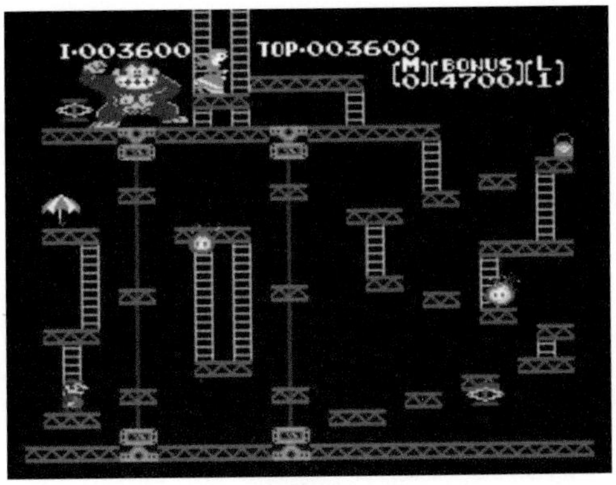

Nintendo of America, Inc.

Donkey Kong—one of the first platformers.

Platformers have clearly identifiable characters that are given a simple mission at the beginning of play. For example, in *Donkey Kong*, Mario must get the girl back from the gorilla.

As the missions unfold and challenges become more intense, the game itself becomes a type of story.

While *Ms. Pac-Man* is an action game that rewards the player with a mini-romance-movie about Pac-Man and Ms. Pac-Man, we should consider what the story is in terms of playing the game. What is *Ms. Pac-Man* really about?

The platformer genre has evolved into 3D games such as *Sly Cooper*.

Sucker Punch/Sony Computer Entertainment of America

Like Pac-Man, Ms. Pac-Man's main goal is to consume power pills for food. It's a story about consumption. It's a story of survival—since Ms. Pac-Man faces death around every corner—and it is a story about the sweet rewards of life represented in the game by the fruit that gives the player bonus points. It can be a story about many things. Power, survival, and joy are ideas or themes that represent the story. Themes about trust or honesty might be difficult to incorporate into an action game, but they might provide an interesting point of entry when considering making an action game.

Shooters

The term *shooter* refers to a game in which the player carries and uses a weapon—often a gun or other projectile. The shooter subgenre breaks down further into two different types of shooters based on the character's *point-of-view.*

Sometimes a game with weapons such as a sword, shield, or other armory is called a "hack-and-slash" game because of the combat style—but it is still a type of shooter. The choice of first-person versus third-person point-of-view in a shooter can change the experience for the player. Let's take a close look at each.

First-Person Shooter (FPS)

The *first-person shooter (FPS)*—as found in games such as *Halo, Metroid,* and *Doom*—is played with a first-person point-of-view (POV). The player is given a brief description, usually in a mini-movie, of the main character, location, and situation

Half-Life 2 is an example of a first-person shooter.

Valve

(often showing the character in third-person POV). After all of the information has been provided, the POV switches to first-person—and the player "becomes" the character. Everything the player sees from then on is from the character's POV.

In *Halo 2*, cooperative play is incorporated into the first-person perspective. As many as 16 players can play the same game at the same time online. Players will encounter one another as they might in a real-life game of paintball. These team efforts are often referred to as "Capture the Flag," while an individual playing another individual is often referred to as a "Deathmatch."

Ben Bourbon

The popular real-world game paintball offers a real-world first-person shooter game experience.

Cooperative Competition?

Recently, colleges have begun intercollegiate *Halo* competitions. Teams of players representing their schools fight others in military-type situations. For schools that have little or no budget for sports, *Halo* offers an alternative to more costly competitions. At larger schools such as USC it is said that students will choose a dorm based on their *Halo* team.

If you want to build a game that makes the player feel more directly part of the action, an FPS is a good choice—since it places the players directly into the action, giving them the feeling that they are truly "inside" the game.

Third-Person Shooter (TPS)

Not surprisingly, the other shooter sub-genre is the *third-person shooter (TPS)*. This form of play provides a wider field of vision and allows players to see their characters. Many third-person games offer camera movement similar to the first-person perspective—yet in the third-person perspective, it is easier to see and understand the player situation in context of the game location. This can be very useful during the execution of game tasks.

Survival-horror game *Resident Evil 4* is also considered a third-person shooter.

Capcom Entertainment, Inc.

First- and Third-Person Shooters Combined?

In the game *Crimson Sky: High Road to Revenge,* the player flies a plane and engages the enemy in first person. When the player lands the plane to receive orders for new missions, the perspective switches to third person. This back and forth perspective offers both worlds to the player.

Both *first-person* and *third-person* shooters are some of the most popular games in today's game market. If you were going to make a shooter, which perspective would you emphasize?

Racing

The racing subgenre is dependent on the same twitch muscles as any other action game and, while the goal may not be to kill or be killed, it is still about victory or defeat. Racing games often allow the player to toggle between first- and third-person points-of-view. Players may compete against the game itself or other players. Racing was among the first video games in arcades. From Atari's *Night Driver* all the way to the new competitive console releases *Gran Turismo 4* (PS2) and *Forza Motorsport* (Xbox), these games remain exceedingly popular in homes and arcades all over the world.

Nintendo of America, Inc.

Mario Kart: Double Dash is a popular racing game featuring the Mario Bros. (Mario and Luigi).

In the racing game *Cart Fury: Championship Racing,* the player may choose a car and a well-known race car driver. From this real-world association, the story is already set in forward motion. If the player chooses to be Mario Andretti, for example, that player knows Andretti to be among the best drivers. The player also knows that Andretti only drives in the top competitions around the world. This external information fills out the story as the game is played. In this case, the theme is about excellence.

Due to the great popularity of racing games, we can conclude that not only will they be even more realistic in style in the future, but also that there will be plenty of racing games to come!

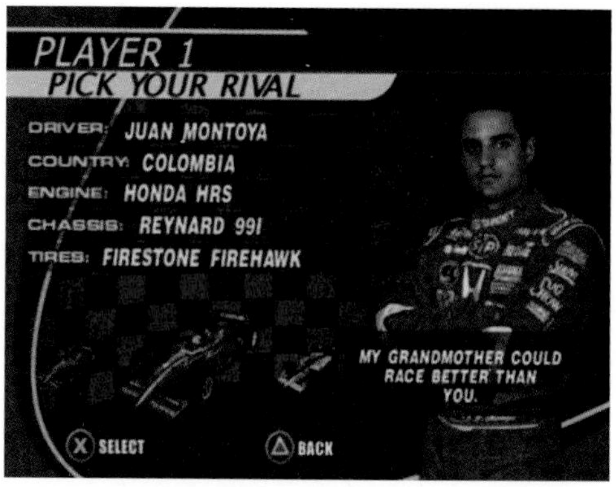

Midway

Cart Fury offers real-world characters and conditions to help drive the story forward.

Eidos

Backyard Wrestling offers the over-the-top fun of big-time wrestling.

Fighting

Fighting games also depend on the player's good reflexes—and, often, a buddy to play against. These games offer social interaction and variations in story content. For example, compare the classic martial arts fighting game, *Soul Calibur,* and the rambunctious *Backyard Wrestling*. Fighting games are normally shown in a third-person side view.

First-Person Fight?

Although a side view is most common in fighting games, think about a fighting game using a first-person perspective. Would it provide a more interesting experience than the traditional side view of other fighting games?

Often, moves found in fighting games are also found in large action games and add great variety for the player.

In *War of the Monsters*, we see again the pre-existing narrative. Even though the monsters are not classic monsters from other fictional stories, they bring to mind associated images. Players may choose monsters that look like the classic Godzilla or King Kong. In this case the preexisting narrative association is from real-world fiction. Godzilla versus King Kong is a fun way to tell a story whose thematic tones are about dominance.

Action games are ripe with possibilities for stories. Be sure to understand what idea you are trying to promote, and the action of the game is sure to be thrilling!

Pacing and Genre-Specific Storytelling

In a fast-paced game (head-to-head fighting), much of the story happens between intense gameplay or is conveyed through character design, art, and attitudes—as well as dialog snippets during the experience. The slower the pace of the game, the more important story and character issues are to filling out the overall experience. Some genres are more open-ended, and the characters carve out their own stories based on their decisions; how the world reacts to the characters' actions is the basis for this kind of storytelling. In any genre, seamlessly integrating the story into all aspects of the game (AI, art, character design, music, ambient sound) so that the different components are each enhancing the experience—and moving the player toward the same emotional state—gives the best experience.

— Mark Terrano (Technical Game Manager, Xbox–Microsoft)

Adventure

Something else our cave ancestors probably did was to explore the world around them to find food and shelter. As we evolved throughout history, exploration brought us deep into the jungles, fueled the discovery of the Americas, and even landed us on the moon. Today we still explore untouched regions of the planet and travel far into the cosmos. Exploration may bring goods and trade—but it seems, in spite of material gain, human nature is driven by a need to explore and understand the world.

Unfortunately, sometimes modern life, with its time and financial restrictions, gives us little opportunity to realize our desire to explore. Certainly, sitting at home watching TV is no way to turn this natural penchant toward exploration into adventure—but, lucky for us, playing a game can. It is our desire for exploration and discovery that is the basis for *adventure* games.

The first adventure game was *Colossal Cave Adventure*—a text-based mainframe computer game that allowed the player to explore and find treasure. While the desire for exploration is a key component in adventure games, this is only part of the challenge. Puzzles, mazes, and rewards inspire the need for further play.

Eventually, graphics were added to these text adventures, and *Myst* became the most popular adventure game of all time. *Myst* went beyond puzzles and mazes and added an element of story for the player.

The Mystery of *Mystery House*

In 1980, *Mystery House*, created by Roberta Williams—one of the first women to co-found a game company (Sierra On-Line)—was the first computer game to use text and graphics. The game is set inside a Victorian mansion with seven other people. As players explore the house, they are quick to learn the people they share the house with are being murdered. The goal of the game is to find the murderer before the murderer finds the player! Roberta Williams was inspired to create *Mystery House* after playing the very text-adventure game, *Colossal Cave Adventure.*

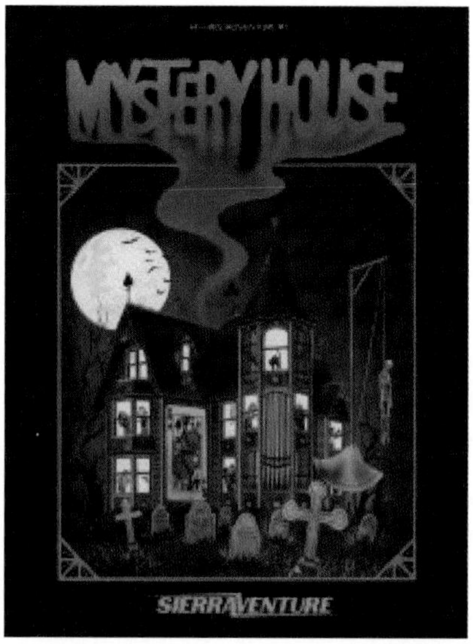

Vivendi Universal Games

Unlike action games where the story is the play experience, adventure games usually offer their own rich storylines that can intrigue and nudge the player forward to find out "what happened." To make the story experience more compelling, it is useful for the game developer to know the entire story—while only exposing certain elements to the player. Revealing small but interesting clues in the same way a mystery novel might give the reader a series of hints is a way to keep the player captivated. The difference is that the player takes part in an active search instead of being fed clues sequentially as a reader would experience in a novel.

::::: How Big Is the Mystery of *Myst*?

Cyan (the creators of *Myst*) felt that the game itself must contain a complete story, even if the player never learns it entirely. This contributes to an unconscious awareness of a "bigger picture," driving the curiosity of the player even more. Doing this adds an intangible richness to the game and story. Within the game, the player runs across many clues from a story that happened before the game began. Pieces of the mystery unfold to the player in parts and are necessary to complete the game even if the whole story is not ever completely revealed.

Cyan Worlds, Inc.

While there are often puzzles throughout adventure games, the revealing of the storyline contributes to the riddle of the entire game, making gameplay engaging and compelling until a satisfying conclusion is reached. A story that would work well with the adventure genre is one that works like a mystery.

Tom Clancy's Splinter Cell offers action and adventure.

Ubisoft

Action-Adventure

The only hybrid to distinguish itself as a genre in its own right, *action-adventure* calls for quick reflexive action to combat enemies as well as reflective thought to negotiate the environment through puzzles, mazes, and navigational exploration. Action-adventure games allow the player time to delve into the world, discover a character, and approach the story.

Combining action and adventure is a great way to get the best of both worlds and keep the game interesting for the player. Since action-adventure uses both the reflexive response of action games and the reflective thought of adventure games, this hybrid can be used quite effectively when it comes to storytelling. Offering moments of action can give the player a sense of pace, time restriction, and usually life-or-death circumstances that convey the immediacy of the situation in that part of the story. The adventure part of the game offers a slower pace, but it can be mentally stimulating, giving the story depth and resonance that enriches the action part of the gameplay.

:::::Direct Experience in *Area 51*

In a first-person shooter game such as *Area 51*, the story itself unfolds directly for the player. Pace, time, visual cues, and other characters contribute to a direct experience. The story is told within the game through dialog from other characters, surrounding environments, and challenges—allowing the player to experience walking in the main character's shoes rather than seeing the character as distinct and separate.

Midway

Ethan Cole, the character in the game *Area 51*, is a soldier and a scientist. He isn't a classic hero like James Bond or a superhero like Spiderman, but he is a guy who just happens to be in the wrong place at the wrong time. It is this everyday type of character who helps make the story more direct and the experience more personal.

Third-person narratives offer yet another way of telling stories, and third-person point-of-view (POV) games often have much more of a cinematic feel. Since the player can see the character, the experience, although still personal, is less direct. The player knows what he or she, as the hero, looks like and what powers the character has.

The third-person POV offers a different game experience. Seeing the character helps the player bond with the character more than in a first-person game. Mini-movies placed within the game take the player out of gameplay to watch a preordained storyline. While some may get impatient watching these plot points, others find it helps to create a better experience by filling out the world and allowing players to try on a different but well-developed persona.

Real-World Lara Croft?

Identifying with a character so strongly that the player wants to be the character is a common result of third-person action-adventure games. In the game *Tomb Raider*, the player identifies with Lara Croft, the game's super-cool hero. Wildly popular among both men and women, Lara has been franchised into novels and movies and even inspired costumes. Some people identify with Lara so strongly that they take on the role in the real world—attending parties, clubs, and bars as Lara Croft.

If you are a player who likes epic storytelling within the confines of an action-adventure game, third-person might be the right choice for you. The third-person POV gives way to a more movie-like experience. Although this type of game usually tells a linear story as well as provides linear play, it allows a designer to create a character's appearance, which can significantly contribute to the story experience. While character appearance will be discussed in later chapters, it is important to note that the look of the character usually has to do with the character's history—which contributes to the character's story.

The Pain of *Max Payne*

The game *Max Payne* mixes the playing experience of a video game with the reading experience of a graphic novel. This valiant attempt made for an interesting hybrid of media but many game designers these days are looking beyond traditional storytelling media and creating stories specifically made for the game experience. As games and stories continue to evolve, we will see less of these hybrids and more stories designed with the player in mind.

Choosing either first- or third-person POV can both alter the story and the manner in which the player receives information. Consider POV as you determine the type of story you want to tell and how you want to tell it.

Massively Multiplayer Online Games (MMOGs): A Genre-Specific Technology Platform

As discussed in Chapter 1, Aristotle believed drama to be the most direct response to humanity's need to imitate experience. While Aristotle developed this notion over 2,500 years ago, the sentiment fits nicely into the game genre of *massively multiplayer online games (MMOGs)*. These games offer real-world emotions even if the game itself is fantasy.

Blizzard Entertainment, Inc.

World of Warcraft allows players from all over the world to interact and play together. This is an excellent example of an MMOG.

MMOGs are games that players from around the world may compete in, online, in a persistent-state world (PSW). In other words, players can log in and play anytime of day from anywhere. One of the advantages of an MMOG is the unpredictability of human nature. Since most other characters are other players, there is the very real sense that anything can happen. MMOGs often use other genres in order to create a game. Under the MMOG umbrella, one can develop first-person shooter (MMOFPS), role-playing (MMORPG), real-time strategy (MMORTS), and even puzzle (MMOPG) games.

While we can never know if Aristotle would agree, MMOGs appear to be the most modern, direct response to humanity's need to imitate experience, because they actively approach games in a way that is akin to life.

Don't Force Story into Genre

The problem is that "story" has been injected into every single genre. This means that I can't just fly my spacecraft around (like in *Asteroids*)—but I must first listen to some horrible story about the galaxy in threat. Then I can play. Story for story's sake is a real downer. I don't mind people trying to inject story into all genres—but if it's not working, then forget it and go back to pure gameplay. The player will thank you.

— *David Perry (President, Shiny Entertainment)*

Bill Brown on Enhancing an MMOG through Music:::::

Bill Brown (Composer, Bill Brown Music Inc.)

Bill Brown has composed music for directors and producers including Steven Spielberg, Oliver Stone, Clive Barker, Michael Crichton, Gus Van Sant, Michael Mann, and Tom Clancy. His evocative, powerful orchestral scores continue to gain special recognition and awards in the industry, including three nominations for BAFTA Awards in the music category. Bill is the Director of Music for Soundelux Design Music Group in Hollywood, CA, and he has composed and produced music for theatrical releases such as *Any Given Sunday, Ali, and Finding Forrester.* Bill has also scored television films such as *Scorcher and Trapped,* and games including Tom Clancy's *Rainbow Six* series, *The Sum of All Fears, Lineage II: The Chaotic Chronicle, Return to Castle Wolfenstein, and Command & Conquer: Generals.* In 2005, Bill started his own company, Bill Brown Music, Inc. He currently lives in Los Angeles, CA, and is represented by First Artists Management. Bill is currently the composer for the hit CBS television series, *CSI: NY.*

My score for the massively multiplayer online role-playing game (MMORPG) *Lineage II* arcs over narrative content that has been continually updated from its creation in 2002 to the present. In this online game, hundreds of thousands of people (per game server) help to create their experience and stories through the epic fantasy world that the developers at NCsoft created and continually update. Players from all over the world pay a monthly fee to log in, and are then able to select a class of character and develop that character into more powerful classes, in real time, inside a world with complex political and economic systems. The narrative within the game is essentially a co-creation of the players (characters) and developers—and it continues to evolve and change synergistically with each update. The world is huge relative to the player and their experience, and the gameplay can last many years.

It's not always as easy to connect with a character in writing for games because the character usually becomes defined as the game unfolds through gameplay. Most of the time, I'm writing the music as the game is being created. I usually work with narrative from the game design, the story behind the gameplay, and any images or game builds that are available to me. It's freeing as well because I can bring my own experience to the project and add a dimension to it that might not have been there.

What is wonderful about writing for an MMORPG is that the story takes on a life if its own. It's my job as composer to help the players connect to their own experience of the game. Each character can travel anywhere in the world, and develop in whatever way they are moved to—interacting with the world and each other in their own unique way. As the composer, I help bring that world and experience to life—and bring added drama and emotion to it.

Creating for this fantasy world is freeing musically because of the nature of the narrative—the organic flow of the journey. The music can be magical, suspenseful, exciting, visceral, emotional, joyful, surreal, exotic, dramatic, and more. The real essence of music for any media is its innate ability to circumvent the mind, and touch the human spirit directly. As the players' stories unfold through MMOG gameplay, they have their own connection to the experience. The purpose of the music is to not stand out from the game and entertain—but to pull the players deeper into their experience of the game and accompany a magical exploration of the world.

Puzzle

Although puzzles are found in many genres, *puzzle* games involve puzzle-solving as the primary activity. Games such as *Tetris* offer a fast-paced experience of an action game, while others such as *Scrabble* offer the need for more reflective thought. Usually a puzzle game offers an individual experience and no character to control—but games such as *Puzzle Pirates* offer puzzle-solving fun in a competitive story-laden environment.

::::: Virtual Inebriation?

Three Rings Design

While virtual drinking in games such as *Puzzle Pirates* may not be quite as fun as real-world drinking games, at least you can drive home safely afterward. The irony, of course, is that if you are playing a game online, you are most likely already home!

Within the game *Puzzle Pirates*, puzzles simulate real-world challenges such as drinking games. In the drinking game, two players attempt to solve a series of puzzles. Each time a player fails to solve a puzzle, he or she either loses a turn or a skill required to compete successfully. This is done to simulate the drinking experience.

Many movies and TV shows offer puzzles for the characters to figure out making the story more intriguing. While puzzles are fun all by themselves, think about how they can be used in a storytelling experience.

Genres & Depth of Story

Some genres, such as puzzle games, don't need a story to make them viable. Others, like role-playing games (RPGs), would be empty and unplayable without a story. Single-player shooters tend to have linear, minimal story elements. The more rigidly a game adheres to a specific genre, the more linear or obvious the story tends to be. Lately the genres have been bending and morphing, and multi-genre games are becoming more and more common.

—Amy Albertson (Level Designer, Ubisoft Entertainment)

Role-Playing

A *role-playing game (RPG)* allows a player to take on a character such as a wizard, warrior, or welfare recipient and actively develop that character throughout the game. From the first *pencil-and-paper* games such as *Dungeons & Dragons*®, computer and video games have developed rich and fantastic worlds that allow the player to develop a working relationship with his or her character on the way to a goal—which might be as simple as retrieving a single material item or as grandiose as saving the universe.

:::::: *Dungeons & Dragons*®: The First RPG

Chris Brooks (http://www.chrisbrooks.org)

In 1974, a new type of game appeared on the horizon. *Dungeons & Dragons*®, a game without a playing board (known as a paper-and-pencil or tabletop game), where players can build their own characters, became a worldwide phenomenon. Soon other role-playing games (RPGs) followed suit, and real-world adventures began to emerge. By the time electronic games appeared, the idea of the player as a character had been firmly embedded in the world of games, and player control became the ultimate experience.

NCsoft

Character advancement through combat plays a large part in the RPG *Tabula Rasa*.

Role-playing games (RPGs) offer a rich world with all the classic elements of storytelling. RPGs allow the player to develop a character throughout the game. The fun of RPGs comes from the character getting to negotiate a complex story and choosing a way of advancing toward a goal. The game developer in this instance must focus on the elements of the game landscape to help convey the story so the player can have a fulfilling experience. The RPG is an ever-growing phenomenon and is seen not only in video games but also in real-world RPGs.

In a massively multiplayer online role-playing game (MMORPG), the player's character exists in a persistent-state world (PSW) and is given challenges to complete. An advantage to creating an MMORPG is its social aspect and the possibility of using teams and cooperation. A story requiring several characters to solve a problem—making a statement about cooperative living and the importance of the collective whole—could be told through an MMORPG. Another fun factor in MMORPGs is that players can develop more than one character and continue with the ongoing storyline.

Imagine a story that you could return to time and again and actively participate in the story. MMORPGs offer this opportunity and are definitely a great way to build interesting and dynamic stories that never end.

"Form—Not Formula"

There are conventions in every genre. These are the elements that people expect when they read a mystery, or watch a comedy, or play a military tech-thriller game. The game designer's choice of genre compels a good writer to make choices that fit the expectations of the story receiver... even as we plot to surprise them. Genre conventions are the "form" aspect of art form. They provide the framework to hang your story. My advice is to use them wisely and break away from them with caution, or your game narrative will become unfocused. The type of game will also greatly affect how you tell your story. An intense FPS is like a Michael Bay movie—90 percent action. Its convention is to keep moving, keep crashing, keep getting bigger, and keep up the body count! That's what's expected. It's a far cry from *Jak and Daxter* where we are adventuring in a fantastical world, and the sightseeing exploration is a large part of the experience. Or taken to a further extreme, a *Final Fantasy* game where the story is huge, and pages of expository dialogue carve out the world and character in exquisite Tolkienesque detail. RPG people want the story front and center. They love that. They pay for that. In contrast, many FPS players pay for action, action, and more action, with a little story thrown in on the side. Of course, there's a whole spectrum in between. But remember, all conventions are meant to be stretched and all rules are meant to be broken. As Robert McKee states, "It's about form—not formula."

— E. Daniel Arey (Creative Director, Naughty Dog Studios/SCEA)

City of Players?

In *City of Heroes* (pictured), players become superheroes and can work together to defeat evil. Players earn hero powers throughout the game, and they may play cooperatively to rid the city of villains. Players may also fight villains individually but may not be successful. If a player is tired of doing good all of the time, he or she can now work with other villains to defeat good in the upcoming game, *City of Villains*.

NCsoft

Chris Avellone on Genres & Story Expectations:::::

Chris Avellone (Chief Creative Officer & Lead Designer, Obsidian Entertainment)

Chris Avellone wanted to make computer role-playing games (RPGs) ever since he saw one of his friends playing *Bard's Tale 2* on a Commodore. He went to the College of William and Mary where he got a piece of paper that claims he has a Bachelor's degree in English. He started writing a bunch of short stories and RPG material after graduation—some of which got published. (Most of it didn't.) The submissions that were accepted were enough to get him hired at Interplay, and he worked there for 7-8 years before co-founding Obsidian Entertainment with a bunch of other ex-Interplayers and ex-Black Islanders who'd also worked there a long time. Chris has worked on *Starfleet Academy, Die by the Sword, Conquest of the New World, Red Asphalt, Planescape: Torment, Fallout 2, Icewind Dale 1, Icewind Dale: Heart of Winter, Icewind Dale: Trials of the Luremaster, Icewind Dale 2, Baldur's Gate: Dark Alliance, Lionheart, Champions of Norrath, and Star Wars Knights of the Old Republic II: The Sith Lords.* He is currently a designer on *Neverwinter Nights 2* Chris' mom still isn't exactly clear on what he does on a day-to-day basis, and neither is he.

Players expect an engaging story when playing role-playing games (RPGs). When players encounter characters with depth and hidden agendas, come across interesting plot elements (and twists), and experience a rich game world with lots of backstory, they are challenged to think at a higher level while playing. Suddenly an NPC you meet isn't just someone who gives you a quest. You have to figure out how and why he wants you to do it; what the consequences might be morally, reputation-wise, and financially; and what impact the quest may have on the game world itself. In RPGs, there's much more time to experience the story at your own pace. Players can explore, speak to anyone in the game world, and generally ease their way into their new environment. Players are much more tolerant of cut-scenes, slower pacing, slow introduction of information (and a lot more of it), and plenty of side quests and other "detour" elements.

Those who play first-person shooters (FPSs) usually have much less patience for the presentation of story, so it's best to communicate the story and background in a way that never slows down the action or impedes the character's movement. In an FPS, the information can be communicated through voice recordings, ghostly images, or other means that never slow down the action or get in the way of the shooting and killing.

As for adventure games, the story's the thing. It's very linear, and there's one way to solve it—putting the right object in the right place, asking a character in the game the right question, or solving the right puzzle to get the next element of the story that carries you on to the next challenge.

Simulation & Sports

Just as the name implies, *simulation* games simulate real-life experiences using real-world rules. Of the many applications of simulations, two lead the market: vehicle and sport. Vehicle simulations emulate complicated machinery and are a first-person experience. Sports games simulate real-world games such as football, basketball, or baseball, and are almost always from a third-person point-of-view. Many sports games showcase real-world sports figures such as John Madden to sell the game.

Simulations also emulate real-world experience in games such as *Sim City*. Many simulation games are also used as "serious games"—which offer training to people such as medical emergency personnel and the military, as well as offer teaching games that promote and advance societal change. (In fact, the Serious Games Summit, held in Washington, DC every fall, maintains that an entirely new market has emerged that is largely associated with simulation games.)

Electronic Arts

Neversoft Entertainment/Activision

Sim City and even sports games such as *Tony Hawk* can be considered "simulation" games because they simulate real-world processes.

Sheldon Pacotti on Game Genres::::

Sheldon Pacotti (Game Designer, Secret Level)

Sheldon Pacotti currently works as a game writer/designer. His most well-known project, *Deus Ex,* has come to be regarded as the PC Game of the Year for 2000, winning that award from over 35 publications. It also won many awards for the story and the writing, including awards from IGN and GamersPulse. The sequel, *Invisible War,* released in 2003, has likewise won many awards, including Best Story of 2003 from IGN and a nomination for Best Writing at the IGDA Developer's Choice Awards. His most recent project is *America's Army: Rise of a Soldier.*

Genre is a necessary evil in any cultural marketplace. It's the way consumers make sense of what would otherwise be a bewildering range of products. You can work against genre but never without genre, in games or in any other medium. I don't feel that genres hurt game stories; *games* hurt game stories—by narrowing a player character's scope of action, range of emotion, and sense of possibility. We don't ever ask "What was the 'game story' of *Civilization*?" Nor do we say, "Wow, Will Wright wrote a great 'game story' when he made *The Sims*." That's because the games that "do storytelling" well don't tell stories; they create spaces of possibility. We won't be concerned about cheesy genre video game stories anymore when the games themselves stop borrowing stories from other media and begin creating their own.

Turn-Based Strategy (TBS)

Turn-based strategy is defined by an interval that gives the player time to think strategically before making important decisions. In TBS games, resource management is essential and involves decisions such as what types of resources to create, when to deploy them, and how to use them to the greatest advantage. The ability to take time in making decisions offers great appeal to players.

:::::*Alpha Centauri:* Enhancing a Strategy Game with Story

Stories are uncommon in turn-based strategy games—but Firaxis' *Alpha Centauri* was especially enhanced by its story. The game used an interesting method of telling its tale. Whenever a new technology was researched or a building was purchased for the first time, an audio quote from one of the game's characters was played. Through these snippets alone, which were well voice-acted, the game managed to create interesting characters and an intriguing story that provided unusual depth for a strategy game. Though certainly many other games, particularly some RPGs, have more engrossing stories, I feel that *Alpha Centauri* is a terrific example of using story to enhance the player's experience.

Firaxis Games

— Kevin Saunders (Lead Designer, Obsidian Entertainment)

Firaxis Games

Sid Meier's Gettysburg is a strategy game with a military backdrop.

Strategy

Strategy games involve managing resources in order to win. Strategy games are either turn-based or real time. Often, many of these games deal with military strategy as the mechanic, but, more often than not, the backdrop is a historical event or war.

When thinking about a strategy game, consider what experience you are trying to create. Since turn-based strategy offers different experiences for the player, let's take a look at both.

Lucien Soulban on Story Elements in All Genres:::::

Lucien Soulban hails from the paper-and-pen role-playing industry where he wrote and co-wrote over 80 books and helped launch three role-playing games including White Wolf's award-winning *Orpheus.* Lucien wrote the script for Relic Entertainment's *Dawn of War* and *Winter Assault,* as well as A2M's *Chicken Little and Kim Possible 3 & 4.* February 2005 also saw the release of Lucien's first novel, *Blood In, Blood Out.* Lucien is now a scriptwriter for Ubisoft Montreal.

Lucien Soulban (Scriptwriter & Novelist, Ubisoft Montreal)

Most role-playing games (RPGs) tell stories on a global or epic scale and how one's character becomes a lynchpin in those events. In this case, RPGs encourage storytelling through the journey of one character. We discover the world and ourselves at the same time the character does. As the character evolves, we cheat to quantify that growth through the discovery of new powers or acquisition of pets and allies.

The same can't be said for most first-person shooters (FPSs)—notwithstanding a few gems—which literally plant you in the head of the character, but not in the mindset. In an FPS, the main character is often faceless—a blank slate for the player to overwrite. Story in these situations is often badly handled because the player may grow frustrated with what the character does or says—or the player simply remains detached from the hero. Stories in FPSs are thus seen and treated (especially by companies) as placeholders for action sequences.

The interesting stories are those told for real-time strategy (RTS) games. There seem to be two versions of the story in most RTS cases: one told on the macro-battlefield scale that treats armies/nations/planets as characters, and another one told in the cut-scenes between the characters leading the aforementioned factions. The opportunity to tell deep and enriching stories is far greater in RTSs than RPGs—simply because the RTS automatically provides two layers of story, and thus two levels of personality to the characters themselves. The character is no longer as lost in the world as he might be in RPGs. The character is a force to be reckoned with and thus engaging to players.

Real-Time Strategy (RTS)

Real-time strategy offers real-time action. When making strategic decisions, the element of restricted time offers a more realist sense of action. For example, if you were a general in a war and had to make strategic decisions regarding your attack, the enemy might not allow you to take your time to make the best choice. Rather you would have to make the best choice given your current time constraints.

::::: Can Strategy Go Beyond War and History?

There are other settings and stories that could use strategy. A fantasy world might provide interesting story elements, or perhaps a sci-fi setting. For example, a lunar colony might have limited resources such as oxygen that players would have to manipulate in order to survive. Everyday we are faced with issues of time and resource management that could be exploited for compelling game stories.

Maxis/Electronic Arts

The *Sims* uses everyday time issues and management problems to fill out the story for the characters. This is a great example of how strategy games do not have to be military games.

Kevin Saunders on Genre-Specific Storytelling :::::

Kevin Saunders programmed his first game, a 'port' of Intellivision's *Astrosmash,* on a ZX81 at the age of six. His official career as a game designer evolved from his graduate research in environmental engineering. This research included lab experiments that required 24-hour monitoring over two- to three-day periods. These lengthy experiments gave Kevin the time to explore the world of online games and led to an opportunity to work on Nexon's *Nexus: The Kingdom of the Winds,* which launched in 1998 and became one of the world's earliest massively multiplayer online games (MMOGs). Kevin subsequently designed and produced *Shattered Galaxy,* the world's first massively multiplayer online real-time strategy (MMORTS) game. Kevin worked as a Game Designer at Electronic Arts (*Command & Conquer Generals: Zero Hour* and *The Lord of the Rings: The Battle for Middle-earth*). He is currently at Obsidian Entertainment, as Senior Designer on *Knights of the Old Republic II: The Sith Lords,* and is now Lead Designer on an undisclosed project. Kevin earned his Master of Engineering degree from Cornell University.

Kevin Saunders (Lead Designer, Obsidian Entertainment)

Different genres entertain players in different ways. Though the word "genre" means something different when applied to movies, I believe the term is similar in this regard. Sometimes the moviegoer is interested in a comedy, or a horror movie, or a drama. Though these genres have similarities, movies of each kind typically tell their stories in different ways.

Similarly, sometimes the gamer is interested in a first-person shooter (FPS), role-playing game (RPG), or real-time strategy (RTS) experience. Much like movie genres, each game genre has its own appeal—its own way in which it provides entertainment. Therefore, each game genre is best complemented by a certain type of storytelling. For example, one appeal of an FPS is fast-paced action—so any story in an FPS must be designed to support that type of gameplay. In general, however, the method of storytelling used depends more on the specific flavor of the game itself rather than its genre. *Doom 3* and *Far Cry* are both FPS games, but the latter has a story while the former doesn't particularly. Both were well-received by players.

If you want to explore a story idea that includes the elements of strategy, look into this genre. It offers exciting game and story possibilities that will remain at the heart of games!

While there are many different ways to exploit story through game genres, try to find a genre that conveys what you are trying to say as a developer. This will help to make the most of each genre and make the playing experience more fulfilling for both game developer and player.

In this chapter we've learned about the many types of game genres that can be used in storytelling and how each might support a particular type of gameplay. Now that we have an understanding of what game genres are available, let's take a look at how all stories are built and how they might be integrated into game-story design.

:::CHAPTER REVIEW:::

1. Each popular game genre incorporates certain elements that might be used in a "template" for other games in that same genre. Choose a popular game genre (such as FPS, RPG, RTS, action-adventure, simulation, or sports) and discuss five features that apply to all games across that genre.

2. Most game genres reflect style of play rather than setting or storyline. Choose a genre that is usually associated with film (such as science fiction, romantic comedy, film noir, mockumentary, western, military drama) and come up with a game storyline that reflects that genre. What elements would you incorporate into your game that could be used in a "template" for your chosen genre for subsequent games?

3. Some game genres have adopted new characteristics over the course of game-development history. In fact, the newer adventure games (some of which are included in the action-adventure genre hybrid) do not share much with the classical adventure game genre. Some players have asserted that the new incarnation of the genre has focused on visual impact and repeated reflexive keystrokes at the expense of in-depth storylines. How has the adventure genre evolved over the years? Discuss three characteristics that have changed, and three characteristics that have remained the same. How can classic adventure game elements be brought back into newer adventure games while keeping the genre fresh?

4. You've learned about several genres in this chapter. It's time to test your game genre knowledge while creating something new! First, combine two genres discussed in the reading to create a new hybrid (mixed) genre. What type of game would you create for this new genre? List five unique features of the game and discuss what would motivate players to try your game. Next, create a brand new game genre that is distinct from those discussed in the reading. What type of player might be interested in playing a game in your genre? Finally, take a pre-existing game and change its genre. Discuss its original and "new" genre—and determine what features you would need to change in the game in order to accommodate this new genre.

5. Play and analyze a digital game for at least four hours. Rate the game on a scale from 1 to 10—with 10 being "perfect." Include the following in your analysis: title, development studio, publisher, genre, player mode (single or multiplayer?), intended audience (type of player), rating, story structure, and character development. Does the story have dramatic impact? Do you as a player have any perceived control over the storyline? How do the story elements add or detract from the game's "fun factor"? What suggestions would you make for improvement?

CHAPTER 3

Building Your Story:

how to construct a story from concept to execution

Key Chapter Questions

- What is a concept, and where does it come from?
- How does context work in terms of story, and why is it important?
- What is the significance of a premise, backstory, and synopsis?
- What are some common philosophical themes used in games?
- How do game stories differ from traditional stories?

Coming up with story ideas may be easy for some people and difficult for others. The idea may come from a philosophical belief. It may come from a "what if" type of concept. It may even come from Aunt Fanny's second husband and his affinity for blown glass horseshoes—in which case it might be a character-driven story. There are stories all around us, every day. We read them, we watch them, and we experience them. Sometimes they can come from looking at the world in an entirely different way—such as from the point of view of an ant, as in the movie *A Bug's Life*—or from going into the mind of enemies, as in the recent game *Psychonauts*. Stories can be small and quirky or they can be big and explosive. They can be about real people or superheroes—but, most importantly, they are usually about what the writer thinks, believes, and feels. Stories are always about what the writer feels he or she *must* say. In short, stories, as well as games, are about the passions of the creators. The following pages offer ways to start getting those stories up on their feet and out into the world.

Concept

A *concept* is an abstract thought or generic notion generalized from a particular area. It is the very first kernel of an idea. It can be as simple as a single word or a drawing. It is the conception, the beginning, the first step on your way to a story—and it is usually the device that keeps the story moving.

Story Engine

The *story engine* is the vehicle that drives the concept through the story. The concept is the fuel for the engine. A common writer's mistake is to use a gag or vignette and assume it illustrates an entire story when it does not. This attempt at a story fails because there is not enough of a concept to fuel the story engine. In a game, the story engine is important because it needs to illustrate the entire story while supporting the gameplay.

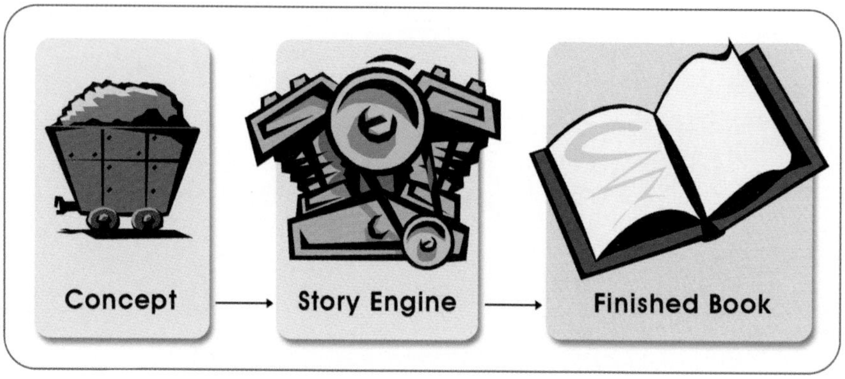

Per Olin

Hard-Coded for Storytelling

In the past, games were first an innovation oddity, then a fad, then a pastime, and now a mainstream entertainment medium. As we have expanded our market to encompass the larger audience, we have added to the experience by creating more engaging scenarios that mimic other art forms that our audience expects and understands. This has inevitably led to stories taking a stronger central role.

But I feel it goes deeper than that. Humans crave stories as a means of understanding and learning. It is coded into our DNA. Storytelling provides reason, context, meaning, and a framework for making sense of the world around us. It was only a matter of time before games demanded the same framework. In games these stories provide meaning for the actions we take on screen, and this leads to a much deeper emotional experience.

Storytelling in games adds layers of complexity just below the surface. Like a fine wine, good narrative adds nuance that enhances—if only subliminally—the total experience for the player. In the end, stories provide logic, cause, and effect—and that magic energy of pathos that is the human experience.

— E. Daniel Arey (Creative Director, Naughty Dog Studios/SCEA)

The following are a few concepts from popular television series and movies:

1. A prototypical villain who is really a hero
2. Point of view from a sea creature
3. Cheerleading superhero

Recognize any of these concepts? While they might sound familiar, they could be any number of stories because the concept, at first, covers a broad canvas. Once we have the concept, it's time to start developing it into a fuller concept called a *springboard*.

Springboard

In the world of television animation, it is typical for a writer to be asked to come up with several *springboards*—simple ideas that can be developed further. A springboard is usually used for an episode of an established show but can also be a way of generating ideas. For our purposes, we will use the term to further the concepts mentioned above:

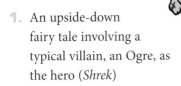

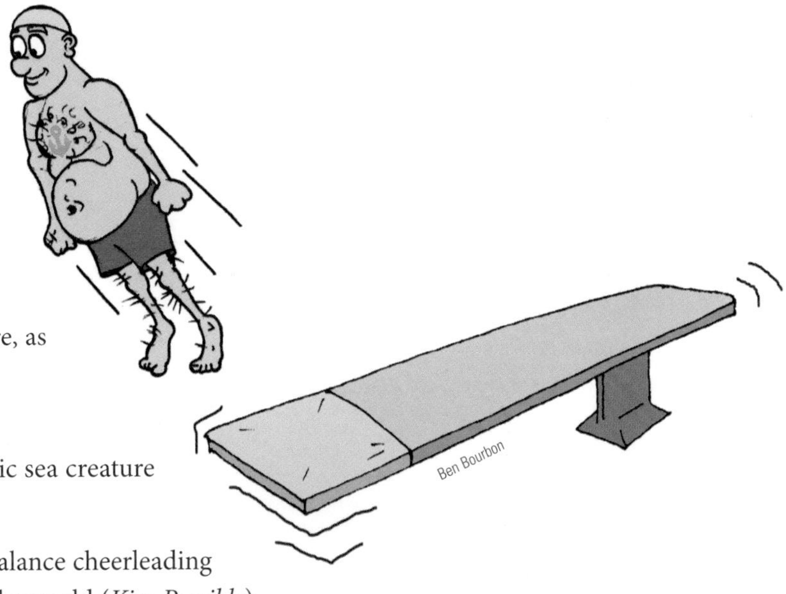

1. An upside-down fairy tale involving a typical villain, an Ogre, as the hero (*Shrek*)
2. The adventures of an irrepressibly optimistic sea creature (*SpongeBob*)
3. A teenage spy must balance cheerleading practice with saving the world (*Kim Possible*)

How to Generate a Springboard

Think of several games you haven't seen that you would like to develop and play. Take about 5 minutes and write down 5-10 springboards. While you may not like all of them, there are bound to be a few that you will want to investigate further.

Even though these concepts are for animated television and film projects, springboards can also be used for game ideas. Coming up with ideas like this is similar to brainstorming. Springboards, however, tend to be directed, specific, single ideas.

Setting

The setting is the world in which the story takes place. The world itself can be as robust as Harry Potter's Hogwarts or as stark as Mad Max's Australia, but either way, the setting should feed the narrative in subtle yet concrete ways. For example, *Mad Max* takes place in a future, post-apocalyptic world where the cordiality of civilization is gone. The setting is a desert, a barren environment where only the very toughest survive. The stark backdrop contributes to the story as much as the characters do. In games, where sometimes characters do not exist, setting becomes an essential part of the storytelling process.

BioWare Corp.

The lush gardens in the Imperial City add to the rich setting of *Jade Empire.*

> I like video game stories that make me feel like I am a part of a place bigger than myself—when I look around and see and hear a world that is nothing like my own. *The Legend of Zelda, Star Wars: Knights of the Old Republic,* and the *Oddworld* series are examples of this. Each of these games has stories that take twists and turns and engulf you in them.
>
> — *Kofi Jamal (Game Art & Design student)*

Suspension of Disbelief

Suspension of disbelief means that the creator of the story or game must make the audience or player forget the rules of real-world logic. For example, when we see Superman fly, we are suspending our rational thinking in order to enjoy the pleasures of the story. This is more difficult to achieve than it seems—because even within fantasy worlds there are still rules to which the characters and players must consistently adhere.

The setting can be realistic and mimic real-world rules—or there can be suspension of disbelief, as in the setting for *The Lord of the Rings.* In some cases, suspension of disbelief combines with realistic elements—such as in the game and the movie *Spiderman,* a real-world setting that includes a fantastic hero and surreal circumstances.

Spiderman: Fantasy & Reality?

While the characters in *Spiderman* cause the audience to suspend disbelief, the world itself offers familiar real-world appeal. This combination of fantasy and reality gives the audience an element of the extraordinary within the confines of the mundane. The delicate balance of the Spiderman world is especially interesting because it is important for the audience to accept that even in our everyday lives there is the possibility for the extraordinary. Another benefit from this dualistic setting is that the stakes are personal and often involve everyday people such as ourselves. In the films or in the game, the audience or players can identify with these everyday situations, therefore making the experience more compelling. When you are thinking of stories in general—and especially stories for games–consider your setting and how it supports story, game and what you as a creator are trying to say.

When you consider setting, you must also consider the context of the story. Let's say that you want your game or story to take place in ancient Rome. If so, we must understand what this setting means in terms of the story's context.

Developing a Cinematic Experience

I've yet to experience a game story that moves me anything like a quality movie does. I've never been brought to tears by a game; I've not even been close. Characters tend to be the same: You want to like them, but they are just not "alive" yet—and they *always* break the suspension of disbelief, bumping into stuff or getting stuck on stairs. I think when we get better acting, dialogue, and scores working together (like in movies), we will get a much richer emotional ride.

— David Perry (President, Shiny Entertainment)

Context

The *context* of a story has a direct effect on the story, so let's begin with learning the definition of context.

In Hollywood, budding screenwriters are often told to follow the "party rule" when writing a scene: "Come late. Leave early." For example, if the relevant information of the scene doesn't happen until after a character walks through a door and has eaten a bag of chips, then don't write the character coming in and having a bag of chips and waiting to get to the important part of the scene. Start writing the scene after the last chip has been eaten.

Ben Bourbon

This guest doesn't know the "party rule"!

Ben Bourbon

The same goes for ending a scene. Do not have characters linger in the scene. Get out as quickly as possible after the pertinent information is revealed. This is good advice, especially when writing within the tight confines of a screenplay and especially important when writing informative scenes within games. However, the reason this rule works so well has to do with context—which briefly explains what happened before as well as what might happen after. If we are watching a movie and we see a big guy with a big knife hide behind a door—and then we see a woman come through the door—we might naturally assume that the big guy with the big knife has mal intent planned for the next scene.

If the pertinent elements in the scene are…

- Big guy
- Big knife
- Woman
- Doorway

…then the sequence might play out like this:

```
INT. KITCHEN - NIGHT

In a kitchen, a MAN rummages though drawers. He
finds a big knife. The noise of a car pulling
into the driveway chases the man behind the
kitchen door as he quickly douses the lights.

                                        CUT TO:

EXT. DARK HOUSE - NIGHT

A WOMAN, just returning from a hard day's
work, gets out of her car. She looks to the
dark house, pausing a moment as if she feels
something isn't right.

                                        CUT TO:

INT. KITCHEN - NIGHT

The Man with the knife lies in wait behind the
door. He breathes heavily.
```

CUT TO:

EXT. DARK HOUSE - NIGHT

The Woman walks in through the kitchen door . . .

In the last scene of this sequence, where the woman walks into the kitchen, the audience knows there is a man behind the door with a knife. We know that he is not there to fix the plumbing. We know from the previous scenes that the woman is in peril.

Now let's take a quick look at the same elements of the scene in a different context.

INT. KITCHEN - NIGHT

A MAN fishes through a drawer, finally pulling out a big knife. He goes to the refrigerator and grabs some carrots. He starts chopping the carrots when suddenly he hears a car pull into the drive. Quickly he douses the lights.

CUT TO:

EXT. DARK HOUSE - NIGHT

A WOMAN, just retuning from a hard day's work, gets out of her car. She looks to the dark house, pausing a moment as if she feels something isn't right.

CUT TO:

INT. KITCHEN - NIGHT

The Man puts the knife down, lights some candles on a small cupcake, and hides. He looks back to the table with the cupcake, sees the knife, and grabs it.

CUT TO:

EXT. DARK HOUSE - NIGHT

The Woman walks in through the kitchen door...

Due to the context of what we saw the man doing with the knife, we certainly wouldn't expect him to be capable of mal intent. In fact, this is probably a romantic situation where in the third scene of the sequence the woman will walk through the door and be surprised by her boyfriend's attempt at a romantic birthday dinner. Same basic elements; completely different context.

The broader sense of the entire piece can also be covered by context. If the historical context is World War II in Berlin and we know a character is Jewish, then we can assume that the character is in danger of being taken away by German officers of the Third Reich because we understand story in the context of history.

Context is used to center the audience. If you were watching a movie about Spartacus, the Roman slave who led a revolt against the empire, you would never expect to see Spartacus pull out an AK-47 assault riffle and start mowing down the Roman guard. It would be out of context and would in fact change the meaning of your story. If you want your story to be about alternative realities or time travel, then it might be fun to give Spartacus an advanced weapon, but it would no longer be a story about the ancient Roman Empire.

Midway

The context of the game *Area 51* comes from the the urban legend surrounding the real-world Area 51.

The concept of context exists in all stories—even in game story. Back in the first chapter, we briefly touched on urban legend. In the game *Area 51*, the context comes from the urban legend surrounding the mythical Area 51. Urban legend says that Area 51 is the infamous research facility in which the United States government houses aliens from other planets, as well as myriad of information on all things supernatural. Even though the game setting is science fiction, a player of *Area 51* will understand the context of the story and can expect to see many of the myths of Area 51 come to life in the game. Once we have established the context of a story, it is then that we can start to think about the backstory.

Backstory

Although it is sometimes true that *backstory* is not seen within the confines of story, it is also true that you cannot have a story without a backstory. Wherever your story starts, there is always what happened before. What happened before the dinosaurs? Walking fish. What happened before the walking fish? Swimming fish. What happened before swimming fish? Multi-celled organisms. What happened before

Ben Bourbon

multi-celled organisms? Single-celled organisms. And so on—all the way back to the big bang (or however the universe began), and even that has a backstory; we just don't know it yet.

Let's move up a few million millennia to the day when Julius Caesar crossed the Rubicon. For those of you shy in your historical knowledge of Western civilization: Before Julius Caesar became Emperor of Rome, he was perceived as a threat to the Roman state, the Roman Senate, and Pompey the Great—Caesar's son-in-law and ally-turned-power-hungry-enemy. To confine Caesar's influence within Rome, the Senators forbade Caesar from coming into Italy from the province of Gaul. The barrier they set was in fact the Rubicon River. The story of how Caesar came to power begins the day he crosses the Rubicon and enters Italy with his army. The backstory is one of family, hated enemies, and political intrigue—important elements to the dominant story of war, conquest, and power.

In the case of Julius Caesar, and in all stories, the backstory is relevant because it lets the audience know why Julius Caesar is doing what he is doing. It lets the audience know what kind of obstacles and enemies Caesar will face when he enters the city of Rome. Further, Caesar had just spent the previous five years honing his strategy and hardening his army, offering more backstory. Now the audience also knows not only what our hero is up against, but what he is capable of doing—thus setting the stage for dramatic and dynamic storytelling. While it will be exciting to see the war, elements of character and conflict are dependent on the backstory.

Story without Backstory?

Do you think there is a way to tell a story without backstory? As a simple exercise, try to take two characters and place them in an argument. It can be any two characters—husband and wife, best friends, hated enemies, total strangers, God and the devil. Now give them an argument about anything. Soon you will see the elements of backstory creeping into the argument—even if that backstory occurred just five minutes prior to the meeting of the characters.

Now that we've talked about backstory in terms of classic storytelling and movies, let's take a quick look at how it applies to games.

We use backstory in games the same way you might in a movie, novel, or play—but, rather than informing an audience about a character, backstory informs a player about a situation. In short, it orients the players. It helps them understand what they are capable of (skills and weapons) and what they are up against (enemies and environment).

Firaxis Games

In Sid Meier's game, *Gettysburg*, the year 1863 is the backstory.

In *Gettysburg*, a game created by Sid Meier, the context is the Civil War. The backstory of the game is the United States in the year 1863, and it focuses on the events leading to the three-day battle fought on the rugged terrain around Gettysburg, Pennsylvania. The story and game very specifically focus on the three-day conflict at Gettysburg.

How does backstory affect playing the game *Gettysburg*? During the days leading up to the battle, it is certain that each army, the Union North and the Confederate South, had a given amount of ammunition, men, and food available. What resources they had on the day the battle began has a direct effect on how to play, since the game is one of history, strategy, and resource management.

::::: Backstory Feeds the Story of *Myst*

Cyan Worlds, Inc.

The documents in this scene from *Myst* offer players backstory information that serve as valuable clues to solving the riddle of the game.

In the adventure game *Myst*, the information given from the backstory propels the story and adds intrigue to keep the player moving throughout the game. The backstory, found in several journals and books throughout the game, offers the player a *non-linear* way to explore the story. Interestingly, the mystery the player is trying to solve is more about what has happened on the island of *Myst* over the ages. It is the player's job to use the clues found in the journals and books to complete the game. Although there are many endings possible in *Myst*, there is only one satisfying answer to the story and the game.

In a movie, novel, or play, the backstory is usually told throughout the story. In a game, however, the player needs to be oriented quickly. For this reason, the backstory is often explained on the back of the game's packaging, in the manual, or within an introductory cinematic sequence.

Premise

In any movie theater in the United States, there are movie posters or "one sheets." On these posters are graphics, actors, MPAA ratings, and credits. There is also what is referred to as a "tag line." A tag line is a quick couple of sentences that gives the prospective audience information about the theme or idea behind the movie.

In games, the tag line found on the packaging is called the *premise*. Although the premise can be written from any point of view, a way to actively engage the consumer is by focusing on consumers as players and addressing them in second-person voice. Here are a few examples.

1. *Ratchet and Clank – Up your Arsenal*: Blast away through huge galactic battlefields as you discover new worlds to blow up! Jump into armored vehicles with a teammate or go it alone with all new power-packed weapons.
2. *Ghosthunter*: You are Officer Lazarus Jones of the Detroit Police Department—and a late-night disturbance call leads you to an abandoned school, the site of a gruesome murder spree some 10 years past. What should have been a routine run descends into a disaster of supernatural proportions when hordes of tortured souls are accidentally unleashed. It's now your job to hunt and capture the undead before they achieve their ultimate vengeance on the world of the living.
3. *Prince of Persia – The Sands of Time*: Deceived by the traitorous Vizier, you are led to unleash the Sands of Time curse upon the Sultan's Kingdom. With little but an ancient dagger and a devious princess to aid you, you must undo your fatal error.

This small summary should not only address the player directly, it should also give the player an idea of what the game is about in terms of setting, character, and how the game is played. While this is the official definition of "premise" in the game industry, it does little for us when we are generating ideas into a cohesive story structure. In other words, Alvin Sergeant, writer of *Spiderman 2*, most likely does not think about the tag line for the movie poster. Instead, he thinks about story ideas.

A premise by Hollywood definition is a complete story idea encapsulating some kind of story arc. We will discuss arc later—but suffice it to say, arc is the way a story develops and grows. And yes, there are arcs in games!

Remember the springboards we came up with? Let's see how they might be made into full premises.

1. **Springboard**: An upside-down fairy tale involving the typical villain, an Ogre, as the Hero.

   Premise: A surly and reclusive ogre and his chatty donkey set out to save their forest home. While doing so, the Ogre finds love and lives happily ever after in spite of the fact he is not the typical "Charming" Hero. (*Shrek*)

2. **Springboard**: The adventures of an irrepressibly optimistic sea creatures.

   Premise: A sea sponge who wears pants and hangs out with his best friend, a starfish, engage in wacky misadventures on the ocean floor, as well as on dry land. (*SpongeBob*)

3. **Springboard**: A Teenage spy must balance cheerleading practice with saving the world.

   Premise: Teenager Kim Possible not only must contend with life as a high school cheerleader during the day, but she is also a Super Spy charged with saving the world every night. When will she ever have time for homework? (*Kim Possible*)

Clearly, the premise gives us a more rounded idea of what the story is about. From this more rounded idea, it is much easier to jump into the synopsis.

Synopsis or Treatment

We've considered a springboard, looked at setting and context, determined the backstory, and developed a premise. Now let's dig a little deeper. As your story and game develops, it naturally needs to move into more detail. Technically, in Hollywood and other media, a *synopsis* is a summary of a piece of work after it is written. A summary of the projected work is usually called a *treatment*. To be sure, the terms synopsis and treatment (and even premise), are brandished around quite loosely in Hollywood, and they are often interchangeable. For our purposes, we will use the term synopsis as a document of the projected story of the game. A game synopsis is the fuller detail of the game and story. It includes elements that pertain to how the game is played, but for now let's just concentrate on story.

A story synopsis is a loose document that roughly outlines a story. It can run from just a few to 20-plus pages—but it's best not to add too much detail just yet. All we are trying to achieve in the synopsis is the broad idea of the story, the principle characters, and the major plot points.

Now let's go back to our buddy, Julius Caesar, and break down what the story elements are thus far.

- **Springboard:** A story about Julius Caesar *before* he becomes Emperor of Rome. Perhaps even how he became emperor.
- **Setting:** Italy and Rome.
- **Context:** Ancient Rome.
- **Backstory:** In 71 B.C., Pompey the Great returned victorious to Rome after having put down a threatening rebellion in Spain. At the same time, Marcus Licinius Crassus, a rich patrician, suppressed the slave revolt led by Spartacus. Pompey and Crassus both ran for the consulship—an office held by two men—in 70 B.C. Pompey, who was ineligible for consulship, somehow still managed to win with the help of Julius Caesar. Crassus became the other consul. Ten years later, when Caesar returned to Rome, Caesar joined forces with Crassus and Pompey in a three-way alliance known as the First Triumvirate. Caesar gave his daughter, Julia, to Pompey for marriage—an act of good will—but soon the Roman Senate became leery of Caesar's lust for power. They sent him to conquer Gaul, thereby keeping him out of Rome and Roman politics. When Crassus was killed in battle in 53 B.C., the Senate instated Pompey the Great to rule all of Rome—an idea that did not sit well with the ambitious Julius Caesar.
- **Premise:** Young General Julius Caesar has just crossed the Rubicon and started civil war in the greatest empire of all time, Rome. First family—then hated enemy—Pompey the Great is given the power to control and protect all of Rome because his troops far outnumber those of Caesar's. Permission from the Roman Senate, backed by numerous legions, still prove a difficult match for the ambitious Julius Caesar and no match against the tide of destiny.

Per Olin

Julius Caesar crosses the Rubicon from his intriguing backstory into his personal triumph and world history.

As you can see, there is a clear starting point. There is mention of what Caesar is up against, as well as an allusion to the final outcome. These few sentences offer a full vision of the story. A premise for a game would read basically the same way except from the second-person perspective.

Use of Language

Take note of the language "the tide of destiny," "hated enemy," and "greatest empire of all time." Certainly, you could express these ideas in a more mundane way—without all the exaggeration! The premise, however—whether it is on the back of the box or in a design document—is meant to enthrall, intrigue, and (most of all) sell the idea, story, or game to the prospective player.

- **Game-Style Premise**: You are the young, ambitious General Julius Caesar, and you have just crossed the Rubicon River to start civil war in the greatest empire of all time, Rome. Your hated enemy, Pompey the Great, was given the power to control and protect all of Rome because his troops far outnumber yours. Permission from the Roman Senate, backed by numerous legions, still prove a difficult match for your ambitious nature and no match against the tide of your destiny.

- **Synopsis:** On the foggy banks of the Rubicon River, Julius Caesar, one of the three leaders of Rome, keeps watch at the head of his small legion of soldiers. With a single word, he commands the troops across the water and thus hurls the empire into a turbulent civil war, while civilization itself hangs in the balance. In order to defeat his enemy, Pompey, Caesar acts swiftly and decisively by placing his men throughout Northern Italy—while Pompey gathers his numerous but far-flung legions. City after city is conquered, and town after town falls to Caesar. Many are without resistance until Rome herself lays at risk. Within weeks, the Senate and Pompey evacuate Rome—leaving in their wake the bloody warning that any who stay within the city will be considered Caesar's ally and Pompey's enemy. Pompey's retreat eastward is a strategic one, since his intent is to draw Caesar to Asia where Pompey has many allies in the form of powerful kingdoms. Unfortunately for Pompey, during the scramble to evacuate Rome, he and the senators forget to take the vast amounts of treasure stored under the temple of Saturn. Caesar is quick to discover the plunder, which significantly increases his war purse. For another six months, Caesar relentlessly pursues Pompey—eventually crushing the last of his armies in Spain. The defeated Senate has no choice but to instate Caesar as head consul and dictator of all of Rome.

Naturally, the story of Caesar goes forward all the way until his death, but in this case we are only talking about the civil war as the story.

Bad Endings

If you don't know how the story of Caesar ends, let's just say it isn't pretty. Continually threatened by his power, the Senate eventually assassinates Julius Caesar, and the famous quote, "Et tu, Brute?" ("And you also, Brutus?"), is uttered. From this bloody act of violence, the empire again goes into turbulent battle with characters such as Brutus, Octavius, and Marc Anthony—making even more material for dramatic, engaging stories.

The above synopsis follows history pretty accurately, but let's not forget: the fun of stories is the fiction of stories. If you wanted to tell a story about an alternate reality in the Roman Empire—one where the slave Spartacus does indeed have an AK-47 assault rifle—then that context would be written in the synopsis.

Now that we have a synopsis—the basic story document—the next item we need to assess is the theme.

Theme

Ben Bourbon

A story about war might include a theme about the desire for power and the horrors of human conflict.

Before you even start thinking about context, backstory, or story, you might feel that you want to write a story about a particular theme. A theme is what the story is really about. For the purposes of this exercise, let's assume you want to write about war—what war means on different levels, and who it affects. Maybe it's a commentary on the politics of war, where old men talk while young men die. Maybe your commentary isn't against war but rather about the sorrows of war—and how war is an unfortunate but sometimes necessary event in the course of human history marching toward emancipation. Whatever your opinion, whatever you want the story to be about, that is your theme—and you can aim toward that theme before you even put one word on paper.

As you write, something interesting starts to happen. The story begins to tell you what it's about rather than you imposing your opinion on the story. While this may feel like you are losing control of what you want, it is actually a very good sign—because it means the story is alive, active, and kicking. You may have wanted to write a story about war, so you'll choose to make your point through the backdrop of the Roman civil war. A story about war taking place against history's most bloody and war driven society is a good idea, but you may soon realize that the real story is about power. All of the characters in your story want power. When they achieve power, it begins to change and corrupt them. Then you start to write toward a theme that is about power. Again, it changes into a story about control. Ultimately you may realize through your story that there is no such thing as control—because destiny will unfold in spite of our greatest efforts, and there you have it: a story of Julius Caesar becomes a story about destiny.

Playwright and director David Mamet once said that you write your first draft about something you choose. Then during the process, you figure out it's about something altogether different. Your next draft will then be about that altogether different topic—but it too becomes about something different. This process continues on until you truly understand what you are trying to say and what your story is really about for you, the characters, and the audience.

This may sound daunting. But just as you feel you have lost complete control of your story, you will figure out what you are really trying to say—finally wrangling its elements to create a great story with a clear and concise theme.

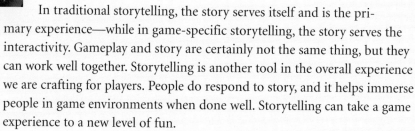

Gordon Walton on Storytelling as a Game Development Tool :::::

Gordon Walton has been authoring games and managing game development since 1977. His most recent position was Vice President and Executive Producer for *Star Wars Galaxies* and an unannounced project at Sony Online Entertainment. Prior to joining Sony Online Entertainment, Gordon was Vice President and Executive Producer of *The Sims Online* at Electronic Arts/Maxis, and also at Origin Systems managing *Ultima Online*. He also served as Senior VP of Kesmai Studios, where he oversaw the development of *Air Warrior* and *Multiplayer Battletech*. Gordon has owned and managed two development companies and has been development manager for Three-Sixty Pacific and Konami of America. He has personally developed over 30 games and has overseen the development of hundreds more.

Gordon Walton (Consultant & Producer)

In traditional storytelling, the story serves itself and is the primary experience—while in game-specific storytelling, the story serves the interactivity. Gameplay and story are certainly not the same thing, but they can work well together. Storytelling is another tool in the overall experience we are crafting for players. People do respond to story, and it helps immerse people in game environments when done well. Storytelling can take a game experience to a new level of fun.

Traditional Structures

Traditional story structure is very popular when writing screenplays. It is a time-tested technique that, when applied properly, offers solid story results. Unfortunately, there are elements to storytelling that are intangible, and even when a writer follows the rules, the results can sometimes be lackluster. Even so, one thing that all good stories have in common is a solid structure. Let's take a quick look at some of the different structures used today.

Three-Act Story Structure

Many in the "indie" film camp refer to the three-act story structure as "formula" —and formula is viewed as negative. While the concept behind a formula is to produce several products that are consistently of high quality, anyone who has spent time looking over movies in a video store knows that the quality of movies is any-

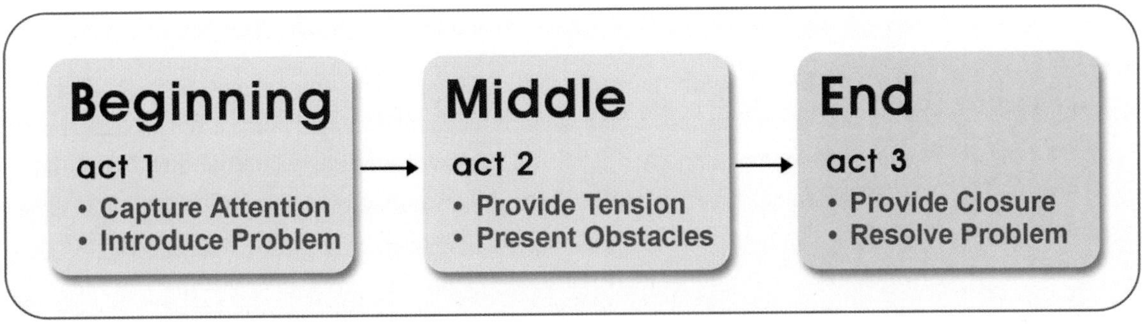

Per Olin

The three-act structure is what is commonly used in Hollywood feature films.

thing but consistent. Some films use structure well, while others fail miserably. The nature of writing and creating a movie is far more complex than a simple formula. Furthermore, if one were to analyze a blockbuster film against a good independent film, there would still be a definable structure. Some argue that films such as *Pulp Fiction* and *Memento* break from structure, but they don't really. They are very clever in their disguise of it, but it is still there. The following are the basics of what the three acts cover:

Beginning **(Act 1):** The beginning of a story introduces the main characters, usually the hero (protagonist) first. Act 1 should also set up allies, the villain (antagonist), and the world where the main character lives. Most importantly, the first act establishes the hero's problem and goal. By the end of the act, the hero is faced with a choice or placed in a completely different situation than where he has been before.

Middle **(Act 2):** As the character begins to adjust to his newfound situation, he faces obstacle after obstacle—usually set into place by the villain. These obstacles keep the hero from solving his problem and achieving his goal. This act is where the bulk of the story is told and where the character experiences the personal growth needed to solve the problem and accomplish the goal. The middle act is different than the first or the third act because it is twice as long—usually about 60 pages—and it deals with character growth and story plot. Therefore, it is a difficult act to negotiate for a lot of writers.

End **(Act 3):** The story ends when the character achieves the goal and solves the problem–but in the interim, something else has happened. He or she has changed for having had the experience. This is character arc—something we will talk about later. For now, Act 3, from a strictly structural point of view, is where the characters and story reach a new equilibrium—a new balance and a new life.

Three-Act Structure in *Ms. Pac-Man*

Namco's *Ms. Pac-Man* incorporated a familiar idea from movies: the three-act structure. The game uses mini-movies that appear between game levels to "reward" players for completing each level. The story follows Pac-Man and the soon-to-be Ms. Pac-Man as they meet (boy meets girl), chase (boy loses girl and attempts to get her back), and eventually have baby Pac (obviously, boy got girl back). While fun to watch, *Ms. Pac-Man* dictates a predetermined story. The story disrupts the experience as the player momentarily must watch rather than play the game.

Three-act structure has been used for many years and does provide an overview of what is needed within a screenplay. However, the three-act structure is only one way to look at structure, and when you are writing your story—especially a story for a game—it is helpful to look at other structures as well.

The Hero's Journey

Joseph Campbell's The Hero's Journey offers another storytelling structure. This classic story theory applies to many storytelling media and looks at how all stories throughout human history follow the same basic patterns. Most commonly seen in screenplay format, Christopher Vogler applies Campbell's Hero's Journey to screenwriting and has instituted.

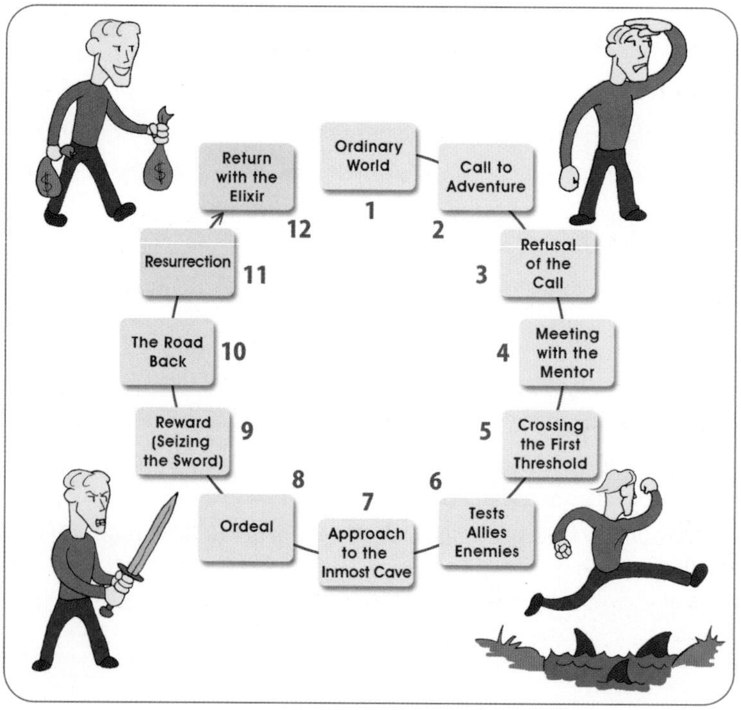

Per Olin

The twelve steps of the Hero's Journey changes the Hero inexorably before his return home.

1. **Ordinary World**: The hero's ordinary world is established. Everyday life and surroundings are introduced.
2. **Call to Adventure**: The hero is introduced to an alternate world and is asked to go on a quest or journey.
3. **Refusal**: The hero refuses the call because he is not willing to sacrifice his comfortable and ordinary surroundings. The hero is uncomfortable, however, with his refusal.
4. **Meeting with the Mentor**: The hero receives information that is relevant to the quest and his need to go.
5. **Crossing the First Threshold**: The hero has abandoned his initial refusal because of the information received. He embarks on the journey, commits to the adventure, and enters the special world.
6. **Tests, Allies and Enemies**: The hero's mettle is tested through a series of challenges. Through this period, the hero meets allies and enemies.
7. **Approach the Innermost Cave**: More tests, a period of supreme wonder and/or terror. Preparations are made for the ordeal.
8. **Ordeal**: The biggest challenge the hero faces thus far. The hero must defeat the "big" villain.
9. **Reward (Seizing the Sword)**: The hero receives a reward. It feels like the end of the story, but it usually isn't!
10. **The Road Back**: Once the Ordeal is over, the hero has the choice to stay in the special world or return to the ordinary world. Most choose to return.
11. **Resurrection**: The Hero must face death one more time in another ordeal known as the climax. It is here where the hero demonstrates that he has been changed by the journey and resurrected into a fully realized person.
12. **Return with the Elixir**: The hero finally returns home, but he is forever changed from the experience. If he is a true hero, he returns with an elixir from the special world that will help those he originally left behind.

The three-act and "hero's journey" scenarios are two basic storytelling structures that are used in film and in other linear media. Unfortunately, they don't offer the variation needed for games and can feel restrictive in the context of a game. For an alternative, let's look to the structure of series television.

Allen Varney on the Unimportance of Traditional Storytelling in Games:::::

Allen Varney (Freelance Writer & Game Designer)

Allen Varney is a freelance writer and game designer in Austin, Texas. In addition to computer game design work for Origin Systems, Looking Glass, and Interplay, he also designed an online business leadership simulation, *Executive Challenge*, which has been utilized by major companies and business schools nationwide. In the paper-and-dice role-playing area, Varney is best known as the designer of the 2004 edition of the classic satirical science-fiction role-playing game, *Paranoia.*

Note: Although the authors feel that traditional storytelling plays an important role in game stories. Allen offers an interesting counter argument.

Storytelling, in the sense we usually understand it, is unimportant to the game experience. A game's exploratory path can include story-like elements such as surprise and a sense of wonder, and it can borrow the tools of film and stories to create them. These elements can produce the same emotional effects they would produce in a good story—the first time you see them. But a good game should be at least theoretically replayable—at which point the player correctly understands these story-like elements as just another type of set dressing.

Stories and games are two different experiences. Good stories and good games both foster a sense of immersion. However, a game's immersion bears only cosmetic similarities to the immersion we feel when lost in a good story. The two brain-states—player and listener—are irreconcilably different. In a game we are active; in a story, passive.

A parallel discussion has proceeded for decades in the science-fiction field: whether good characterization is important to a good science-fiction story. Obviously, no one objects to well-developed characters—but the question is, does deep characterization contribute to the particular virtues of science fiction vs. other genres? Does it have anything to do with the experience, the brain-state you seek in reading a sci-fi story? William Gibson said it seemed "like grafting mosquitoes to wheat plants."

In the same way, the virtues of traditional storytelling are not the virtues of good games—and the two work at cross-purposes.

Episodic

In a network television series, there are usually 22 episodes throughout a season. Each episode uses the same characters and locations but addresses a different story every week. These stories can be totally independent of each other. In the classic comedy series, *Seinfeld*, for example, Jerry, George, Elaine, and Kramer live in small apartments, eat at Monk's Restaurant, and work in Manhattan—but each week they face a new set of problems that are completely different than those of the week before.

Per Olin

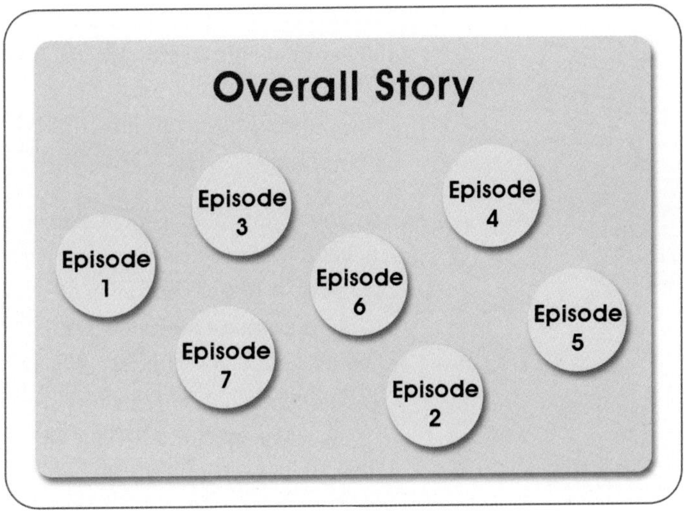

In episodic structure, many small stories can be told while maintaining an overall story.

The Evolution of *Buffy the Vampire Slayer*

In the hit television show *Buffy the Vampire Slayer*, Buffy and her posse of good guys (known as "The Scoobies") had to fight vampires, monsters, and demons every week in a self-contained storyline. In addition, there was usually a single villain plotting end-of-the-world–style domination. Each year of the show the cast of characters had to discover the villain and his evil plot and foil it by the end of the season. Not only did the characters experience growth and change throughout the years, the show was often noted for its great use of literary devices such as theme and metaphor. *Buffy the Vampire Slayer* is an excellent example of how small stories and larger stories can be used simultaneously and provide an alternate to traditional three-act structure.

Alternately, television took on a new way of telling stories with Steven Bochco's *Hill Street Blues*. Using the same approach as writing a novel, not only did each episode have its own standalone story, it also had an overriding story that was addressed each week throughout the season (year). This is known as serialized writing and it freed writers to build more complex and interesting storylines and enrich their stories with vivid, human characters capable of change and growth. Nowadays, most one-hour shows are serialized with—a standalone story for the casual audience and a larger overriding story for the committed audience.

Earlier we referred to the Hollywood structure as being in three acts. In television, acts are thought of differently. At the end of each act, there is a plot point usually in the form of a cliffhanger. The show will go to commercial and come back to reveal how the hero gets out of trouble. Each style of show uses a different format.

:::::: Cliffhangers

A cliffhanger is an ending that is left unresolved, usually with extreme consequences for the hero. It teases the audience to come back next week to see what happens. The name "cliffhanger" came from the film serials of the 1920s and 1930s where the hero was often left hanging by his fingertips on the edge of the cliff, uncertain of his fate. If the audience wanted to see what happened, they would have to return and pay another nickel.

Ben Bourbon

Within this format, the stories are broken down into A-story, B-story, and sometimes a C-runner. In the feature film format, they are called plot and sub-plot, but they are the same thing.

Main storyline (A-story)

The A-story will involve the main characters and take up most of the time. In a police show, they will usually be the "case" the cops are working on.

B-story

The B-story covers secondary, or supporting characters. This helps the flow of the story by allowing implied time to pass between scenes. It also takes the focus off of the main characters. If the story is intense drama, the B-story can add comic relief and relieve the tension.

Per Olin

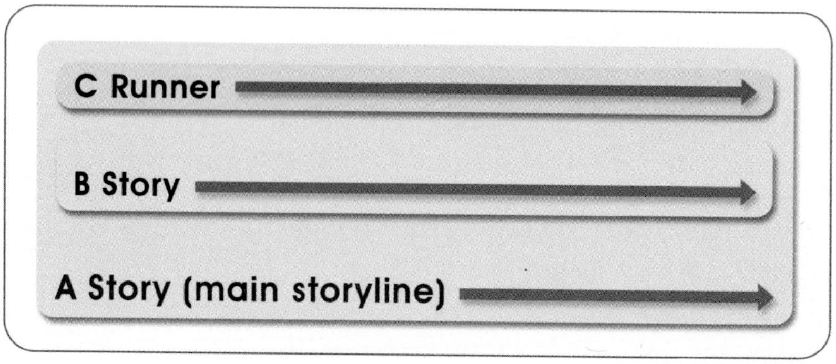

C-runner

A C-runner is usually found in a half-hour situation comedy and is a gag that runs throughout the episode but isn't really a story.

The purpose of looking at television structure is to consider a different way to tell a story and to offer greater storytelling flexibility. When you are writing a story for your game, be sure to consider using more than the typical three acts. Episodic and serialized story structure can offer reliable alternatives to the classic structures and may even be more suitable to game stories.

> *Final Fantasy VII* still remains fresh after all these years in terms of story and characterization. It was one of the first games where these factors came together for me. The complex story and cliffhanger situations kept the purpose for the action in view as did its vivid characterization. . . . Despite other flaws in the overall storyline logic, the characterization created a 'pit bull' of a game that dragged millions of players into its world and kept them through the finale.
>
> *— Howard Kinyon (Game Art & Design student)*

Frank Gilson on the Importance & Role of Game Story::::

At Wizards of the Coast, Frank T. Gilson manages game design and development in the R&D department. Frank Gilson was Producer at Atari's Santa Monica office—managing aspects of third-party development, contracting with talent (such as composers and writers), and overseeing external development. Prior to working at Atari, Frank was Associate Producer at Blizzard for *Warcraft III: Reign of Chaos* and the expansion, *Frozen Throne*. He also worked in Quality Assurance as QA Technical Engineer (*Diablo 2*), QA Lead Analyst (*Starcraft: Brood War*), and QA Analyst (*Starcraft and Mac Diablo*). Prior to joining the game industry, Frank was a graduate student at UC Irvine in Mathematical Behavioral Sciences, studying formal models for economics, voter choice, and psychology.

Frank T. Gilson (Senior Developer for Online Games, Wizards of the Coast)

A modern game needs to get everything right to be a true success. Visuals, sound, gameplay, and story must all be of high quality.

Story is a very important element of a game. It helps to immerse the player in the game experience and keep interest high. Part of the reward for completing a game is experiencing its story. Games that provide the best value for entertainment dollars spent are also replayable. Game storytelling must provide for this kind of 're-reading'.

Games should offer the writer the ability to set a stage, place characters, launch events, and have it *all* react to the player.

Devices for Execution

Earlier in this chapter we looked at the broad strokes of figuring out what your story is about and how to structure it, but the real challenge of storytelling is in its execution. In the following pages, we will look at some storytelling devices that will help you tell a better story.

> *Grim Fandango* is, in my opinion, a near-perfect game story. It plays to the strengths of the medium, immerses the player in the lead character, and really gives the player an emotional connection to what's going on. The first time I played it, I sat there and thought, 'Oh, *this* is what I'm supposed to be doing.'
>
> *— Richard Dansky (Central Clancy Writer, Ubisoft/Red Storm Entertainment)*

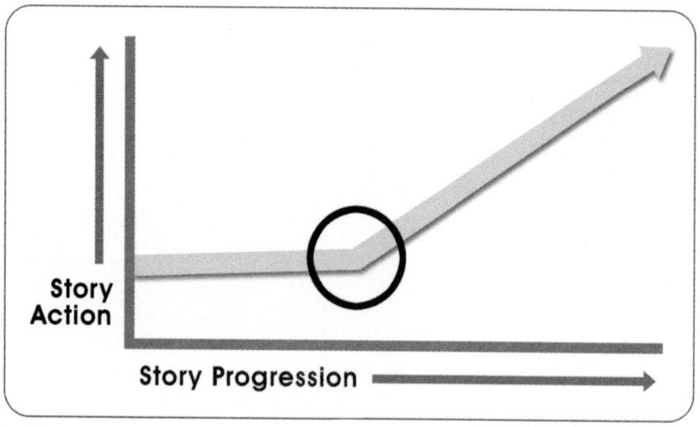

Per Olin

Inciting Incident

In every story there is the one thing—a moment, an action, a line of dialogue—that sets the wheels of the story turning. It is where the story truly begins. The inciting incident defines that one moment. It is the moment the hero is thrust into the story and hopefully irrevocably changed.

Sunset Boulevard and *Silent Hill*: Comparing Inciting Incidents

The film *Sunset Boulevard* starts with the murder of the main character—who also happens to be narrating from beyond the grave. While the murder seems to be what incites the *telling* of the story, the story itself is actually incited by one simple random action—a flat tire. When the lead character, Joe Gillis, gets a flat tire on Sunset Boulevard, he finds his way up to a Beverly Hills mansion to get help. What happens from there becomes the story that will eventually result in his death.

Now let's compare the inciting incident in *Sunset Boulevard* to the inciting incident in the game, *Silent Hill*. When main character Harry Mason takes a late vacation to Silent Hill with his daughter, Cheryl, they arrive late in the evening. Suddenly a shadow appears in front of Harry's car and causes him to crash. When Harry awakens from unconsciousness, Cheryl is gone. While it may seem Cheryl's disappearance is the inciting incident, the actual incident is the shadow that caused them to crash. Because of this, Harry is incited to the action of finding his daughter.

The inciting incident doesn't necessarily have to be in the form of a physical action—which can be as large as an explosion, or as subtle as the glances of the star-crossed lovers in *Romeo and Juliet*. An inciting incident can also occur in verbal or non-verbal dialogue. The look on an actor's face can be as inciting as a spoken line of dialogue. Whatever the writer chooses to use, it must be a single moment that provokes the character to a choice. From the choice comes the action that usually brings another choice—leading to even further action, revealing the plot points and eventually the story.

Earlier in this chapter, we followed the exploits of Julius Caesar. You may think that the inciting incident in that story is Julius crossing the Rubicon. If we go just a little deeper into the backstory, however, we might remember that the reason Caesar crosses the Rubicon is because the Roman Senate instates Pompey the Great as ruler of the empire. This action on the part of the Senate incites Caesar to the choice, then to the action of crossing the river.

Ben Bourbon

Is it the first move that incites action in the game of chess, or the decision of the player to play the game that incites action?

In the game of chess, the inciting incident could be construed as the first piece moved because it incites the game. If no one ever moved the chess piece, then no one would ever play and there would be no game, no conflict, no story. The incident, however, could have happened before moving the first piece. It might be the moment the two competitors meet. It can be a bet. It can be as simple as two friends seeing a chessboard and the sight of it provoking them to sit down and play.

In video games, it appears that the inciting incident is just a matter of the player picking up the device to play. In other words, the player incites play and therefore incites action and story. In a game, the player sometimes has to retrieve something in order to move ahead, and this incites the player to play further. How to make the player pick up the game in the first place is another problem that can be tackled through compelling content. Starting with a good story will help in creating a good game.

Foreshadowing

Sometimes a story will reveal itself through *foreshadowing* coming events. In other words, subtle suggestions will be shown to the audience giving them an inkling of the story that is about to unfold. While it is usually not obvious at the time, the signs will become clear in retrospect.

Midway

The remnants of infected soldiers found in *Area 51* foreshadow things to come.

The reason writers use foreshadowing is to keep the audience interested and to build tension. If a story does not alert the audience that conflict is on the horizon, what keeps them in their seats? How does the tension build? What is the coming disaster? Without the use of foreshadow, the piece will quickly become boring.

Foreshadowing in games can be exceptionally useful because it draws the player into play.

Now that we have provoked action from our hero—and hinted at the problems to come—let's make it even harder for him.

Conflict

Conflict in a story is essential to keep the action moving forward. Sometimes a character may not want to face conflict but will have no choice and therefore will move the action and the story toward its inevitable conclusion. There are several ways to look at *conflict*, but two of the basics are external conflict and internal conflict.

Internal

Internal conflict is usually a psychological deficiency that keeps the character from what he or she really needs. A character may want a million dollars but he may need to be loved. The desire for money becomes about what the character is missing in life. Internal conflict gives us some great movies but not necessarily great games.

Later, we will discuss whether internal conflict is needed in game characters—but let's initially focus on external conflict in stories.

Capcom Entertainment, Inc.

Dante from the *Devil May Cry* series is an internally-conflicted character who is half-demon yet fights for good—not evil.

External

KOEI Co., Ltd.

Combat with enemies in *Samurai Warriors* provides external conflict.

External conflict takes the form of something physical that stops a character from achieving a goal. A minefield between the character and his goal is an example of external conflict. Another person keeping the character from achieving a goal is also external conflict. If a villain places a minefield in front of a pot of gold and the villain knows the hero needs the gold to further his goal, then this is a clear case of external conflict. When the hero finally makes it across the minefield, the villain may physically place himself in front of the pot of gold to keep the hero from getting it. As you can see, conflict is comprised of *desire* on the part of the hero and *opposition* from the villain.

In the game *Donkey Kong*, main character Mario (a carpenter) *wants* to save his girlfriend, Pauline, from the wicked Donkey Kong who has stolen her. Donkey Kong, of course, *opposes* Mario by throwing *obstacles* (external conflict) such as barrels, fire, and springs in the path of Mario. Mario must take *action* either by jumping over the obstacles or by using his weapon, a hammer, to destroy them. As the game progresses, the obstacles don't change but they do increase in pace and volume. To make matters worse, each time Mario gets closer to his *want*, Pauline, Donkey Kong climbs to another level, again *opposing* Mario. Mario, again, must take *action* by climbing to the next level to achieve his want.

After about four levels of this external conflict, Mario finally faces the villain, Donkey Kong, in the final battle over Pauline.

In all stories, external conflict always comes from a *want* that is *opposed*. Therefore, *action* ensues. External conflict *always* manifests in an action. In games, the *want* of the character becomes the *want* of the player. The *opposition*, provided by the villain, becomes the obstacle (external conflict) that the player faces in order to win the game.

Now that we have considered want and opposition being the definition of conflict, let's take a look at what drives those forces.

Unity of Opposites

The *unity of opposites* is usually defined as two characters wanting the same thing. In *Raiders of the Lost Ark*, Indiana Jones (hero) and Belloch (villain) both want the Ark of the Covenant. In this story, both sides are unrelenting. There is no

Three Rings Design

The "unity of opposites" is prevalent in *Puzzle Pirates* because everyone is always fighting over the same booty!

compromise that can be reached. Both characters, because of the unity of opposites, will drive the conflict until there is one resolution.

In games, the unity of opposites can be demonstrated in various ways. In the game *Donkey Kong*, both Mario and Donkey Kong want Pauline.

In the game *Pac-Man*, Pac-Man wants to eat all of the power pills. The ghosts want to stop Pac-Man from eating the power pills. To win and go on to the next level, Pac-Man must consume all of the power pills before being destroyed by the ghosts.

In the MMORPG *Puzzle Pirates*, teams of players go after the same treasure and sometimes compete for each other's ships. Even though the entity competing might be a team of players, the common goal for one team might be the same as the goal for another team.

Another way to demonstrate the unity of opposites is in a typical racing game. Players race cars against each other or the game. There can only be one winner, but all players want the same thing in order to achieve first place in the race.

Using the *unity of opposites* is a great device for both story and gameplay. It keeps the goals focused and the action simple yet compelling. Think about how this device can work in your favor when creating your game story.

Goals

In storytelling, it is always good to allow characters to have specific goals. Rather than have a character say he needs to find his friends, have him say, "I need to find my friends, Goo and Prickle." Further, discuss why they need the specific goal: "I need to find my friends, Goo and Prickle, because they have been kidnapped by the Blockheads." What the character does to achieve the goal becomes the story. In the above-mentioned example from the game *Gumby and the Astrobots*, the main character, Gumby, must find his friends who have been hidden in magical books by the Blockheads. His attempt to find his friends creates the game as well as the story.

In *The Legend of Zelda* series, Link's overall goal is to rescue Zelda—and save the world. In order to achieve this goal, Link must embark on a series of adventures—engaging in battle with many different creatures.

If you provide your character with strong goals, you will be certain to give the player a good game and story experience.

MacGuffin

The "master of suspense," Alfred Hitchcock originally coined the term *MacGuffin*. In a 1966 interview with director Francois Truffault, Hitchcock explained the MacGuffin by recounting the tale of a Scotsman traveling aboard a train with a device–which he called a MacGuffin–for catching lions in the highlands. One of the passengers promptly pointed out that lions do not reside in the Highlands. "In that case," the Scotsman replied, "the device is not a MacGuffin."

Blizzard Entertainment, Inc.

Items found during side quests in games such as *World of Warcraft* are types of MacGuffins.

The MacGuffin is the physical manifestation of a goal and—like the object of a scavenger hunt—the one thing everyone in the story is trying to find. In the movie *The Maltese Falcon*, the MacGuffin is the statue of the falcon. A MacGuffin keeps the eye of the spectator/audience centered, while at the same time giving the characters something to do. It is a plot-enabling device that often means nothing in terms of story but everything in terms of plot. In the same way, the use of the MacGuffin can serve as a function in games and game story by simply giving the player something to do, but a MacGuffin can also be used in a different way. In MMOGs, questing or going after a specific item within the larger world of the game provides the player with a goal. The specific item they are after could be considered the MacGuffin. For example, in the game *World of Warcraft*, a player will be sent on a quest to retrieve an item. Within that quest, a mini-story will unfold as the player goes for the item/MacGuffin. While the quest for the item might be important, the story the player experiences while on the quest is what is satisfying about the game.

Ticking Clock

In order to add immediacy to a story, many writers employ the element of a *ticking clock*. The main character is given an amount of time to reach a goal, usually in the first act. If the character fails to complete the goal in the time allowed, the consequences are often deadly. Think of the movie *Armageddon*. The main characters have to stop the asteroid from hitting earth. Since the asteroid is streaking toward earth at mach speed, this pending disaster imposes its own "ticking clock."

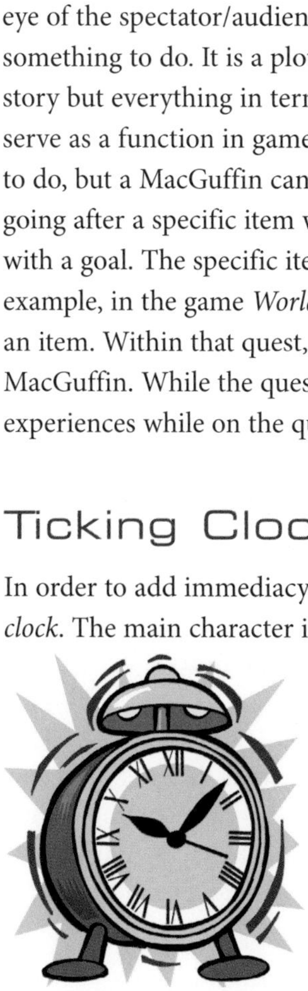

In games, the use of a ticking clock is employed when a player is given only a certain amount of time to complete a task. In Chapter 2, you learned about real-time and turn-based time intervals. The "ticking clock" device introduces a new time interval—known as *time limited*—in which the game (or a portion of the game) is bound by time constraints. Ticking clocks help add to the pace of the story and the game. Use a ticking clock to add tension and drama to your game.

The Problem with Game Story

Story—for the sake of story—does not really have a place in video games unless you can merge the story with the experience. In those cases, you get something very special. But if that is not your aim, then forget trying to tell a story *and* make a game—and instead just *make a great game.* It's a hell of a lot easier to just focus on one task.

Most people do not buy games for a story. They buy games for an experience—and even a fantastic experience with little-to-no story can be more fun and more successful than a story-based game that is not firing on all cylinders. . . . That said, I think story games represent the future of the medium. Right now, we are learning the tools that will let us tell satisfying stories within the interactive structure. Once we master that toolset—and then provide trained authors with it—I feel the audience for games will expand to a more mainstream crowd because the experiences will be emotional and satisfying on a level beyond pure mechanics. But we are not there yet—and, sales-wise, there is no benefit to doing a story-based game. I do them because I love them and feel compelled to do so.

— David Jaffe (Creative Director-Internal Development Studio, Sony Computer Entertainment Santa Monica)

Story versus Plot

A story can be many things. It can be a personal story of how you came to be where you are today. Maybe your family came from another country and your grandfather had to work hard to learn English to send your father to school, where he met your mother, married, and eventually had you. Story can also involve news that follows certain timely events. Let's say a man escapes from jail. He steals someone's car. The cops chase him. He hits a fire hydrant. The streets flood. The interstate is closed for safety reasons, causing you to be stuck in traffic and late for your very first important job interview. When you do finally get to the office, the job has been filled—so in frustration you take to a life of crime and get put in jail, where you meet the guy who caused you to miss out on your very first job.

> Traditional stories thrive on embellishment, while game-specific stories suffer from it.
>
> *— Lucien Soulban (Scriptwriter & Novelist, Ubisoft Montreal)*

A story can be a fictional telling of events. These stories are found in plays, films, television, and games. Although they are fictional, they are often linked to universal truths. What all types of stories have in common is that they are *causal.* Something happens that causes something else to happen.

What's Your Story?

Everybody has a story that they have lived. If you are alive right now then your story continues to grow. Think about your personal story and what, up until this point in your life, it is about. How would you execute it in a fictional story? What might be your theme?

The *personal* story involves how you came to exist: your history. If we gave this story a theme, it might be the benefits of perseverance, the struggle of the American dream, or the gift of the generations that came before.

Now let's take a look at the second example: the *news* story. Although this example is quite ridiculous, think what it might be about. Maybe it's about how we are all interconnected and how one thing, no matter how small, will have a profound effect on something far away and seemingly unrelated.

Both of these examples are stories. They say something, they are about something, and they hopefully mean something.

Plot Points

A plot is not a story. It only serves to help reveal a story. Let's say you have a favorite coat. You want to see the coat, so you hold it up to yourself—but then you can't see it. You choose to put the coat on a hanger so you can look at it without interference. The coat itself is the story while the hanger represents the plot. In other words, the plot is the structure from which you hang the story. If you had no hanger for your coat, it would be a crumpled mess in the corner and you might never see it for all its beauty. If you have no plot, your story will lie in a crumpled mess and no one will ever see it, know about it, or hear what you are trying to say.

The Butterfly Effect

The term "butterfly effect" was coined by MIT mathematician and meteorologist Edward Lorenz as a tenet of "chaos theory." The term was later popularized in Chaos: The Making of a New Science by journalist James Gleick. Originating from an old Chinese maxim, the "butterfly effect" states that "the flapping of a butterfly's wings in China could cause tiny atmospheric changes which over a period of time could affect weather patterns in New York." It is this same idea that defines stories as causal. In good stories and games, the smallest of actions could have significant repercussions later on.

In our story about the criminal, the plot plays out like this:

Ben Bourbon

- First plot point— Criminal breaks out of jail
- Second plot point—Criminal steals car
- Third plot point—Criminal hits fire hydrant
- Fourth plot point—Water floods streets
- Fifth plot point—You get caught in a major traffic jam
- Sixth plot point—You miss job interview
- Seventh plot point—You turn to a life of crime
- Eight plot point—You are arrested
- Ninth plot point—You meet criminal responsible for making you miss your first interview
- Tenth plot point—The two of you begin planning a jail-break

Each plot point builds the story in a particular way and gives direction to the unveiling of the story. While a story is a causal path in its entirety, each point in time that causes further action is a plot point.

In a good story, plot is directed from the character and that character causes the next action based on his personality traits. Julius Caesar, for example, chooses to challenge the legions of Pompey because he is an ambitious man. If he were a slacker who would rather be drinking wine and eating pasta, Caesar would never have become a threat to the Senate, and they would never have tried to stop him, so there may never have been (for better or worse) a line of emperors protecting the cradle of western civilization. We would have long ago been taken over by the barbarians, and life as we know it today might not exist. *Why?* Because of whom Julius Caesar was. He was not a slacker. He was an ambitious man who not only pushed his own story, but that of the entire world.

It is important to recognize that plot points (or plot turns) in a story come from character(s). In games, however, it is vital to recognize that players create plot turns by making choices and applying strategies to address obstacles in their paths. Theoretically, each choice the player makes should create and cause the story. If a player comes to a fork in the road, then he will have to make a choice. From that choice, the plot point is forming the player's own personal story in the game. However, the fork in the road (the challenge or obstacle) is created by the game developer.

Plot Twists

It has been said that plot is the drugged meat the thief tosses to the guard dogs while the house is being robbed. Interpretation: The reader follows the plot, but the experience of the story is what is important. The same can be said for plot twists.

The Plot Thickens

Again, we can use chess to demonstrate story devices in game. In the game of chess, each individual piece that is moved is the plot point created by the player. The whole game, including mistakes, triumphs, and strategy, constitutes the story.

It is the writer's job to guide an audience toward a logical conclusion, but a plot that tells the player, reader, or audience exactly where it is going lacks tension and will find the seats in the theater—or the console controllers—quickly vacated. In a narrative, an author needs to direct the player, reader, or audience, but how do you do this without giving away the satisfying and surprising ending? There are a couple of techniques.

Red Herring

Typically used in mysteries, a *red herring* is a device that is used to take the audience off track. It is a misleading clue or series of clues that leads an audience toward a specific conclusion, but not the right one. Games can use red herrings quite effectively, offering clues that may or may not win the game but will keep the player guessing and moving forward. In the game *Myst*, there are several directions a player can follow via clues left throughout the game, but there is only one right answer and one satisfying ending. These clues act as red herrings in the game.

Ben Bourbon

Reversals

Reversal is often used as a comedic device, but it can work well in all dramatic structure. When a story is going in an expected direction—and the audience knows it is headed in that particular direction—try to think of a completely opposite direction and start to drive the scene away from what is expected. Never let your audience know where you are going until you get there. This keeps the conclusion fresh, clever, and surprising.

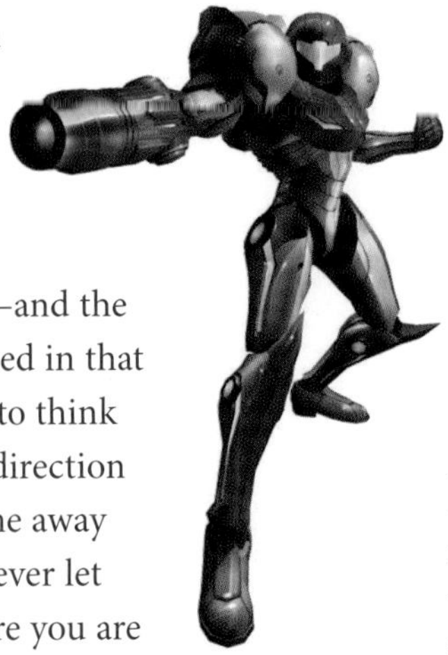

Nintendo of America, Inc.

Nintendo of America, Inc.

In *Metroid*, the player is often surprised to learn the character he or she has been playing is female. This is a good example of how a game element can be a fun and surprising reversal.

Line of Action

Several plot points in a row might make a story, but will it be an interesting story? Here is where plot can help build the dramatic tension of a story. In traditional storytelling, as we've discussed, the story should come directly from character.

As the story progresses, the action of both story and gameplay should increase. Each plot point should drive the action forward and increase the intensity of situation (or gameplay) upward.

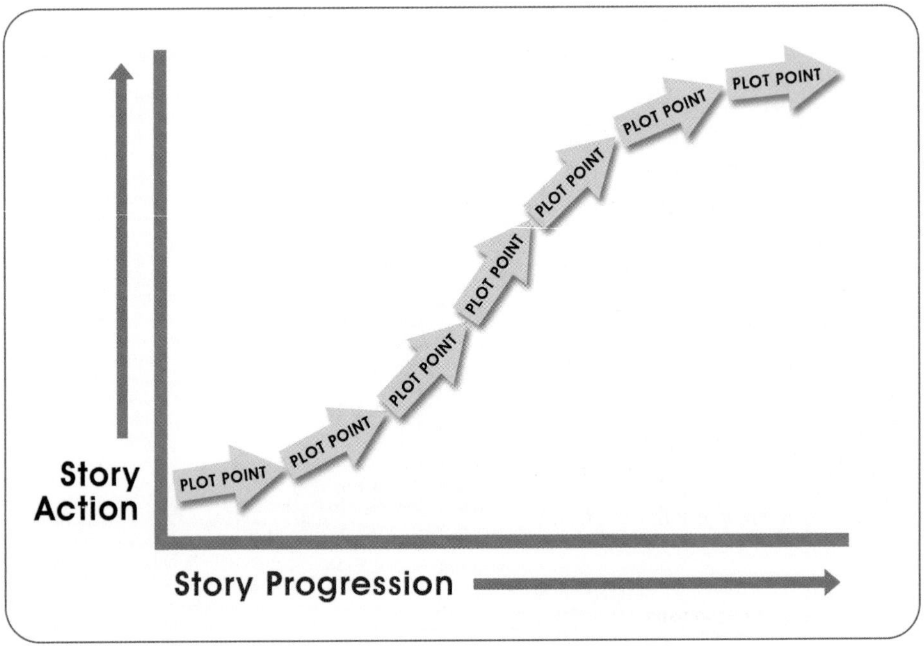

Per Olin

Throughout the story there is what is called a *line of action*—which is made up of plot points—but a series of plot points may or may not make up an interesting story. Let's look at a flat line of action.

1. You take your dog for a walk.
2. Because you take your dog for a walk, you meet up with a neighbor.
3. The neighbor tells you that there is a block party next week.
4. You continue your walk. But because you have spent time talking to one neighbor, another has arrived home from work.
5. You tell this neighbor that there is a block party next week. He thanks you.
6. You arrive back at your house and give your dog a biscuit.

Not very interesting, but is it a plot? You, the character, did initiate the action—a walk. Going on the walk caused you to talk to one neighbor. Stopping to talk to that neighbor gave the appropriate amount of time, which allowed the other neighbor to get home. You took the action of talking to that neighbor. You went home. So yes, it could be a plot—but one action did not deny other actions. This is where a rising line of action keeps the story interesting.

A line of action begins with something happening. It could be the inciting incident. After the thing happens the hero must make a choice. The hero can refuse the call, or he may want to jump in and immediately try to fix the problem. If the hero refuses the call, the refusal can make matters worse until the hero can no longer deny the call. Either way, the minute the hero makes a choice, there will be repercussions that will cause bigger problems. The hero will have to address these problems, too. The line of action will continue in this way. However, in order to build the action, each choice has to lead to the next action and must also eliminate choices—forcing the hero further into the story. If you do not force the action in this way, the dramatic tension will fail to build—and if dramatic action fails to build, your audience will lose interest.

Refusal of the Call
You have one opportunity to take out the garbage, but you refuse the call.
Your house smells bad - really bad.
People refuse to visit you.
People refuse to date you.
You have no social life.
You die alone.
RIP

Keep the action and tension moving forward and upward in your story.

Per Olin

It can be argued that—even with the elimination of choices—the tension will not build. Let's take a look at this in the most mundane of situations:

1. You have one opportunity to take out the garbage, but you refuse the call.
2. Your house smells bad—really bad.
3. People refuse to visit you.
4. People refuse to date you.
5. You have no social life.
6. You die alone.

Who wants to die alone? Not taking out the trash is a ridiculous example of how to drive the line of action up toward the climatic conclusion. Now let's take a look at another example that is far more serious.

High Stakes

"Make the stakes higher" is a mantra of Hollywood, but what does this mean? Simply, what is there to lose? In the film *Armageddon*, what is at stake is the entire planet. Complete annihilation awaits if the hero does not succeed. These are pretty high stakes and a lot of pressure for the hero, but remember that personal stakes can be just as effective. If the hero has a girlfriend or a child to lose, this can be just as devastating personally and often more satisfying to the audience, who can more readily identify with personal stakes.

In the film *Sophie's Choice*, the stakes are as high and the choice as difficult as they can be. A woman in a concentration camp must decide which of her two children will live. If she fails to choose, both children will die. Not a choice one ever wants to make—and a choice that will haunt the surviving characters throughout the story. As grim as this story is, it demonstrates the type of choices that will drive the line of action upward because the choices are irrevocable. Once made, you cannot go back and change the outcome. Furthermore, to do nothing becomes as irrevocable as doing something.

In video games, it seems that nothing is irrevocable because players can repeat situations and challenges. Try to think of three compelling story situations that might be considered irrevocable but would still work in a game. This might be a difficult task, but if you can achieve it, it would up the stakes and tension for the player and create an interesting game experience.

Climax

Eventually the line of action will conclude into a *climax*—a final battle where the story will definitively end and the problem will be resolved. The moments leading up to this are where the most intense action happens. In three-act structure it is the final 25-30 pages. In the hero's journey, it is the ordeal through the resurrection. In a game, it is in the final moves that will lead to victory or defeat. The rising action in a racing game comes usually when two or more competitors are vying for the first-place position. They drive as aggressively as possible without crashing. Who will win and how they achieve it drives the tension, causes the action to rise, and leads to the climax.

::::: Persistent-State Worlds: Where's the Climax?

In the massively multiplayer online game (MMOG) *City of Heroes*, the world is persistent–meaning it is available to players 24/7. Essentially there is never a climax to the story because the story does not end. Within the game, however, there are mini-stories and goals that do provide dramatic "mini-endings." In the case of *City of Heroes*, going after a particular villain or villains will end that particular adventure but not the entire game. After the goal is completed, the player can go and find a new task that will also offer a climactic ending.

NCsoft

Obviously you wouldn't want to get to the end of a movie, book or game and find no ending or even worse, find a disappointing end. As you construct your story and game design, carefully place the story elements and plot points so that in the end, there is a logical progression of action and dramatic tension that offers satisfying climax.

Deus Ex Machina

The translation of *deus ex machina* is "god from the machine"–but what it relates to is the unsatisfying resolution of a story by some god-given miracle. Imagine this:

You're watching a movie where the hero and villain are finally battling. The hero is losing—but you know he will eventually win. Then all of a sudden, the villain suffers a heart attack and dies. The hero wins the battle, but not because he was the superior fighter. Now think of this in terms of a video game. You are in the final boss fight when a bolt of lightning strikes the boss and you win, not because you were good enough, but rather because of this random event. Would that be a fun conclusion to a game you may have just spent 20 hours playing? Probably not. While this seems obvious, this is often the case where a writer finds himself using this maneuver to get him out of trouble. Maybe he's written himself into a corner. Maybe the characters aren't true or developed. In any case, it is a quick out that should be avoided in good storytelling.

As you can see, there a many parts to creating a traditional story and much can be applied to game stories as well. Game stories, however, are even more involved than traditional stories and offer other ways of telling stories. This new type of storytelling will actively engage the player. In the next chapter, we will look at the way games offer a different story experience for the player.

:::CHAPTER REVIEW:::

1. Watch a movie or read a book and make note of how the screenwriter or author makes use of traditional storytelling devices such as the 3-act structure and hero's journey. (Hollywood focuses so heavily on the 3-act structure that each act is associated with a particular time length! For a 2-hour film, the acts are usually 30, 60, and 30 minutes, respectively.) As you watch or read, notice what happens in the plot during the three acts. The first act should set up all the story elements—including introducing the storyline and characters. The second act should develop the story and present the story's major conflict. Finally, the third act should intensify the drama and end up resolving the conflict. After making note of where these acts begin and end, determine whether the hero's journey is being utilized in the story.

2. Develop a broad concept for an original game idea and turn it into a springboard. Then create a more formal *premise* (also known as a *high concept*) for your idea. Your premise should be written in 2nd-person voice—addressing the player directly—and it should be no more than three sentences in length. Your premise also needs to "sell' the game to the prospective player by revealing the game's dramatic elements and "fun factor"!

3. Create a backstory and synopsis for an original game idea. Make sure that both relate to the premise you created in the previous exercise. The backstory should address what happens before the game begins. It should be no longer than one paragraph—around 3-5 sentences. The synopsis should address what happens while the game is being played. It should be at least one paragraph long—and it may be several paragraphs long, depending upon your storyline's complexity. Your synopsis should *not* read like a scripted story. Remember: You can have several different endings in a game—and your characters can go down different paths in the story! Do not get bogged down in details associated with plot points.

4. Add a series of three plot twists to your game's overall storyline by utilizing some of the devices discussed in the chapter (such as red herring, reversal, or line of action). In what ways do these plot twists enrich your storyline, and how might they affect the way your game is played?

5. Expand on your storyline by creating an outline of your story's "acts." Incorporate story layers into your outline by identifying an A-story, B-story, and C-runner. How can these three elements work together to make your story more rich and complex, and how might they affect the way your game is played?

4

CHAPTER

Game Storytelling Devices:

integrating game-specific elements into a story

Key Chapter Questions

- How is player control incorporated into a game story?
- How can players take ownership over a game's dramatic elements?
- How can cinematics and cut-scenes make or break a game?
- How does the Schrodinger's cat scenario illustrate game-specific storytelling?
- How can game storytelling devices be used to express emotional content?

If a tree falls in the forest and no one hears it, does it make a noise? If we humans do not observe a series of events, is there a definable story? If Einstein believed that we change the universe simply by observing it, then it must be argued that story can only be created by our very existence. When you watch a film, you become an *observer*—allowing the film's story and characters to play out in front of you. When you play a game, you no longer watch—but you *play*, becoming a *participant* in the game's storyline and character roles. Gameplay facilitates this transformation from observer to participant—but it also can allow you to become a *creator* or *author* in the process. As players, we can trigger events that happen in the game's story by making choices—deciding the fate of the game's characters.

As cliché as it may sound, I always love to conquer evil and save the world. The idea never seems to grow old. . . . But one element that needs to stop is the idea of helpless women being kidnapped to some castle/fortress/hideout.

— Isabel Davila (Game Art & Design student)

Conveying Information

The way a reader receives information while reading a book is sequential. When a viewer looks at a painting or a photograph, the information relayed is simultaneous. All of the information in the picture is given immediately. If there is a story being represented by a piece of visual art, we presume to understand the story immediately because all of the information is available. We can fill in the blanks with our own imaginations.

ICO: Playing the Story

There was a fascinating game called *ICO* created a few years ago for Sony. You played a kid wandering through this castle with a white ghost girl. Then a dark hole would open up on the floor and try to pull her in with a dark shadow-like arm. It was that simple: You had to save the girl, or you failed the game. There's the story: *Boy meets girl, ground shadow wants girl, boy must defend girl.* Simple. And the players feel like they were making the decision to play out that story. How to make that happen in a more complex story is the bigger challenge.

— Mike Daley (Freelance Writing Producer, Blindlight)

This can be broken down further. A novel is sequential; a photograph is simultaneous; but a movie is both because, as we look at the images on the screen, everything on the screen serves the story. In fact, everything on the screen tells the story, but only in part because we must wait for the next piece of information to be given to us. The director and editor have chosen the next bit of information that they want us to see. If a character walks into a dark room and turns on the light, and the character reacts, we want to know what the character is looking at—but we won't be able to, if the editor chooses to cut to another scene.

New Narrative Forms in Games

I want to help make games branch out to involve other forms of narrative—mystery, dark humor, and comedy, for instance. We need our *Citizen Kane* moment, and more importantly, our nonlinear *Pulp Fiction, Memento,* or *Usual Suspects* game. Anything but another game story about armor-clad space marines fighting off aliens from hell. Game creators need to stop hitting the same note over and over. There's a whole symphony of game narrative experiences out there!

— E. Daniel Arey (Creative Director, Naughty Dog Studios/SCEA)

In games, the story is told both sequentially and simultaneously like it is in a movie—but the player can also move around, change the perspective, and sometimes control the camera. This gives the player simultaneous information as he looks at each image and sequential information of his own design. Beyond this, players can make decisions that may affect the storyline; in this way, players can be thought of as co-authors of the game experience and storyline. What the player chooses and how that affects the story is what separates game storytelling from other, more traditional forms of storytelling. Hollywood developers have struggled with the in-game story conundrum for some time, and many have based the idea on the Hollywood model, trying to insert a linear story into a game. Often cinema-driven devices such as the following are employed.

Cinematics

In games, *cinematics* are used to tell a story visually to a player. Cinematics often appear at the beginning and end of a game to illustrate the game's backstory and conclusion, respectively. They can also appear between levels. This device is used in the game, *Prince of Persia: The Sands of Time*—in which the game periodically stops to tell the adventurous story of the Prince.

> *Warcraft 3: Reign of Chaos* has the best game story: a royal test of loyalty and control and the enraged power struggle of bloodlust between orc brothers—provoked by immortal, demonic enemies. Not to mention the best-looking cinematics to ever grace our screens, period!
>
> — *Charlie Yee (Interactive Media student)*

Often in games where there is a direct storyline that the player must follow, there is also a direct game path, usually incorporated from one level to the next level. If a player gets from point A to point B, he might get another piece of the story—and sometimes this piece of the story offers a doorway to the next level.

Per Olin

Cinematics often stop the action to tell a predetermined story, which often disrupts the flow of the game.

Ubisoft

Cinematics are a common storytelling device used in *The Prince of Persia: The Sands of Time.*

There is little player choice involved in games with linear storylines—and there's no control when it comes to story. The player is spoon-fed the story line. While this is the reason we go to see movies, for many it is not the reason to play games—especially since the cinematic stops the action of the game and interrupts the flow of play. Just for fun, let's imagine something like this happening in the real world:

You are walking down a dark alley when a ninja materializes in front of you. You have a bad feeling about this. You can either fight or you can run. Let's say you run, but the ninja is on your tail. Unbeknownst to you, you are the chosen one. If you realize your full potential, the forces of evil will fail—but right now you don't care about that. You only know that you must escape. Eventually, you run right past a store with televisions in the window. You stop and watch your favorite commercial. The ninja decides to stop, too. Even though evil will prevail if you are caught, the ninja knows it's your favorite commercial so he'll wait for you. As you watch, you realize it's not a commercial but instead a mini-movie about you—and, although it may tell you something, it doesn't help your current situation. When the mini-movie is over, you continue to run. The ninja also continues after you.

Fantasy elements aside, we would never see this happen in real life. We would never see this happen in a scene from an action movie. So why would anyone want to put it into an interactive experience? To be fair, most cinematics do come at more opportune times so that they do not disrupt the flow of the game—but, even so, they tend to pull a player away from the game experience.

Cinematics sometimes use a different technological engine to drive them and are often produced away from the game-development process. These mini-movies are sometimes outsourced to animation production houses.

Nintendo of America, Inc.

Cut-Scenes

Cut-scenes are similar to cinematics, but they tend to disrupt the game's action —forcing the player to watch. To their benefit, cut-scenes can offer information that is useful to the player immediately or much later in the game.

Cut-scenes are used in games such as *The Legend of Zelda: Twilight Princess* to convey a mysterious mood.

Now let's look at our ninja situation again as if it were a cut-scene. You are running down the street, away from the ninja. You see another warrior, but this guy is dressed in white. You stop to ask where you can get help. The white warrior quickly tells you how to get away from the ninja, or maybe even how to defeat him. You follow the white warrior's advice. That quick interaction would more likely be a cut-scene than a full cinematic.

Cut-Scenes

When we first started writing for games we would surprise the producers by saying, "We hate cut-scenes." They assumed that's all we would want to do. But we wanted to be part of the game—not a cut-scene the player would skip over with his "A" button. How can we make this interactive, and still take them through the story we want to tell? A simple step in this process was to push for more ambient dialogue. In *Shrek*, we knew kids would skip through the cut-scenes, so we were more worried about the gameplay dialogue sounding like the characters in the movie and setting the tone for that game.

— Mike Daley (Freelance Writing Producer, Blindlight)

Triggered Events

A story in a movie, play, or novel is a specific sequence of events—usually told from the most distant to the most recent. There are characters, usually including a hero and villain, and as the story plays out the audience is allowed to witness the conflict. Ideally, an in-game story also deals with a specific set of events—but, unlike the movie, the events could unfold in a different sequence depending on player choice. These events could also represent alternate possibilities that may or may not happen—depending on which events are "triggered" by the player. One player could trigger a certain subset of events or story elements, while another player could trigger a completely different subset. Even one player, upon replaying the game, could make different choices and thereby trigger different realities!

Pre-planned events that are triggered by either time or a player's interaction are known as *triggered events,* which can be as simple as trap doors opening once players walk over them. A *scripted event* is also triggered, but can involve a more extensive sequence, such as scripted dialogue. In the case of our ninja situation, if you were to approach the white warrior more than one time, you might get different dialogue telling you the same general thing, but instead of triggering a cut-scene, the next time it would trigger a scripted event. These scripted events sometimes break the fourth wall and speak to us directly as the player—but does the fourth wall actually exist, since the player is an active part of the narrative?

The Fourth Wall

In the theatre, the fourth wall implies that there is an invisible wall that the audience peers through to watch the action of a play. If a character addresses the audience directly, it's called breaking the fourth wall—which usually takes the viewer out of the experience of the story. When used as a storytelling device throughout a story, it is considered a form of narration but for the most part, breaking the fourth wall is often considered taboo in writing.

This Hollywood style of predetermined events and story points helps to tell a story to a player. This technique is still prevalent and has created many successful games, in spite of the fact that the player loses control over the story. There is, however, a new way of telling stories that is specific to games.

Mark Terrano on Developing the Story around the Player::::

Mark Terrano works in the Xbox Advanced Technology Group as a Technical Game Manager. In this role, he is able to work with game developers worldwide to help them make the best possible Xbox games. Previously he worked with Ensemble Studios on the *Age of Empires* series as a designer and programmer. He was also a network specialist involved in every area of computing from stock markets to oil pipelines. When not working, he enjoys Seattle, playing music, and—of course—all kinds of games.

Cyrus Kanga

Mark Terrano (Technical Game Manager, Xbox–Microsoft)

Many developers seem to lose continuity throughout the process. If the story is developed by one group and the action is developed by another, the elements just don't squeeze together at the end to make a great experience. Every element should reflect the story, respect the characters and the world, and work to create the desired experience. Try to tell the story through the action and the decisions of the player—not through long expositions.

With very well-defined storylines you can get into the situation where players are wondering if they should do what the characters would do, or what they themselves would do when faced with that particular story. I think if you make the experience about the players—about their choices and actions—then you can make a much more compelling experience. It is easy for designers to become so enamored with their world or story that they stop thinking about how to evoke it in the player's mind.

Player Control

The essential difference between traditional stories and game stories is putting authorship into the hands of the player. There are many ways developers can achieve this, so let's take a look at how a player can actually create his own story within a game.

Over the centuries of storytelling, we as audience members started out observing a distant stage. With movies, the big screen takes us to the very edge of the action. Now, with electronic games, we are allowed to enter and engage in the story—making the audience (the player) a participant.

> The more we expect players to get involved, the less we can use the word "storytelling" but "story-enabling."
>
> — *David Perry (President, Shiny Entertainment)*

To allow the player to be involved in the action, *player control* is essential. Imagine being at a sports event as a spectator. Now imagine that it's not just any sports event, but a very special event where the players are allowed to fly. You are so exhilarated that you run onto the field and splat, you hit an invisible wall. You can't play the game, so you watch—but, after a while, watching people fly isn't any fun. Wouldn't you rather fly than *watch* people fly?

Ben Bourbon

Ben Bourbon

In the early days of drama, the actors wore masks so that the audience, who sat a great distance away, could see the faces of the characters. With today's video games, the audience actually gets to enter the story space and contribute to the story outcome.

Player Control in Non-Linear Storytelling

For games with non-linear (or seemingly non-linear) stories, the primary difference is interactivity. The player is provided with choices of how to proceed. These options need to make sense and have to be entertaining and worthwhile. In traditional storytelling, the writer decides how the main character will act in each situation, while in games with non-linear stories, the player must always feel that their decisions are driving the story (whether or not this is true).

— *Kevin Saunders*
(Lead Designer, Obsidian Entertainment)

BioWare Corp.

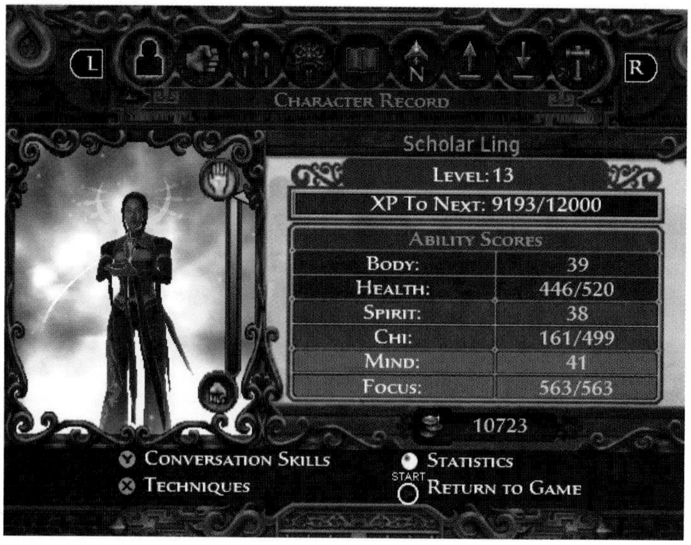

In the game *Jade Empire*, players have the opportunity to customize their characters.

Character Customization

In role-playing games (RPGs), players are allowed to *customize* their characters. Choosing specific attributes and characteristics gives players certain advantages and helps them advance their characters more effectively.

Character customization is one way to offer players control. By actively creating the character's qualities, the player feels like he has created a character within a story. Promoting the feeling of control is very attractive for players.

Amy Albertson on Players Building Their Own Rides::::

Amy Albertson has been wandering around in game industry corridors for a little over a decade. She's done testing, story localization/editing, level design, game design, system scripting, voice work, and story writing for Sega of America, the 3DO Company, Crystal Dynamics, and Midway Studios Austin. She currently works for Ubisoft Entertainment in Montreal.

Amy Albertson (Level Designer, Ubisoft Entertainment)

In traditional narrative, the reader's or listener's path is predetermined and usually linear. The most active party is the author; the audience is invited to immerse itself in a universe with predetermined plot points, like riding an amusement park ride. Early on, game storytelling followed the same model, except the player has been expected to provide the engine to power the narrative along the rails.

Recently, there has been movement toward allowing players to build their own rides—and the new challenge for design is to create intuitive, adaptable tools for players to construct their own rich and satisfying narrative experiences.

Players want the tools to build their own stories. A game is not a book or a film. The industry is still young, and the doors are starting to open on the possibilities specific to the medium. In a game players can become anyone, explore choices and repercussions, or learn, fight, and build a virtual life in a created world.

Game narratives will eventually depend more on providing choices that the player can build upon to create a satisfying story that isn't like anyone else's.

Plot

Players can often choose their own path throughout a game, thus creating their own plot and experiencing their own personal story. Plot is usually broken down into plot points that define the action of the story. Each plot point is usually a definitive action that furthers the story.

Thinking in terms of the game of chess, the action of taking another player's piece is a plot point, although each move a player makes may not be an actual plot point. In an action-adventure game, choosing to go down a particular hallway is not a plot point, but defeating an enemy at the end of the hallway is a plot point. The action in a game builds until a plot point can be executed that allows the player and the story to move forward.

The player, no matter how simple the game is, gets to make *choices*. Even in *Pac-Man,* the player controls Pac-Man's direction. If the player makes Pac-Man turn in the wrong direction, Pac-Man might die—but that is the consequence of the choice the player has made.

The Illusion of Control

In today's pop-psychology world, the trend is to let children think they have control. If your goal is to get a child to wear a sweater, you might offer the child a choice between the pink sweater and the blue one. The child feels empowered by making a choice, and your goal of getting him to wear a sweater is satisfied. This is very similar to games. Developers must allow players to make choices, yet still keep them pursuing the main objective of the game and story.

Offering choice to the player is the main reason game stories and traditional stories are different. If the choices you offer the player are interesting choices, you are on your way to a great game.

Consequences

What do we get from choices? *Consequences.* Ideally, these consequences lead to more choices for the player. This initiates the building of a story within the game—and allows for compelling gameplay. In the game *Fable*, the idea is that each choice the player makes will affect the story of the game. If a player chooses to do something evil and gains evil points, then the player will be limited in other choices, such as the ability to fall in love. In the *Fable* world, girls don't ever fall in love with bad boys.

Engagement and Interactivity

While playing a game, a player might be able to *engage* with game-generated characters known as non-player characters (NPCs). The player will be able to interact with the environment and might either cooperate with other players or compete against them. All of this engagement is what makes games interactive. Games by their very nature are interactive because the player must engage in them to play. It is this interactive quality that makes the player both the storyteller as well as an audience member.

Three Rings Design

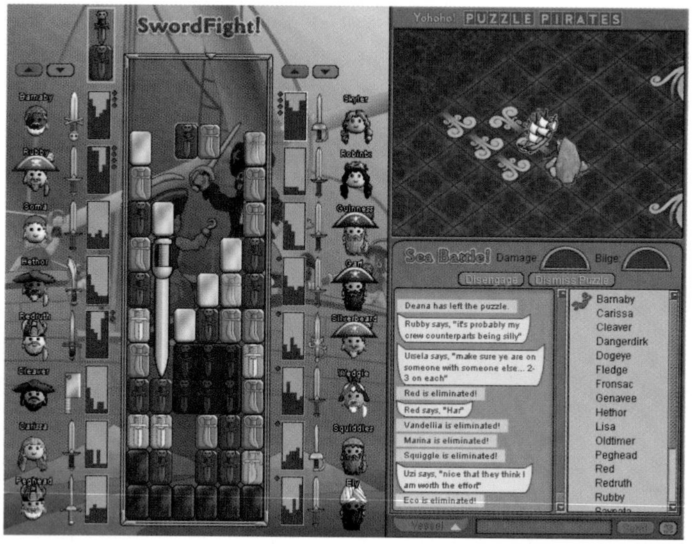

Collaboration is essential to reach a goal in games such as *Puzzle Pirates*.

Collaboration

In many types of games, *collaboration* with other players contributes to the game, since all players will have their own ideas on how to play and win the game. Sometimes collaboration becomes even more necessary, since problems need to be solved through all players, not just individual players.

Collaborative Jam

An interesting way to consider collaborative story development is to gather some friends around. On a sheet of paper, come up with a random sentence. A novel or book is always a good place to look for the random sentence, but don't let that limit you; it can be anything from anywhere. From the sentence, write a paragraph. Then allow the next person to read the paragraph and write the next paragraph. By the end of this exercise, you will have an interesting story full of twists and turns.

Collaboration brings a fun social element to a game as well as offers interesting solutions to large challenges.

Player control comes down to handing players the "reins" of the story so that they may drive the action in a way that is compelling and fun. As a game developer, the trick is to allow the player enough freedom to engage in the story and yet keep the elements of the story flowing so that game does not become stagnant. It's a delicate balance—but if done successfully, it can allow players to feel they are truly part of the game world.

Immersion

The objective behind writing an engaging story, building interesting worlds, and giving the player control leads to one conclusion: *immersion*. In order for the player to get the most out of the game experience, it is necessary to make the player feel as much a part of the world as possible—thereby giving the player a presence within the game world and the game story. To achieve this, imitation of the real world is necessary. This is not to say that players shouldn't *suspend disbelief* or that the stories can't be fictionalized. Fantasy, sci-fi, and horror can and should be used, but there are basic real-world rules that help add to the immersive experience of a game.

Repetition

When an NPC speaks to a player, the NPC should *never* repeat himself. In the real world, people don't repeat themselves—usually. Avoiding *repetition* is not as easy as it sounds. It involves making sure that the artificial intelligence (AI) system is working at a fairly high level. Whether or not your team can prevent this NPC repetition, it's important to be aware of the problem and try to avoid it in any way possible. Each time the player returns to an environment, the player should have a different experience.

Writers as Programmers

Writers may have to become programmers of sorts—not in the hard-coding style of programming itself, but as a way of helping form elaborate artificial intelligence (AI) or world skeletons. More companies are pushing for sandbox—or partially immersive—environments, thus allowing the player to tell his own story within an existing framework. In some games, this comes down to a limited selection of choices and the limits of technology. Eventually, however, every word or action may have consequence in an environment. Writers may need to create in-depth personas or story frameworks so that the AI reacts to a given situation with a wide array or responses. It could boil down to AI responses no longer being a matter of Choice A, B, or C—but rather based on context and even evolution.

— Lucien Soulban (Scriptwriter & Novelist, Ubisoft Montreal)

Consistency

In all narratives, there is the need for a *consistent* world and rules that play out logically. This may seem a simple task—but consistency is often the bane of many writers' existence. Consistency in games is even more essential, since players may take a break from play: a few minutes, a few days—or even longer.

Flow

The flow of the game story is essential to the player experience. If the player must stop play to load a level or watch a cinematic, this disrupts the flow and takes the player out of the immersive moment. Many players who play the game *Max Payne* feel that the excessive use of cut-scenes disrupts the flow of the game, since the player loses control during the cut-scenes. In life, we do not stop what we are doing so that we can watch a video of ourselves doing something, so why should a developer want to add this to an immersive experience?

Non-Linearity

While all stories are linear in retrospect, they take on a type of non-linearity as they are being created. The moment before a player makes a decision is the moment of non-linearity. All options are open to the player. Remember the ninja chase earlier in this chapter? The moment before you decide to run or to fight is the non-linear moment. In games, it should always come down to the choices available to the player. The availability of choice offers a non-linear path, imitates the complexity of real life, and adds to the immersive experience.

:::: Schrödinger's Cat

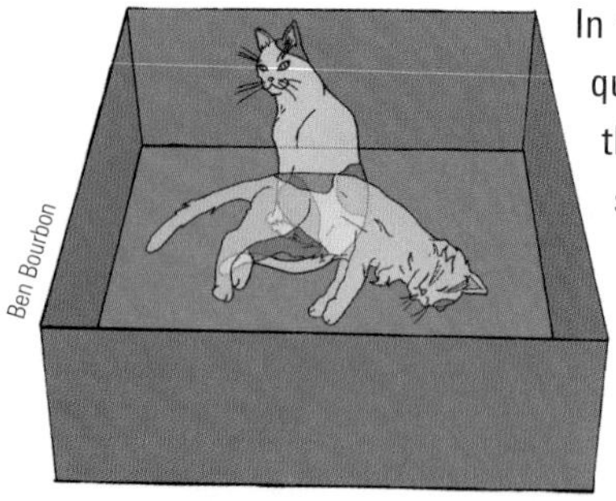

In quantum reality, Shrodinger's cat is both alive and dead, simultaneously.

In the Schrödinger's Cat paradox—developed by Erwin Schrödinger to illustrate quantum reality—a cat lives in a box. Within the box is a triggered device that feeds the cat either poison or cat food—but this cat is a quantum cat in a quantum box, so the device feeds the cat both poison and food at the same time. The result is that the cat is both alive and dead at the same time, meaning that both possibilities—even contradictory ones—can co-exist within a quantum world.

Once we look inside the box, the cat appears to be either alive or dead, since our observation changes the observed. In other words, we can only understand contradictory ideas as "either-or"—not *both*. Due to this, we cannot see the cat as alive and dead at the same time as he is in quantum reality—but rather *either* alive *or* dead. Thus, our observation changes what is observed. Now let's think about this as non-linear storytelling. Directly before the choice is made, the story is non-linear; both possibilities exist. Once the player makes his choice, the path becomes linear—at least, in retrospect.

Mark Soderwall on Game Story Categories:::::

Mark Soderwall has worked in the game industry for 14 years. In that time, he has directed and created 3D/2D art content and animation for over 21 published titles. His career began by chance—after winning a Fiction & Fantasy Art competition in California in the late 1980s, right after graduating from high school. One of the judges on the panel owned a game studio that created content exclusively for the Nintendo Entertainment System (NES). Mark became hooked, and gained even more experience and creative understanding of innovative CG tools, techniques, and technologies with every title he completed. This momentum only fueled his resolve to push the limits of CG art and animation in every company he has worked for over the next decade. Mark has held exciting positions in numerous interactive development and publishing studios throughout the industry. These include Art Director at Virgin Interactive Entertainment, Senior Lead Artist for Electronic Arts, Canada, and Senior Art Director at Atari. Mark also gives back what he has learned by moonlighting as a professional instructor of advanced 3D character animation and compositing at the Art Institute of California, Orange County.

Mark Soderwall (Creative Consultant & Art Director)

Storytelling in a traditional sense is very linear: You start from a point "A" and inevitably arrive at a point "B." However, stories in a game environment usually take on a very non-linear path—allowing the gamer to interactively affect the progression, pacing, and potential conclusion of a story.

Many games are designed around a central story or theme in order to maintain continuity and direction. However, there is usually enough latitude designed into a game's story foundation for players to create or manipulate certain features, characters, or outcomes. This gives players a greater opportunity to place their personal footprint in a game world—allowing for a greater sense of immersion, interactivity, and entertainment.

Games can be broken up into a few specific categories as they relate to story:

- *Sandbox:* A game designed to let the players create their own stories, pacing, and conclusions. Sandbox games allow for a lot of player freedom (e.g., *Grand Theft Auto*).
- *Rail:* A game that follows a linear gameplay style and focuses less on story. These games might give the illustion of choice yet all the while directing and manipulating a player's forward momentum to a pre-determined conclusion

or outcome. Many first-person shooters and driving/racing games are good examples. All "rail" games follow a linear play style and focus less on story.

- *Lock & Key:* A game that combines player freedom with a storyline. Lock and Key games give the player the freedom to explore and create but still require a percentage of the story to be followed or discovered in order to move forward into the game.

I feel that story plays a critical role in any game environment. Even if a game has no objective story tied to it, I still have to create characters, environments, and style guides with some semblance of continuity and foundation to help give the game at the very least visual objectivity or story.

> I think the real indicator will be when somebody confesses that they cried at level 17.
>
> — *Steven Spielberg*

Emotional Content

In the quote to the left, Steven Spielberg was commenting on whether games could be a storytelling art form the way a novel, play, or film is. He seems to suggest that if someone cries, it constitutes art. Certainly crying does not constitute art, or many a Hallmark commercial would play in the Louvre. What crying does speak to, however, is the manipulation of human emotion. In films, the narrative is directed to move the audience in a specific way. In games, since the player helps to create the narrative, the act of manipulation is difficult to maneuver. So how do we make games worthy of emotional investment? By adding the element of human experience.

Experiential Storytelling

When writing in any storytelling medium, the idea is to make the story experiential. To achieve this, you must direct the action toward human experience and to the foundation of human experience—emotion.

If we see a character that is hungry. We can relate to that character because we have been hungry ourselves. If the character is starving, we can still relate to the character because—although we may never have experienced true starvation—we have experienced the lesser form of the want: hunger. If we see a character that is poor and wants a lot of money, we can relate to that character because most people think about money throughout their lives. Perhaps some of us have experienced not being able to make rent or pay our bills. Some people think about money too much, which can turn into greed. When we watch a greedy character, we can relate—but we might make judgments because we know that greed usually leads to a bad end.

Goals

Just as a character in a movie has goals, game developers must provide goals for the players to keep them engaged. In order to make the goals meaningful, it helps to tie them to human wants and needs.

If the goal is simply to collect a gold nugget so that you earn a point, that works—but if the nugget has the added power to save lives, this is more important to a player emotionally because human life is valued in the real world.

Wants and Needs

Electronic Arts

The Sims gives the player a strategic look at wants and needs.

Since preservation of our own life is innate, a primary *want* in a game is to survive. We may also have wants for many other things, but right now let's concentrate on the basic want: survival. In order to satisfy the want, we will have to address our *need.* The want fulfills the need. We *want* to stay alive, so we *need* to eat and drink. We *want* to procreate, so we *need* to find a mate.

To illustrate this, let's think about the typical hack-and-slash game and its objective: to stay alive. However, what if you have been fighting bosses for several hours and your health points are dangerously low? You need health. This creates a *need* and a *want.* You want to stay alive. You need to find health to do so. This keeps you hooked throughout the game.

While want and need make up most of the human existence, there is also the further extension of need: desire.

Desire

Capcom Entertainment, Inc.

The classic hack-and-slash game, *Maximo vs. The Army of Zin* clearly shows a want and a need.

If want expresses a need, *desire* expresses longing—the normal but sometimes destructive human emotion for something that may not be attainable. If you want money to live happily, that's one thing—but if you long for riches and nothing else, you may die alone and miserable. You may also die happy and fulfilled by your riches, but that outcome is unlikely.

In traditional stories, the desire of the character is often used as a plot device or a goal, but the character that chases his desire is flawed and his desire is usually an expression of that flaw. Wanting only money and having the single-minded pursuit of money, for example, extinguishes all the possibilities for other riches in life. A character on his way to quenching his desire for money might learn that love is more important than money. Desire sometimes takes us beyond what is normal and healthy—but, if we can instill desire within the player, this might be a way to evoke emotion from a game.

Thinking in terms of want, need, and desire, let's go a step deeper and look into a few basic human emotions.

Cyan Worlds, Inc.

Myst inspires curiosity in the player by offering clues leading to a rich story.

Curiosity

Curiosity is an emotion that can bring about destruction as well as great good. If Einstein hadn't been curious about the power in the atom, we might not have nuclear weapons. On the other hand, if Sir Alexander Fleming had not been curious about how to fight bacterial infection, he might not have discovered penicillin and we might not have cures for many of the world's diseases.

Inspiring curiosity in games is essential for all gameplay. If the player is not curious, then why should he continue to play? Fortunately, this is an easier emotion to evoke since most people have an unquenchable amount of curiosity.

Majesco

Environment and story incite fear within the player in *Jaws*.

Fear

Typically, *fear* is a reaction to danger. We see a threat and we feel fear. However, fear can be much more complex than this. Perhaps there isn't a threat, but we might still have fear. What about the fear of loneliness or of rejection? Being alone or being rejected isn't a life-endangering threat—and yet these fears drive us as much as seeing a large shark while we are swimming or a gun pointed in our direction. Exploring fear on a deeper emotional level will give a game texture and complexity.

Some games use suspense, a form of fear, to add atmosphere to the game. If you want to instill fear in a player, danger is a good way to start, but also be sure to consider other fears as well.

Love

Nintendo of America, Inc.

The Legend of Zelda centers around a love story.

Love is the most complex human emotional experience. First, there is no logical reason someone might fall in love with another person. Second, there are several kinds of love: for children, for a mate, for friends. While they are all related the same basic element, there are significant nuances to each. Finally, people often get romantic love confused with lust. Love is an emotional response, while lust is a physical response.

Creating a game around a love story has been done, but only in that the player is told that he loves another character. If you can make your player actually feel love within the story circumstance, then you are on your way to that good cry Spielberg is hoping for in Level 17.

These are just a few of the vast array of human emotions that can be manipulated while trying to create a good game story. Let's take a look at what other emotions we might attempt to evoke from game story.

Virtues & Vices

Ben Bourbon

A compelling game story might evoke one or more of the seven deadly vices in the player.

The seven deadly sins (or "vices") were developed in the middle ages and are defined as transgressions fatal to spiritual growth. We can also look at them as flaws that we are all subject to experiencing. The seven sins express the extremes of emotion. For example, while self-respect is good, pride can get in the way of mending a family argument.

The idea here is to pull these emotions from players through story content. While a writer might give a character the flaw of greed, the game writer and designer's job is harder. They can't just plop an emotion like greed onto a character because the player is the character. It is the game writer and designer's job to create a situation that might make the player *feel* the emotional pull of greed. Let's have a look at the seven deadly sins. Can you think of game situations that might make the player feel every one of these?

1. **Greed:** the overwhelming desire to have more than what is needed
2. **Gluttony:** the act of eating or drinking to excess
3. **Envy:** desire of another's possessions or happiness
4. **Lust:** strong desire for sexual encounters
5. **Sloth:** dislike of work or physical exertion—laziness
6. **Pride:** an attitude shown by people who unjustifiably believe they are better than others—a feeling of superiority
7. **Wrath:** anger marked by the desire for vengeance

Even more difficult emotions to elicit from the player might be the seven heavenly virtues, which are defined as:

Ben Bourbon

A compelling game story might evoke one or more of the seven deadly virtues in the player.

1. **Faith:** trust in something without logical proof
2. **Hope:** a feeling of trust
3. **Charity:** the impartial love of other people
4. **Fortitude:** strength in spite of a difficult and painful situation
5. **Justice:** fair treatment of people
6. **Temperance:** self-restraint
7. **Prudence:** good management of resources

Usually these emotions are saved for the end of the story as the character becomes enlightened. An example of this is in *Star Wars, Episode 4*, when Luke Skywalker learns to use The Force. This is an example of a character experiencing faith. Again, in games, the above-mentioned might be difficult to elicit from players, but if you can achieve this, we are on our way to games becoming a true art form. One game that has made an effort to elicit emotions from the player is *Fable*. The player of *Fable* is given the choice to be good or evil, and this choice will have consequences later on in the game. A player might want to be charitable toward another character to earn good points. Games such as these are raising the bar and helping players become even more emotionally involved in the game and gameplay.

Creating the Emotional Experience

The question remains, how do we get players to experience emotions? The writer/designer doesn't have to spoon feed the player every event; sometimes it's enough to let the player imagine what might be happening.

Ben Bourbon

The shape of the character is the negative space. What isn't there tells us part of the story.

Artists often understand the importance of negative space—which is defined by what is not on the page but what is surrounding it. If a cartoon character crashes through a wall leaving the hole in the shape of himself, the hole is the negative space; the wall is what surrounds it. What is not there is as important as what is there. This technique can be applied to games as well.

Let's say that you want to inspire greed. Perhaps showing riches to a player is enough—but if you show another character with riches, the player may not only feel greed but also envy. The player, having seen what he doesn't have (negative space), will imagine himself with what he desires. The desire will fill with emotions.

Another way to use this technique is to let what is not in the story fill the player's imagination. Since players are humans, they are subject to a myriad of emotional states. Often these emotional states have no basis in logic. In a real-world example, let's say Harry lives in the dorms. Harry is in love with Amy, who also lives in the dorms. Unfortunately, Harry is very shy and won't talk to Amy. When Amy brings home a male visitor, Harry is extremely jealous and can't sleep throughout the night. As it turns out, Harry's imagination got the better of him because the male visitor Amy brought home was her brother, Charlie. Leading players along with red herrings and giving them imperfect information can inspire certain real-life emotions even though the world they are in is virtual.

:::: *Un Chien Andalou:* Chicken or the Egg?

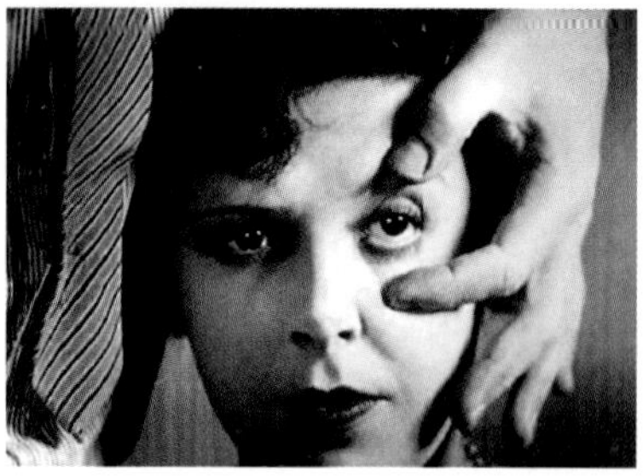

The 1929 film *Un Chien Andalou* by Luis Bunuel and Salvador Dali was made to be completely non-sequential. Every scene is different, and every frame is separate unto itself. However, a narrative still emerges from these seemingly disjointed frames and scenes. So the question becomes: Does our imagination fill in the negative space with story because we are used to seeing stories—or were the filmmakers unable to escape the human necessity of telling a story in spite of their attempt not to?

Human imagination is powerful and should be considered carefully when constructing a game. Be sure to use this to your advantage when creating a game story, and remember, what isn't there is sometimes as important as what is there.

Empathy on the Game Screen

Speaking as both a novelist and a game designer, I feel that we are still in very early, primitive days when it comes to delivering in the new media what the old medium does very well: empathy and a sense of character—a powerful, almost telepathic, illusion that you *are* the main character, with all of the personality quirks and complex emotions of another living person. The best written literature can do this. You can feel another person's pain, whether he or she was an extrapolated historical person or one created by the author's imagination. That depth has yet to be developed on the game screen.

— David Brin (Author, Scientist & Public Speaker)

Layering

Just as you would never take all this emotionally-driven content and drop it into the first act of a movie, neither would you drop it into the first level of a game. It would be too confusing for the player.

The difficulty is how to layer in the emotional content. There has to be time to build emotional bonds with other characters and with the game world. As we discussed, this is partially accomplished with immersion. The further immersed the players are, the more emotionally attached they will become. In the beginning, however, this will be accomplished with the developers delicately choosing where the emotional content should be placed. This will often depend on instinct—the first step to any good art.

Satisfaction

In terms of the spectator or player, all media creates an experience. A novel creates a personal space, a play creates a live space, a movie creates a collective space—and they all provide a specific experience. If the experience is not satisfying, we will feel cheated out of the hours spent engaging with it.

This is even more important when creating a game, since games are dependent on many hours of play. At the end of the game, we want the player to feel satisfied and accomplished. What Spielberg might have been speaking to is the simple yet cathartic moment when the audience feels changed by the experience of seeing the movie. What we are after in terms of story and game is the moment after the players have taken the journey—when they are better for having had the experience.

Interactivity: Getting Closer . . .

The player doesn't want merely to be told a story, but to actively participate in that story. From killing bad guys to solving riddles, the best games make this happen. But as a writer, I feel we still haven't found the way to truly write stories interactively. A game like *Zelda* comes the closest—where the story is out there waiting to be explored and the player can choose when to reach it. Still, the story unfolds as a narrative to be listened to, not a truly interactive experience. There is still a very exciting opportunity here to reinvent storytelling through games.

— *Mike Daley (Freelance Writing Producer, Blindlight)*

The idea of eliciting emotion through gameplay is something that has been talked about in the past by game developers but is just now coming to the forefront as a necessity for creating a rich game experience. Using some of the ideas on emotion discussed in this chapter will help to build an engaging game story.

Throughout this chapter, we looked at the many elements that contribute to a game story—such as cinematics, cut-scenes, player control, immersion, and emotional content. Allowing players to make choices during a game provides them with the illusion of control while still leading them along a great story experience. This delicate balance between choice and manipulation contributes to player's emotional state and the immersive experience. In the following chapters, we will look at character development—another important element that contributes significantly to the overall game experience.

:::CHAPTER REVIEW:::

1. What role do *cut-scenes* play in a game, and how can they sometimes compromise player control and immersion? Choose a cut-scene from a pre-existing game, and identify 3 reasons why you feel the cut-scene is being used in the game. Is the cut-scene necessary? Does it compromise immersion? If you were on the game-development team and were told that the scene had to be removed, what would have to be done in order to ensure that the "reasons" for the cut-scene were still being fulfilled? Create a synopsis for an original cut-scene and discuss why the cut-scene is essential to the game experience.

2. What is the importance of allowing for player control in game stories? Play a game of your choice. At which points in the game are you able to make decisions about which path to take through the story? Are you given the opportunity to create or "co-author" story content in the game?

3. How do game storytelling devices help create *immersion* in the game experience? Were you truly immersed in the last game you played? Discuss at least 3 techniques the developers used to keep you immersed in the game.

4. How do games elicit emotional responses in players? For your original game idea, discuss what emotions you would like your players and characters to experience. How do you plan on using experiential storytelling to enable players to feel truly connected to your game emotionally?

Part II: Character

CHAPTER 5

Character Types: who are your characters?

Key Chapter Questions

- How are archetypes useful?
- What is an avatar?
- What is the difference between a protagonist and a hero character?
- What is the difference between an antagonist and a shadow character?
- What kinds of characters are found only in games?

Characters are the central focus point of most stories and, without them, we as an audience would have a difficult time understanding the action. In games, the player is an active part of the story, but characters are essential to the story as well as to the gameplay. In this chapter, we will take a look at the several types of characters—from classic and contemporary film characters to game characters.

Archetypes

An *archetype* is a universal figure. Just as Carl Jung associated a particular type of story to the human condition, he also devised certain character types known as archetypes. These archetypes are found in mythology and literature and have been used throughout the ages to tell a story, especially ones of epic adventure. Recognizable in stories in every culture and every era, they continue to show themselves throughout all storytelling media, including games.

Capcom Entertainment, Inc.

In *Maximo: Army of Zin,* the main character is a classic hero because we see the story through his point-of-view.

Hero

The *hero* of the story is the main character. The audience primarily sees the story through the point-of-view (POV) of the hero. In the classic Hitchcock movie, *Rear Window,* the hero, Jeff, is housebound with a broken leg. As he recovers, he witnesses the goings on in the next building and comes to realize that a murder has taken place. The POV of *Rear Window* is exclusively through the hero, Jeff. Using this technique, Hitchcock ingeniously gives the audience the feeling of restraint, thus allowing the audience to experience the limitations of the hero and bond with him. All of the action of the story is driven through this one character.

> One of my favorite characters is Cloud from *Final Fantasy VII.* When he tells everyone that none of them actually want to save the world—but they are just doing it for their own personal reasons—it shows that he isn't your typical hero. He's just one pissed-off dude.
>
> — *Brian Dalton (Game Art & Design student)*

The hero, whether in a game or in a movie, is the central focus for the audience as well as for the player. The player and the audience need to identify and bond with the hero in order to create an immersive story experience. Using this model, the hero is always faced with a problem at the beginning of the story. When he embarks on the journey (answers the call), his problem is either emotionally or physically resolved—sometimes both—as a result of his action.

It is important for the player to bond with the character he is playing. Creating an interesting hero with a challenging problem helps the player feel for the character and crafts a better game experience.

Shadow

Vivendi Universal Games

Tyler Durden is the shadow of the main character (Jack) in *Fight Club.*

The *shadow* is usually the main opponent, often known as the villain. The shadow symbolically represents the hero's opposite and is often the cause of the hero's problem. In *Star Wars,* Darth Vader not only represents the shadow character and the dark side of Luke Skywalker (the hero), but Darth—who is indirectly responsible for the death of Luke's aunt and uncle—is the direct cause of the problem Luke faces. Sometimes the shadow is actually a literal manifestation of the hero's dark side. In the movie *Fight Club,* the shadow character, Tyler Durden, is actually a psychological representation of the main character—literally his shadow. This is not a new idea; the classic example of this is Robert Louis Stevenson's novel *Dr. Jekyll and Mr. Hyde.*

Whether your shadow character is good or evil, remember that he is in the story to cause problems for the hero. Without these problems for the hero, not only is the story uninteresting, but there is also no room for the hero to grow.

Mentor

Capcom Entertainment, Inc.

Gen is considered the "wise old man" mentor character in the *Street Fighter* series.

The *mentor* character is usually the older, wiser character guiding the hero toward his destiny. Gandalf the Grey in *The Lord of the Rings: The Fellowship of the Ring* and Morpheus in *The Matrix* are mentor characters. In both cases, Gandalf and Morpheus provide information to the hero about the journey he must take.

Mentor characters who have often experienced similar journeys or who are older and wiser can guide the young hero. Sometimes the mentor is a character that the hero meets along the way, as in the *Star Wars* character Yoda—and sometimes the mentor seeks out the hero for the journey, as we see in *Lord of the Rings.* Often the mentor stays with the hero for part of the journey, but later sacrifices himself for the greater good. While this may leave the hero on his own, it is the only way the hero can realize his full potential. In *Star Wars*, Obi-Wan (Ben) Kenobi stays with the young Luke for the first part of the journey, but soon sacrifices himself, leaving Luke to learn about the Jedi way on his own.

Capcom Entertainment, Inc.

Even the Grim Reaper can be a helper, as in *Maximo: Ghosts to Glory.*

Helpers

Helpers do exactly what you might think: they help the hero during his quest. They support the main character in his goal, and they help him accomplish difficult tasks. Legolas Greenleaf the elf and Gimli the dwarf in *The Lord of the Rings* trilogy are mortal enemies, but they bond together and become allies to the hero, Frodo.

In games, it is important to have helper characters such as mentors who guide the player through the game environment. Think about how you might include helpers in your own game.

Guardian

The *guardian* character often represents another opponent or obstacle for the hero. The guardian sometimes blocks the path of the hero and usually tests him in some way. In the classic Greek tragedy *Oedipus the King*, the guardian is the Sphinx, who blocks the gates to Thebes. He poses the "Riddle of the Sphinx" to Oedipus. Another example of a guardian is the three-headed dog, Fluffy, that guards the Sorcerer's Stone in *Harry Potter & the Sorcerer's Stone.* This is the very stone that Harry needs—and the very stone his opponent is after, too. Sometimes the guardian is not a physical manifestation of an opponent but rather a psychological barrier—such as that doubt or fear that might keep the hero from attempting to accomplish his goal. In the classic novel *The Hobbit*, young hero Bilbo Baggins is constantly second-guessing his decision to go on his quest and often wishes he were back in his home in the warm and comfortable shire.

Ben Bourbon

::::: The Riddle of the Sphinx

As Oedipus goes to enter the city of Thebes, he meets a monstrous Sphinx. In order to pass, Oedipus must solve the riddle or else be devoured by the monster, just as his predecessors have been. The riddle goes like this: "What walks on four legs in the morning, two legs at noon and three legs at night?" Oedipus is quick to answer: A human being, who crawls on all fours as a baby, walks upright as an adult and uses a cane in old age. Upon hearing the answer, the Sphinx kills herself. The Thebans are so happy with Oedipus that they make him their king.

The guardian is especially useful when creating games. Many times a player must defeat a guardian type of character in order to reach another level of play. Making a specific challenge into a guardian character can help fill out your game story.

Trickster

Sometimes a serious threat and ally of the shadow character, the *trickster* is a mischief-maker who usually holds no more power over the hero than other ancillary characters—but he can distract the hero from his main goal. In classic Native American literature, the coyote is the trickster, often shifting shapes to play pranks on the hero.

Tricksters can be fun characters to use in games because they can add the element of surprise to a story. Think of how you might use a trickster in your game. Make sure don't make the character's real intentions too obvious. You want to make sure your players are surprised!

Herald

Sony Computer Entertainment of America

In *God of War,* Athena is a herald character because she supplies information to the main character (Kratos) throughout the game.

Ever think about why some newspapers are called "*The Herald*?" It's because they bring people the news. In the same way, a character that brings news to the hero is called a *herald*. The herald character provides information to the hero, often changing the direction of a story. Often, these characters arrive at the beginning of a story simply to incite the hero to action. In the film *Raiders of the Lost Ark*, when Doctor Marcus Brody shows up and tells Indiana Jones that there is information about the Ark of the Covenant, he is acting as a type of herald. The three witches who tell Macbeth of the coming events are also excellent examples. Heralds can be very useful characters for setting up a story and pointing the hero in the right direction for his journey.

While traditional archetypes are found in almost all stories, character types have evolved and are now represented in a new way. In the next section, we will be looking at contemporary definitions of characters.

Contemporary Character Types

Outside of the Jungian archetypes, there are similar characters more often used in contemporary storytelling. While they seem to represent the same things the Jungians do, there are subtle differences.

Eidos

Protagonist Lara Croft promotes the action of the game and thereby drives the story forward.

Protagonist

Like the hero archetype, the *protagonist* is the main character in any story and the one who promotes the action. In movies, he is the hero, the star, the one we watch, and the one with whom we identify. In single-player games, the protagonist is the player's character. Like the Jungian hero, the protagonist usually starts with a problem—but in contemporary storytelling, the problem can be further broken down into two distinct issues: the conscience, and the unconscious. The conscience problem manifests itself in the form of a want, or goal, which is usually the device that drives the story. The unconscious problem is manifested in the form of a psychological need. The protagonist might want money, but what he needs is to learn how to love. The want is something the protagonist recognizes and desires immediately and often illustrates his conscience problem. Because of the conscience problem (the want), all action comes from the protagonist's pursuit of that want. Remember Caesar? He wants the Roman Empire, and all action comes from his desire of the empire. Caesar didn't wait around for someone to give him the empire; he just went out and took it. He created the action and thereby created the story.

The protagonist is often physically or morally strong. The protagonist may even be a good person, but there is always his Achilles heel—the weakness that leads to the protagonist's eventual downfall. This happens in tragedies when things for the protagonist end badly. Macbeth is an example of an ambitious man coming to a bad end because of his personal weakness. Aristotle defined this as a *tragic flaw*. The protagonist's want is usually is born out of this flaw.

Antihero

An *antihero* is a protagonist who simply does not live a moral life and makes poor choices. As you may remember, Tony Soprano—the "lovable mobster" in the television show *The Sopranos*—is this type of hero. In movies, the *film noir* genre always deals with antiheroes. These people are always morally ambiguous. In the case of film noir, the genre is partly defined by the fact that the story always ends badly for the main character. This offers a sense of justice for the audience. You may think this is a new phenomenon, but antiheroes have been around for a long time. Let's take a look at a classic antihero from everybody's favorite playwright, William Shakespeare.

Vivendi Universal Games

The protagonist in *The Chronicles of Riddick: Escape from Butcher Bay* is an anti-hero.

Macbeth, a Scottish general riding home from a victorious battle with is friend Banquo, comes upon three witches who have the power to divine the future. The witches tell Macbeth that he will be king, but that it will be Banqou's sons who will carry on the royal line and be kings in the future. This is confusing to Macbeth. How can he be king if he's not Banquo's progeny? Macbeth tells his wife, Lady Macbeth, who is so taken with the idea that she helps Macbeth figure out how to fulfill the prophecy. Lady Macbeth decides that the witches must have meant that Macbeth should kill the current king, Duncan. Macbeth is unsure about taking his place in the kingdom in this way. Besides, he figures he won't see King Duncan very soon anyway. Of course, the next day there is an invitation to come to the king's castle. It looks like the three witches were right about Macbeth after all. He and Lady Macbeth accept the invitation and find themselves with the opportunity to kill Duncan. Due to Macbeth's hesitance, Lady Macbeth kills the king. This is an irrevocable act that takes place early on in the play, and one that causes the couple to preemptively kill anyone who might expose or oppose them.

For the rest of the four acts, the play really becomes about the bloody mess these two have created and—although we are watching through the protagonists' POVs—it is not a pretty sight. Like classic film noir, all will end badly for Macbeth and Lady Macbeth. They both go insane from guilt. Lady Macbeth begins to believe that she can still see the King's blood on her hands and yells the famous line "Out, damned spot!" Lady Macbeth eventually dies, while Macbeth is finally beheaded. After the massacre, few are left to run the monarchy except the sons of Banquo, who take over the crown of Scotland. While we may not like the protagonist Macbeth, almost everything we see happens through his POV; therefore he is the protagonist, the one that initiates the action.

These days the antihero has become more likeable. The character of the Bride in *Kill Bill Volume 1 & 2* is an antihero. She is an assassin, a trained killer, and a mother who has been separated from her child. She will go to any lengths to get her child back and lift herself away from the world of assassins. Due to this human link, the audience comes to appreciate this antihero for her skill but also for her want to change for the better, and we root for her to win.

NCsoft

In *City of Villains,* the bad guys are really the co-protagonists.

Co-Protagonists

Sometimes two *co-protagonists* must team up to defeat a common goal. If you remember way back to Chapter 3, Caesar and Pompey were once political allies and needed to stop Crassus from tipping the scales of power in his favor. Caesar was able to pull some political strings to get Pompey elected to power. Later, when Crassus is killed, Pompey and Caesar become enemies. Another example of this is in the movie *Independence Day.* When the entire earth is threatened by alien invaders, all of the nations of the world must band together to fight off the attack. While the story itself is told through the POV of Captain Steven Hiller, it is clear that all countries must team up for the survival of the earth. It is very common to see co-protagonists in massively multiplayer online games (MMOGs). For example, many players ban together to defeat powerful villains in *City of Heroes.* In the MMOG *World of Warcraft,* players join guilds to achieve a common goal.

Allowing two or more players to take on the role of protagonist and cooperate during the game will add another layer of complexity to the game experience.

Antagonist

The *antagonist* is the opponent—the one character who opposes the protagonist's want. While antagonists are not always evil, they do cause conflict for the protagonist. The antagonist simply wants the same things as the protagonist—if you remember, this is called the unity of opposites. They may both be good people, they may both be moral people, but they simply oppose each other. In our ongoing discussion of Caesar and Pompey, you will remember that they both want the same thing—to rule the Roman Empire. While it is arguable that both characters are bad people because of their lust for power and control, in this case it may just be a choice of who is the lesser of the evils. It is important to remember that antagonists, even if they are evil, are monsters that are made—not born. Remember to develop your antagonist just as carefully as you do your protagonist. Make your antagonist believable; give your character dimension. Often a story is only as interesting as the obstacle in front of the protagonist: the antagonist, or an obstacle placed there by the antagonist. Just as there are many antagonists who are not evil, there are always those who are evil. Think about Sauron in *The Lord of the Rings,* or even Voldemort in *Harry Potter.*

Capcom Entertainment, Inc.

Arkham in *Devil May Cry* is an antagonist who is in opposition to Dante, the game's protagonist.

Antagonists are so varied and interesting that several antagonist subtypes have been created—including mistaken, exaggerated, and realistic antagonists.

Mistaken Antagonist

A mistaken antagonist is a character who the audience thinks is the villain but is really innocent. If you remember red herrings from the story execution chapter, a mistaken antagonist is a red herring leading the audience down a path away from the real conclusion. This can also work in reverse. In the movie *The Usual Suspects*, the protagonist, Verbal, is an innocent underling to the evil mastermind, Keyser Söze. The story, all told in flashback, is seen through Verbal's POV—allowing the audience to easily identify with the character. By the end of the movie, Verbal has convinced us that Keyser Söze is just a myth. The interrogating officer releases Verbal. Just as Verbal gets away, it is revealed that Verbal himself was indeed the villain Keyser Söze. The protagonist is actually the hidden, mistaken antagonist.

> I am partial to the concept of the hero turned villain, as they show us that everyone has a breaking point and a dark side which we must constantly battle with for control. . . . An anti-hero or antagonist that appears to be a virtuous hero can be more creative and entertaining than your average good guy.
>
> *— Adam Garner (Game Art & Design student)*

Exaggerated Antagonist

An *exaggerated* antagonist is usually a one-dimensional character who is almost cartoon-like in his presentation of an evil villain. Set in a larger-than-life world, such as Batman's Gotham, these exaggerated antagonists are colorful as well as flamboyant. Quite often they are more colorful and more interesting to watch than the actual hero.

Realistic Antagonist

Realistic antagonists tend to be mild-mannered and nondescript. Vincent, in the movie *Collateral*, is a normal-looking businessman until we find out that he is an assassin. In other movies such as *24-Hour Photo*—about a sociopath who develops photos at a drugstore—the antagonist can be creepy and make the audience feel uncomfortable within a scene. With the use of a device known as *dramatic irony*, the realistic antagonist's intentions are usually not known to the protagonist but are clear to the audience. This helps build tension, because the audience knows where the trouble is heading. A classic realistic antagonist is Alex Forrest in the movie *Fatal Attraction*. Although seemingly normal at the beginning, the audience can watch the character become more evil as the narrative plays out.

Is the Antagonist Always Evil?

In the 1993 movie *The Fugitive*, the Federal Marshall (Samuel Gerard) is the antagonist, even though he is a good guy just trying to do his job. The protagonist, in this case, is Doctor Richard Kimball—the man accused of murdering his own wife and who is sentenced to death. During transport to prison, Kimball escapes. The audience knows that Richard Kimball is innocent, but Federal Marshall Samuel Gerard doesn't. Gerard believes he is after a killer. Richard Kimball wants freedom *in order* to find his wife's killer. Gerard opposes that want because he believes Kimball to be guilty and now an escaped killer.

As you can see there are many types of antagonists. If you are creating an antagonist, make sure that he or she is interesting and causing a lot of problems for the protagonist.

Ancillary Characters

Known as supporting characters, *ancillary characters* run the gamut from nondescript infantryman to sidekick to best friend to love interest. All serve different purposes, but without them there would be much less story to tell. Ancillary characters often take on a life of their own and go beyond helping to drive the primary story—adding both richness and depth to the entire piece.

Pivotal Character

A *pivotal character* is usually close to the protagonist. Sometimes the character is a sidekick, a husband or wife, or even an animal, as in the movie *My Dog Skip*. Often the pivotal character has a story of his or her own, which is usually one of the story's subplots. Within this subplot, there is often a story that reflects the protagonist's story.

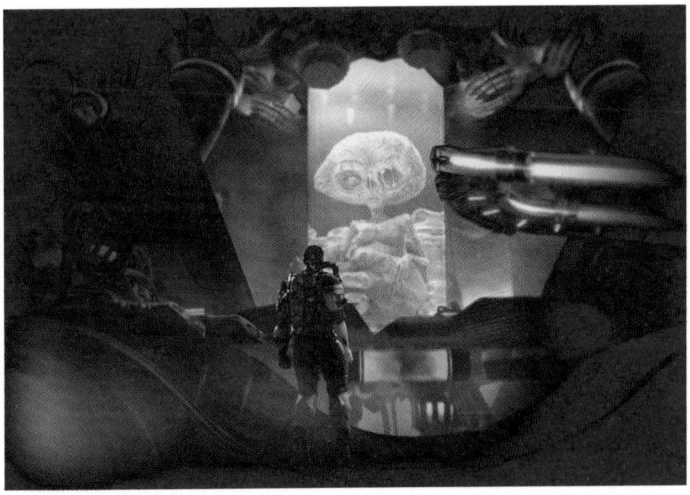
Midway

Edgar is a pivotal character in *Area 51* because he incites Ethan Cole to action.

In the film *When Harry Met Sally*, for example, both protagonists—Harry and Sally—have best friends, Marie and Jess. Harry and Sally decide to set each other up on dates with their friends Marie and Jess. While out on their double date—Harry with Marie, Sally with Jess—Marie and Jess realize that they are attracted to each other instead of their dates, and they end up getting married. This secondary relationship reflects the primary relationship between Harry and Sally who eventually realize they love each other and also end up getting married. A true pivotal character is a character that helps the protagonist see—either by telling or showing —what is wrong in his or her life. The pivotal character helps the protagonist change and grow.

Sidekicks

Capcom Entertainment, Inc.

Lucia becomes Dante's sidekick in *Devil May Cry 2*.

A *sidekick* is a companion to the protagonist. Sidekicks are usually used in classic hero stories. Almost always a pivotal character, the sidekick also serves several other functions within a story. Unlike in a novel—where a character's thoughts can be read by the reader—sidekicks in movies and TV offer important information for the audience. A sidekick is often young and unaware of the burden that the protagonist carries. Not only is this a way to reflect the audience's presence within the story, but it is also a source for the writer to provide informative dialogue from the protagonist to the sidekick, thereby revealing it to the audience.

Another use of a sidekick is to create a vulnerability the villain can exploit to manipulate the hero. A superhero is usually capable of completing any task, but the ever-present sidekick often gets in the way and screws things up for the hero. This always provides new obstacles for the hero to overcome. A sidekick also has an uncanny ability to be in the wrong place at the wrong time. The villain takes full advantage of this by kidnapping the sidekick and threatening to kill the sidekick if the hero does not cooperate. This offers high stakes for the hero, who usually feels strong affection for the sidekick (in spite of his foibles).

Finally, the sidekick can offer *comic relief*. Never as serious or as burdened as the hero, the sidekick can fill in a subplot with comic antics. When this happens, the burdened hero gets a chance to lighten up in the presence of the comical sidekick and offer a view of his normally serious self that the audience would otherwise not get to see. This always endears the audience to the hero.

Lackey

Just as the hero has a sidekick, the villain almost always has a lackey, yes-man, or toady—in other words, a sycophant. This character runs the constant risk of being killed at the whim of the villain. The lackey is not always the brightest bulb in the lamp, but this evil sidekick does serve a very important purpose. The lackey can help the audience better understand the villain—but, more importantly, the villain gives the details of the evil plan to the lackey, so that the audience can hear the evil plan and know what the hero is up against.

Firaxis Games

Troops in military game such as *Sid Meier's Gettysburg* serve as allies.

Allies

As described above, allies are helpers along the way. One step down from the sidekick, allies can come from anywhere and aid the hero's cause. New Yorkers in both *Spiderman* movies become the hero's allies. The armies of trapped souls led by Aragorn in *The Return of the King* are allies. In the famous kid's cartoon *Scooby-Doo,* the Scooby gang—Thelma, Daphne, and Fred—are the allies, while the human character Shaggy is the dog Scooby's sidekick!

Allies not only aid and further the cause of the hero and sidekick, but they are often expendable. The "red shirts" in the original *Star Trek* TV show served as allies, and were always the guys who got killed in the conflict. In a game where the player has control over many characters—as in the strategy game, *Rome: Total War*—the allies, in this case soldiers, are expendable, and are viewed as a resource for the player… a resource best not to waste. The death of allies can serve several purposes: causing guilt and pain for the hero, eliciting an emotional response from the audience, and demonstrating the high stakes in the story.

Henchmen

Henchmen (also known as minions) are in the service of the villain. They serve mostly the same purpose as the allies—but rather than wanting to help for the greater good, they are usually soulless creatures only out to do the bidding of evil. The Orks in *The Lord of the Rings* demonstrate minions perfectly.

Minions and henchmen always make trouble for the hero and his posse. Just as the allies are expendable, so too are the minions—and almost always, their side loses.

Midway

The scientist in *Area 51* is a henchman character.

Mole

In many stories there is the *mole*—the guy who is behaving like he is doing good but who is actually serving the villain. In *The Matrix*, the character of Cypher is the mole. The use of the mole is one of the many ways the villain can stay one step ahead of the hero and cause continuing obstacles along the way.

These contemporary types of characters are found in movies, books, and games, but there are characters that are specific to games. Let's take a look at the characters found exclusively in games.

Game-Specific Characters

All the characters we've discussed can be found in games, but games offer specific challenges when it comes to characters. First of all, a player might be able to play more than one character. Rather than having a single hero, sometimes games offer cooperative play—and every player can be the hero. As discussed earlier, characters in strategy games might only represent resources and not elicit an emotional bond from the player. All of these challenges will be addressed in the following chapter, but for now, let's look at character types that are specific to games.

Player Characters (PCs)

Player characters include all characters the player controls—whether a single character such as Lara Croft in *Tomb Raider*, or several characters such as military troops in strategy games. In MMORPGs, a player might develop (or create) several characters. As you begin to create a player character, consider allowing for plenty of attributes. This will greatly increase the chances of a player wanting to take on the role of the character you created.

Creating (and Selling) a Character

In MMORPGs, it has become popular to create characters and sell them online to other players who want to play at a higher level but not expend the energy to get to that level themselves. Often these "bought characters" don't have the depth of experience of characters that have been carefully developed by their players. Many serious players frown on the practice of buying characters. They feel that an important part of the game experience involves the player learning alongside his or her avatar.

Krisha – one of the world's first avatars.

Avatar

The word *avatar* comes to us through the Hindu religion. It translates as the human incarnation of a deity. Krishna, the Hindus say, is the human form of the God Vishnu. While avatars are here on earth, they never lose their knowledge of their divine nature. Avatars always know they are gods in the form of humans. In games, an avatar has a similar meaning. An avatar in games is the incarnation of the player as a character in the game world. While players can control many characters at once, these characters are not all avatars. The avatar relates to the control and play of only one character at a time. Developing and playing this single character creates a bond between avatar and player, and even in games such as RPGs where the player might develop several characters, only one usually emerges as the player's avatar.

The fun of creating an avatar is to have many choices. If you are developing a game in which players can build their own characters, offer lots of variety. This will insure that the players feel they are taking on unique roles in the game.

Non-Player Characters (NPCs)

Non-player characters (NPCs) are characters that are not controlled by the player. These characters are developed by the game developer and controlled by the game's artificial intelligence (AI) engine. NPCs exist for the player to interact with in some way.

Ultima Underworld: Character Reactivity

In *Ultima Underworld*, I reached almost the end of the game, and had resurrected a non-player character (NPC) who I felt could help me solve the main crisis in the game. When I asked him for help, his only reaction to me was that he *didn't know*. Then, to my shock, *he asked me how I thought I should solve the game*. It became a guessing game with keywords to try and figure out the best way to proceed in the game. It floored and stunned me (and scared me a little) to hear that from an NPC in a game.

— Chris Avellone (Chief Creative Officer & Lead Designer, Obsidian Entertainment)

Boss

A *boss* is a character who offers the player conflict and an obstacle to overcome in order to progress in the game. Bosses are usually defeated through combat—and, as the game builds, each boss becomes more and more difficult to defeat. Usually by the end of the game, the final boss fight takes place between the player and the antagonist of the story.

Many players look for a good boss fight as a way to judge if they like the game. It is important to have challenging bosses—but remember: If the bosses are too difficult to defeat, the player will become frustrated.

Midway

The Theta in *Area 51* is a boss that the player must battle in order to move forward in the game

Ubisoft

The Prince battles a sand monster—an enemy in *Prince of Persia*.

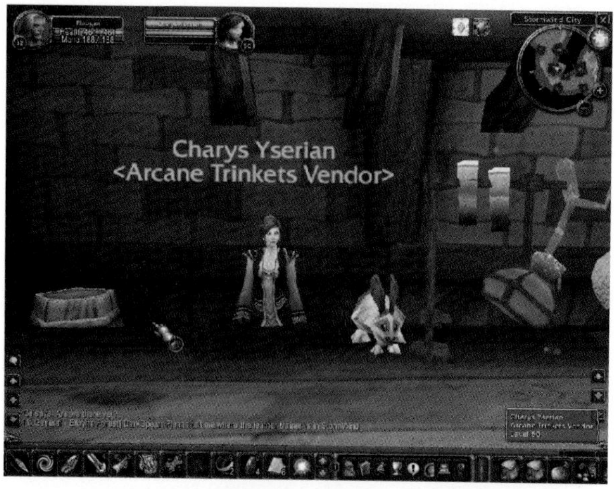

Blizzard Entertainment, Inc.

The pub wench in *World of Warcraft* acts as a helper character.

Sucker Punch/Sony Computer Entertainment of America

In *Sly Cooper 2*, raccoon protagonist Sly and other animal buddies run away from trouble.

Enemies

Enemies are characters who offer more conflict as well as a form of combat that keeps the player busy while trying to achieve the goal. Like the bosses, they are usually defeated in combat. With the use of artificial intelligence (AI)—an area of game programming that focuses on enabling characters and other entities in the game to exhibit intelligent behavior—an enemy can quite often adjust to the player's skill level. In games that require combat, enemies that are challenging to defeat are very important.

Game Helpers

Helper characters provide the player characters with important information on how to play the game or what is happening in the story. They may also prolong your life by selling you much needed food, weapons or other supplies. These NPCs are types of allies, but—unlike allies who often show up at a critical moment—they usually show up once or twice to aid the player. Typically, helper characters stay in one location where the player may return to interact with them.

These are the characters found in games and when developing games they are essential for interesting gameplay. Be sure you understand how these character types work as you design your game.

Animals

Like fables that use animals to tell the story of human frailty, animal representations are still hugely popular today. The Donkey in *Shrek* is a classic example of an *animal* character. Daxter from *Jak and Daxter*, as well as Ratchet from *Ratchet and Clank*, are also animal characters. Animal characters, however, never behave like animals. They are animal representations of humans and human traits. Choosing a specific animal should have meaning for your character. *Sly Cooper* and *Thievius Racoonus* use a raccoon to play the thief. Real raccoons are smart and thieving animals. When developing a character of any kind, it is helpful to think about what kind of animal they might be. If a character is a rat or a snake, think about how that animal represents that character. The reverse is also true. When creating an animal character, try to think what animal best represents the kind of personality traits you are presenting. Doing this will add meaning to your character and make the game experience richer.

Fantasy

Fantasy characters do not have counterparts in the real world. Lara Croft and *God of War*'s Kratos are examples of fantasy characters. These characters were developed specifically for their associated games and do not come from other sources. Developing fantasy characters allows the developer a lot of room for creativity but also demands that the developer pay attention to all the details.

Unlike licensed or historical characters where there is already an idea of the character, a fantasy character has to be built from the ground up. Although it means more work for the development team, building a fantasy character can be creatively satisfying.

Blizzard Entertainment, Inc.

One of the many fantasy characters from *World of Warcraft*.

Licenses

A *licensed* character comes to games from a pre-existing property franchise. Characters like James Bond, Shrek, and the *X-Men*'s Wolverine are all licensed characters. They exist in novels, movies, television shows, comic books, and other media before becoming game characters. Licensed characters are owned by the companies that hold the rights to the characters. To use a licensed character usually involves paying hefty fees and royalties to the owner of the character.

Vivendi Universal Games

Many of the licensed characters in *Chronicles of Riddick: Escape from Butcher Bay* appeared in the original film.

If you have an idea for a game that includes a pre-existing character, it is important to remember that you *must* have permission from the owner of the character rights. Usually these are expensive, and won't necessarily guarantee high sales for your game.

Firaxis Games

The historical figure Gandhi appears as a character in *Civilization IV*.

Historical

Historical characters are real-world people who have existed in a different era. Julius Caesar and Pompey are real people who lived during the reign of the Roman Empire. They are considered historical characters. Thomas Jefferson, Martin Luther, Constantine, and Cleopatra are other examples of historical characters. The beauty of using historical characters is that they don't cost anything to license, and history is rich with people and settings that would make great games!

Lionhead Studios Limited

The wood nymph from *Fable* is an example of a mythic character.

Mythic

Mythic characters exist in myths throughout the world. Games that have been inspired by Greek mythology would include mythic characters such as the Medusa, Cyclops, Centaur, Cupid, and Sphinx. King Arthur is another mythic character. Games that use fantasy backdrops, such as *Fable,* often use mythic characters. Using a mythic character helps define who the character is—but remember, the fun of stories is to tell them in a way that they are uniquely yours.

As you may have noticed, there are many character types to choose from. Usually understanding what your story is will give you a good idea of what your characters are and how they would be effective. Once you have an idea about a character type, it is time to start developing them. In the next chapter we will take a look at how to develop rich and interesting characters.

:::CHAPTER REVIEW:::

1. Choose a character archetype and discuss its significance. Find three well-known characters from books or movies that reflect the archetype you created. What are the qualities that make these characters "fit" the archetype? Create a character based on this archetype for your original game idea.

2. From this chapter, you learned that antagonists can be mistaken, exaggerated, or realistic. Find 4 characters from books or movies that reflect these 4 different types of antagonists. Choose one type and create a character based on it for your original game idea.

3. In what ways can players identify with avatars during a game? How does point-of-view (POV) affect identity? Which POV do you feel helps players identify more with their avatars: first-person or third-person? Which POV will you stress in your own original game?

4. What is the significance of being able to customize a player character? If you were to create a customized character based on yourself, what would it be like? Describe yourself in terms of a game character. What are your physical and personality characteristics, goals and aspirations, strengths and weaknesses, likes and dislikes, hopes and fears, and emotional makeup?

5. What are some of your favorite game characters, and why do you like them? What makes these characters different from those you see in movies, watch on television, or read about in books? While playing a game containing those characters, do you feel you have some control over the characters' actions or reactions?

CHAPTER 6

Character Development:

building compelling characters

Key Chapter Questions

- What are elements of a character backstory?
- How does internal and external conflict differ when developing characters?
- How does character physiology contribute to character development?
- How do you increase dramatic tension using character triangles?
- How do you add dimension to a character?

There are several formulas commonly used to develop characters. Unfortunately, the scope of human behavior is so vast that these formulas often will not be sufficient to develop truly compelling characters. A formulaic application of character has little to do with how to create living, breathing, full-dimensional characters.

Like sculpture, characters must be worked, massaged, and shaped to get the intended result. Just when you think the character you've created is solid, that character will do something unexpected—making the outcome completely original. In games, the player might take on the identity of a character and interact with the storyline and environment. Even with player involvement in character development, it is essential to begin with characters that are already well-developed. Like any storytelling medium, developing well thought-out and fully realized characters takes time, patience, and practice.

Creating a Character Backstory

When creating sculpture, the artist often makes use of an armature—the framework that provides a support core for the clay. When creating a character, it is important to structure an emotional "armature" to make sure your character remains a three-dimensional being and not a blob of mud on the floor.

In Chapter 3, we discussed how the backstory consists of the events leading to the moment the game begins. When we talk about backstory for a character, we are not only talking about the character's history but also the emotional makeup of the character that has led to this particular place in the character's life. When we talk about the story of Caesar, for example, we know that he is ambitious because of his goal to run the empire. Ambition is a good character trait that can cause a lot of conflict. However, it is not enough to simply talk about the fact that Caesar is ambitious; you must also discuss *why* he is ambitious.

Why a person behaves in the way that they do is an entire institution of information. From Sigmund Freud to Carl Jung to Dr. Phil, the study of human behavior is infinite and, in truth, may never be completely understood. When we create characters, however, there are plenty of devices that help us understand the person we are creating. Lajos Egri, author of *The Art of Dramatic Writing*, includes the character's physiology, sociology, and psychology.

Character Physiology

It may seem odd to think about the physiology of character first, but a character's physical traits will actually apply to the development of the character's personality. Later in the chapter, we will discuss the physiology of the character again—since characters are also developed through the art team. For now, let's use physical characteristics to help build the character's backstory.

How does your character look? Is your character short, tall, ugly, or handsome? All of these facts will contribute to how the character behaves. If a man is short, for example, he may have been teased as a child. This in turn may drive him to achieve great financial success, find a trophy wife, and go back to his 25th high school reunion a "winner." His behavior is a direct result of his physiology. What has just been described is commonly known as the Napoleon Complex. Napoleon Bonaparte, it is said, was a very short man. To make up for this seeming inferiority, he decided to take over Europe. Do you think he would have had the same ambition if he had been a tall man? Since there are many factors that contribute to personality, this may be an oversimplified view of a complicated historical character. However, Napoleon may have felt inferior—which could in turn have been a direct result of his physiology.

Think about the story of Cyrano de Bergerac. The entire narrative is driven by the fact that Cyrano has a big nose. Since he has a big nose, he feels inadequate and cannot profess his love to the beautiful Roxanne. When his young comrade Christian falls in love with Roxanne, Cyrano writes letters to her for Christian. Roxanne falls for Christian because of his letters, but Cyrano sees that Christian is a handsome, virile man. Years later, the fact that Cyrano was the author of the letters it is finally revealed—but his insecurity over this physiological deficiency has already ruined his life.

Ben Bourbon

Do you think a tall Napoleon would want to take over the world?

Ben Bourbon

Cyrano de Bergerac's large nose contributes to his personality.

These are just two examples of how the look of the character can help develop the personality of the character. When determining the look of your character, here are a few things to think about:

- Gender
- Age
- Eye and hair color
- Height and weight
- Body type
- Physical appearance (handsome, beautiful, ugly, plain)
- Distinguishing marks and deformities
- Facial expressions
- Nervous ticks
- Gestures
- Health (well, sickly, disabled, gaunt, athletic)
- Genetics (What physical concerns might the character have if his parents genetically "dabbled"? How might this affect his behavior later?)

Let's say you want to develop an exaggerated villain. As you fill out the above list, how do you think these physical attributes might affect his personality? Say for example that you want to make him a hunchback, but a mad-evil-scientist hunchback. Think about how being a hunchback may have made him feel as a child. Would he be lonely?

Would others have teased him? Perhaps it is now his goal to seek revenge for the abuse he experienced as a child by developing a way to make all people hunchbacks.

Physiology contributes significantly to a character's personality. If you want to give specific physical attributes to a character, remember that you do this not only for a good visual appearance, but also to affect his or her psychology.

Character Sociology

In addition to physiology, you need to consider the character's sociological background: where the character comes from, who his parents are, and how he was raised all contribute to the character's personal development. A child born into royalty, for example, is going to have a different sociological outlook than the child of a factory worker. A young child raised in opulent surroundings with every whim fulfilled is going to become a different type of person than a child who has only known poverty.

The job of the writer is to figure out how this background contributes to whom the character is and what he will become. To further explore this idea, consider two different sociological outlooks: a child from abject poverty and a child from unspeakable wealth. Just for the sake of argument, let's say the poor child's parents had only one priority: to send their child to an elite school for his education. Consequently, they worked all the time and eventually sent their son to a prep school. While the intentions of the parents are noble, perhaps this resulted in a child who felt out of his class and constantly embarrassed by his poor upbringing. He might feel his parents abandoned him. What do you think this character might grow up to be? What might his ambitions be?

Now let's look at another child, who is raised in wealth and comfort. This child is given everything, and when his grades aren't good enough, he is still allowed to go to the college of his father's choice. How do you think this character might grow up?

::::: The Sociology of *The Prince and the Pauper*

Ben Bourbon

In the Mark Twain classic novel, *The Prince and the Pauper*, two boys—one the young Prince of Wales, the other a poor citizen of the kingdom—trade clothes as a joke. Unfortunately, the boys are separated—and the young prince must spend most of the story as a pauper. While the point of the tale is about understanding, compassion, and justice, the idea speaks directly to the sociology of the main characters, who have been raised in diametrically opposed worlds. Can you imagine a game that explores this idea? How would you choose to exploit a character's sociology in a game?

Parents and economic background answer only part of the sociological question. Religion, political affiliation, race, and the era in which the character lived help to fill out the canvas of the character's background. Consider what a young, black, Muslim man might have gone through during the 1960s in America. How is his experience going to be different from that of a white, Christian woman from London during the same era? Obviously their experiences are likely so vastly different that this will contribute to their developing different sociological points of view. Also consider the current lifestyle of the character. Things are all important issues to consider when developing a character.

As another example, let's take a look at Caesar. He was raised a Roman, full of Roman pride and arrogance. As a child he lived in a hard world that was built around war and power. His parents were from the Roman elite. Caesar was an ambitious man, and a man with a great love for Rome. If we contrast his upbringing to that of a man born into slavery under the Roman rule, how do you think that character might feel about the Roman Empire? Who do you think that child would grow up to be? Would he honor the freedom of all people? Would he be filled with hate and the need for revenge? It is up to the writer to decide how these characters develop, but having some idea of what they look like and where they come from is a good start. As you work on your character's sociology, try to answer these questions.

- **Economic power:** What social class or caste is your character from? How will this contribute to his understanding of the world? What values will he have as a result of his social status?
- **Family roots:** What is the character's family like? Is he an only child? Does he come form a large family? Were they farmers? Bankers? Factory workers in the city?
- **Marital status:** Not only are we trying to determine if a character is married, try to think about what he thinks about marriage in general.
- **Occupation:** If a character has a particular occupation, try to think about how he feels about it. Does he like his job? Does he want to do better? Is he tired of the high-pressure rat race? If your character is not employed in his ideal job, what might that be?
- **Education:** How far did your character get in school? Is he academically ambitious and has a Ph.D.? Did he quit school at an early age? The education of a character speaks about who that character is. Someone who pursues education for a long time is likely a different type of person than one who quits early to make his fortune in the world.
- **Religion:** What religion does he practice and why? Is religion a passion or an obligation to this character?

- **Race:** While it is easy to assign a race to a character, think about what that means within his environment and historical era.
- **Political affiliations:** Political affiliations can speak volumes about a character. Be sure you understand why your character chooses certain political beliefs.

The sociology of a character is vital to the development process. Understanding the sociology of your characters will help fill out the game landscape with interesting character relationships.

::::: *God of War*: A Violent Yet Sympathetic Kratos

Sony Computer Entertainment of America

I feel that one of the most interesting characters is Kratos in *God of War.* Even though Kratos is a very violent, brutal, and aggressive character, I found that I began to care about him and in some ways almost felt sorry for him. I very quickly overlooked the violent acts he performed and became focused on helping him fulfill his quest to defeat Ares. It was an interesting glimpse into my own psyche; violence in the game didn't affect me as much as it did in the beginning of the game when I first met Kratos' very violent character.

—Shannon Studstill (Director of Production/Producer, Sony Computer Entertainment of America)

Character Psychology

While the physical attributes and sociological background can offer insight as to why a character might behave in a certain way, psychology is the study of that behavior. Behavior is motivated by emotion, and with the study of emotion we are finally getting to who our character is. While no two people will ever react the same way to a given situation, the psychology of a character will help to unify his behavior and make him clear to the audience. If a character were to feel frustrated by his position in life, it might be because he believes that he deserves more. If he fails to go out and pursue what he feels he deserves, this speaks to his psychological identity.

Let's take another look at the classic character Cyrano, who is frustrated by his love for the beautiful Roxanne. Cyrano could confess his feelings to Roxanne but he won't, and he is ultimately incapable of acting on his feelings for her because of his inferiority complex. The reason he has the inferiority complex is a physical attribute—his nose.

Behavior always defines character. Behavior is the single most effective way to establish who a character is, and that behavior usually comes from the development techniques we've listed above. Below are some psychological questions you might answer for your character:

- **Beliefs:** What are the character's values, attitudes, and beliefs? How does the character define right and wrong? Does he see all things in terms of black and white? Is he sincere in his beliefs? Is he a hypocrite?
- **Sex life:** Not only think about how often a character engages in sexual activity, but what does he think about it? If he is promiscuous, does he feel guilt? What is his sexual orientation? How does he feel about that?
- **Temperament:** Is your character easygoing? Quick to temper? Logical or emotional?
- **Attitude:** What is his outlook on life? Is he an optimist or pessimist?
- **Extrovert or Introvert:** Does your character like to be around people or do people make him uncomfortable?
- **Complexes:** Is your character superstitious, compulsive, or neurotic?
- **Intelligence:** Regardless of education, everyone has a given intelligence. How smart is your character? What kind of intelligence (book-smarts, street-smarts, IQ) does he possess?
- **Emotional intelligence:** How does a charter behave emotionally? Does he quickly become jealousy? Is he envious of friends and co-workers? Is he generous or magnanimous?

Citizen Kane (a.k.a. "I Just Wanna Ride my Sled!")

Ben Bourbon

The classic film *Citizen Kane* follows the rags-to-riches tale of Charles Foster Kane. Beginning with Kane's dying word, "Rosebud," the story is told in flashback. Kane is a man of relentless ambition and ruthless business practices—and the film ultimately becomes about a man so lost in his desire for power that he loses all meaning in life and dies alone. In the last shot of the film, the audience sees his childhood toy—a sled with the name Rosebud on it. The entire idea of the film is predicated on the idea that had Charles Foster Kane had a happy childhood, he would not have replaced his need for love with a relentless pursuit of power. His behavior is a direct result of his psychological need.

These lists and techniques help to give you an idea of the character you're developing, but there is part of human psychology that can only be defined as intangible. A man might be an introvert. He might be shy and bookish, but there may not be a definable reason why. The following are ways to further explore your character and ferret out the intangibles that can only come to the writer as the character develops into a fully dimensional person

Character development is being further embraced by the desires to customize individual characters. We want our characters to look, act, and work differently then any other character—since it is our individuality that sets us apart from one another, and we strive to retain it in many forms.

— *Adam Garner (Game Art & Design student)*

Discovering Character

How many times have we heard someone say on a news report: "Gee, he seemed like such a nice guy. I didn't know I was living next door to a psycho killer"? While the above techniques will definitely get you into the neighborhood of the character, what we're really after is getting under the skin of a character—to innately know what, exactly, the character would do in every given situation. In short, how does the writer become the character?

Valve

Gordon Freeman of *Half Life* is a character faced with internal conflict.

Internal Conflict

Have you noticed that the word "conflict" always emerges when discussing story and character? That is because overcoming conflict creates good games, good stories, and interesting characters. While we have discussed external conflict within story and gameplay serving as the physical devices used to delay the character or player from his goal, internal conflict manifests itself in characters in the form of a need. A character might need to overcome a certain fear because this fear has stopped him from improving his life. Cyrano's fear of rejection kept him from telling Roxanne his true feelings. Cyrano's need was to overcome his self-doubt which was related to his nose. The internal conflict manifested itself in the form of fear, which further manifested itself in the form of inaction and ultimately bitter disappointment.

An internal conflict keeps a character from doing what he needs to do. In *Star Wars,* Han Solo struggled with his own selfishness. He needed to overcome his selfish ways, not only to serve the greater good, but also to become a more fully realized person. Overcoming an internal conflict relates to character arc, which we will discuss later in this chapter—but for now, as we discover our characters, it is enough to define what the internal conflict might be and how to find it.

Finding the Conflict: Free Writing

An excellent way to get to know a character is to write about a topic as if you are the character. Write in a first-person perspective. Dedicate an hour a day to write a journal from the point of view of your character. Start with the line, "there is a lot you don't know about me..." and fill out the rest as if the character were confessing his deepest secret to you or even discussing something as mundane as his day at work. At first this may seem to be a silly exercise, but eventually you will start to feel the character bubble up within you. Then, while writing him into a script, his actions will help define the story.

::::: A Struggle with Our Lesser Angels

All characters struggle with internal conflict and the need to do the right thing. The question for game developers is: Does this apply to game characters? Will a player want to make the right choices in a morally themed story? The answer, it seems, is yes. The player wants to become the hero he is playing and will follow the story to achieve this. As games progress, developers need to start thinking about how to allow the player to struggle morally within a story. In the game *Fable*, players are allowed to become good or evil—offering a kind of moral gray area where the player can think, feel, and experience the consequences of his actions.

Lionhead Studios Limited

In *Fable*, players can struggle with whether or not to do the right thing.

Do plenty of free writing for all of your characters. This will give you an intimate knowledge of who they are and what they are capable of doing.

Turning Up the Heat

It is human nature to sit back and pontificate about any given situation. It is easy to see the moral high ground and believe that you would take that road—but the problem is, until you have lived though any given situation, how do you know what you would really do? To demonstrate this, imagine that you were alive in Germany during the war and that you disagreed with the Nazi policy of genocide. Unfortunately, to speak out against it meant that you and your family would probably be killed. Could you do it? We would all like to think we would do the right thing, but life isn't lived in black-and-white— it resides in the gray. In the same way that it is hard to know what you would do in a situation, it is also difficult to know what your character would do until you test their mettle. Placing characters within difficult situations and seeing what they might do is an excellent way to get to know them. The following are a few ways to achieve this.

Capcom Entertainment, Inc.

The players in *Resident Evil: Outbreak* experience their "worst day" when they have to survive by fighting off creatures after a disastrous outbreak caused by a secret biological weapon..

The Worst Day

If you have filled out the physiology, sociology, and psychology lists earlier in this chapter and answered the questions, you will know what your character does for a living. If, for example, your character is Shrek, you know that his job is to be an ogre. If your character is a doctor, then you know that it is his job to save lives.

When actively developing a character, it is interesting to put him or her into stressful situations. One technique is to think about the worst possible day at work. If your character is a lawyer, his worst day might be losing a case—but be sure to take it further. Perhaps not only did he lose the case, but he knows for a fact that the defendant was innocent. Perhaps it wasn't just a case, but the last of the appeals for a stay of execution. The innocent client will be put to death because the lawyer lost the case. That is one seriously bad day. Another example is if the character is a doctor and someone dies. If the character owns a funeral home, then a bad day includes the day that no one dies. If your character is an ogre whose job is to stay under a bridge and be crabby, his worst day is being forced to interact with other forest creatures, including an annoying donkey. Placing your character in this situation adds stress and causes emotions to bubble up to the surface, providing more insight into the character.

Worst Fear Realized

Sony Computer Entertainment of America

In *God of War*, Kratos experiences his worst fear.

Much in the same way you can think about your character's worst possible day at work, also start to consider what is the worst thing that can happen to your character from a psychological point of view. If you have learned from your free writing exercise that your character is claustrophobic, being locked in a small space could be the worst thing to happen—but what does this mean exactly? The rational side of us understands that being in a tightly confined place may not hurt us, so we have to explore what it means in terms of the irrational fear. A small tight place restricts our movement. There may be an issue with oxygen, and ultimately, being in a small place restricts our control over our environment. Even with all of these rational reasons, this still might be looked at in a way that isn't so bad to the objective observer. Now let's take it another step down to the worst-case scenario. Let's think about a small place that is a threat and produces all kinds of anxieties. The scene from *Kill Bill Volume 2,* where the character of the Bride is placed in a wooden coffin and buried alive, demonstrates a worst-fear-realized situation not only for a claustrophobic, but for most people. Finding a situation that is universally disturbing and then honing it into the psychology of your character will offer a way to learn more about him and how he might react in a really bad situation.

Harry Mason, the protagonist of *Silent Hill,* crashes his car. When he awakens he realizes that his daughter is missing. For a parent, this is an example of a worst fear realized. Kratos, the protagonist of *God of War*, also experiences his worst fear—which drives the action of the game's story.

Think about some of the things you are afraid of. Chances are that many other people are afraid of them as well. Now think about your characters and what they might be afraid of. Then, be sure to allow your characters to experience their worst fears. It will be interesting to see what happens.

No Good Choices

Finally, place your character in a scene where there are no good choices—only choices with different, equally bad consequences. What your character might do may be completely different than what you might do or what you would expect the character to do. When this begins to happen, it's a great sign. Once a character surprises the creator, there is the strong possibility that the character is coming to life.

:::: The Lady or the Tiger

Ben Bourbon

Frank R. Stockton's story *The Lady or the Tiger* demonstrates a very bad choice for the main character. The tale is about a young and jealous princess who ends up making a choice about her lover's fate. The handsome suitor is placed in an arena. On one side of him is a hungry tiger, the other a beautiful maiden. The princess must decide whether her lover will be eaten by the tiger, giving him death—or whether he will be allowed to live his life in happiness with the maiden. Either way the jealous princess loses him, so the question becomes, is it worse for you to know another has your true love, or for him to be dead? Both will have psychological consequences on the princess, and neither is a good choice.

Since choice is a big part of story in games, this is an excellent opportunity to give your character and player difficult choices. Difficult choices always make for more conflict, and conflict makes stories exciting.

Compassion

It is important to remember, even when dealing with evil villains, that these monsters are made—not born. All of the elements for building a character contribute to your character's backstory. Try to understand and feel compassion for your character. Try to place yourself in your character's shoes or take your character's side of an argument—even if you completely disagree. This will give you better insight into who your character is and, in turn, will also make your character dimensional and believable. Remember: behavior is a manifestation of who the character is. A character who is a jerk isn't just a jerk. He might be a tortured soul, acting out in the only way he knows how. While some assert that some people are just "born evil", we'll leave that debate to the philosophers. A character who is "born evil" will probably create a very one-dimensional a person rather than a fully realized character. Remember a fully realized character, is an interesting character.

Compassion is a key element when developing your characters. If you don't have any sympathy for your characters, no one else will either.

:::: *Planetfall*'s Floyd: An Endearing Text Adventure Character

Floyd was childlike, playful, and quite whimsical. He wasn't particularly bright, he was frequently annoying, and you often wanted to choke him. However, his desire to play Hider-Go-Seeker or to produce a crayon from some hidden compartment and begin drawing on the walls was amazingly endearing. He was the first game character that I realized I had deep feelings for; when he sacrificed himself to save me, I cried. Really. And the game was a *comedy*! I played it more than 20 years ago, and it's still compelling.

— Patricia Pizer (Lead Designer, 4orty 2wo Entertainment)

Activision

Ancillary Characters

When developing characters for games, sometime the secondary characters are more important than the primary character, since the player takes on the role and will want to experience the role as himself. Pivotal characters in first-person shooters, for example, often deliver the bulk of the story information to the player—so it is important to develop these characters well.

It's About This Doctor...

There is a joke about the actor who plays the doctor in the Tennessee Williams play, *A Streetcar Named Desire*. For those of you who are unfamiliar with the play, at the very end, a doctor arrives, has about three lines, and then leaves. When the actor playing the part is asked what the story is about, he says, "It's about this doctor..." Of course the story isn't about the doctor, but the actor is only supposed to think about the part that he is playing. For that actor, the play is about his character. When developing a character, try to think of it in this way and remember that all characters have a life, a backstory, and an emotional state. All characters can experience pain and pleasure, joy and sadness—and, like people, they are mostly interested in their own lives!

Although sometimes a tedious process, all your characters need attention, especially in games where an actor doesn't necessarily help fill out the role. Carefully and fully develop each character.

Consistency

After you have done your character homework, your character should start behaving in a consistent manner. If your character does not, quickly go back to the beginning and see what you may have forgotten about your character. Often, when a character starts to behave inconsistently, it has more to do with the developers, who interject

Per Olin

One way to make sure your character is behaving consistently is to make sure that—no matter what obstacles appear in his path—he is always moving toward his original goal.

their wishes for the plot, than the character's desires in the story. Spending time with your characters in a thoughtful way should help keep them consistent.

In games, where the development of a character can take as long as three years, the time spent developing and redeveloping can only have a positive effect. Remember, developing a good character takes a great deal of patience.

Character Growth

Now that you have a fully developed character and you know who he is, it's time to think about who he will become. From conflict there is always growth. If your character does not change throughout the story, there needs to be a reason—a message to the audience. If a character cannot change, the message should be a tragic one. If there's absolutely no growth from any characters within a story, this is usually a sign of bad writing—and a writer who doesn't have a handle on his or her characters. The theme of the story should be reflected in the development and change in the characters. If, for example, your theme is about hope, start with a character that is hopeless. If your theme has to do with courage, begin with a character who is a coward. The following are growth patterns that a character can experience within a story.

- Hateful → Loving
- Disillusioned → Hopeful
- Selfish → Selfless
- Indifferent → Caring
- Immature → Mature
- Discontent → Content
- Cautious → Trusting
- Cowardly → Courageous
- Arrogant → Modest
- Dishonorable → Honorable

Character growth is very important. A character that does not grow is a boring character to watch or play.

Character Arc

A *character arc* is a result of the conflicts the protagonist has to overcome in the story. Say, for example, you want to tell a story about courage, so you start with a cowardly character and then present him with challenges throughout the story. Each obstacle that the protagonist must overcome builds his character and makes him ready for the next challenge. When the final battle is set, the main character is no longer a coward and is capable of facing the final challenges to reach his goal. The achievement of the goal may serve the plot, but the story ends up being about what the protagonist needs.

Want (Desire)

As we have discussed before, the protagonist usually has a want at the beginning of a story. Pursuit of this want presents the challenge the protagonist must overcome. During the pursuit of the want, the hero learns that he also needs something.

Unfortunately, it's easy to lose track of the character's desire as the story unfolds. Be sure to keep track of what your character wants. Giving your characters a strong want is a great way to keep the story moving forward.

Nintendo of America, Inc.

In *The Legend Of Zelda*, the hero Link's desire is to save Zelda.

Need

The need comes about as a result of the want. The need defines what the character arc is ultimately about. A man wanting money may find that he needs to be loved. The theme, the arc, and the story is then about recognizing the need for love over the need of material things. As you develop your character, you may learn what it is your character needs. When you do that, you will have a good understanding of how to let your character grow throughout the story.

Ubisoft

In *Prince of Persia: The Sands of Time*, the Prince wants the Dagger of Time (so he impulsively takes it), but what he needs is to grow up. In *Prince of Persia: The Warrior Within*, he apparently has grown up.

Ubisoft

Do Game Characters Experience Growth and Arc?

Since players experience the game's story directly, the use of character arc can be challenging. Often, secondary characters experience character arcs while the player character remains the same. Sometimes the growth in a character comes directly from a player's newfound abilities in how to play the game. In *Halo 2*, the player has the choice to either be Master Chief or The Arbiter. While Master Chief has no backstory or character arc, the introduction of The Arbiter offers a character that experiences significant growth and makes the journey from dilution to truth.

To further understand character growth, it is helpful to develop a character using Abraham Maslow's Hierarchy of Needs model.

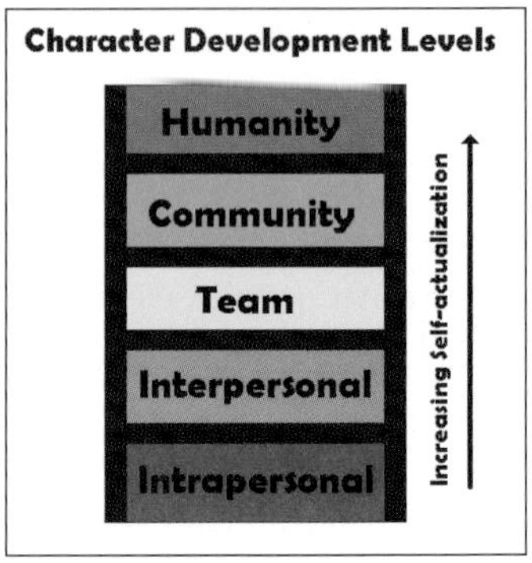

Maslow's hierarchy of needs illustrates the ascent of human growth.

Ubisoft

In *Monster 4x4: Masters of Metal,* the characters are only interested in serving their own desires.

Level 1: Intrapersonal

In this level, the protagonist is only concerned with his or her own needs.

Level 2: Interpersonal

At this level the protagonist bonds with one other character. This character can be a friend, lover, or family member. In terms of character type, the character that the protagonist bonds with is usually a pivotal character.

Ubisoft

The Prince and Princess form an alliance in *The Prince of Persia: The Sands of Time.*

Level 3: Team

In this level, the protagonist bonds with a small group of characters who share common interests. The level fulfills the need to belong. In the game *Grand Theft Auto: San Andreas,* the player is a member of a gang—a primitive type of team.

Level 4: Community

The community represents the larger organized network. A school, city, or company can represent the community.

Blizzard Entertainment, Inc.

In the MMOG *World of Warcraft,* players join guilds. This is a clear representation of the team level.

NCsoft

The city in *City of Heroes* is the community for the characters.

Level 5: Humanity

In the humanity level, the protagonist becomes self-actualized. This occurs when the basic needs of food, shelter, love, and acceptance are met. What it means in terms of behavior is that the protagonist realizes the need to work toward a collective, greater good.

Watching a character go all the way up Maslow's ladder can be interesting and intriguing but difficult in one story. Even so, if your character makes only one jump up the hierarchy, from intrapersonal to interpersonal, the growth can be just as compelling.

Capcom Entertainment, Inc.

Dante, in *Devil May Cry*, fights for all of humanity.

Aaron Marks on Enhancing Character through Music:::::

Practically falling into the game industry seven years ago, Aaron Marks has amassed music and sound design credits on touch-screen arcade games, class II video bingo/slot machines, computer games, console games—and over 70 online casino games. Aaron has also written for *Game Developer Magazine,* Gamasutra.com, and Music4Games.net. He is the author of *The Complete Guide to Game Audio,* an expansive book on all aspects of audio for video games. He is also a member of the advisory board for the Game Audio Network Guild (GANG)—and he continues his pursuit of the ultimate soundscape, creating music and sound for various projects.

Aaron Marks (President/Owner, On Your Mark Music Productions)

As in film, music can add tremendously to the personas of characters in games—and it can let the audience know what to feel about particular characters. For example, dark, menacing music accompanies Darth Vader whenever he appears onscreen—and the audience can detect that this character is pure evil without even knowing anything else about him. Music can be a powerful tool when used correctly, and games can really benefit from this skillful application.

Relationships

As the character goes through various levels of development, you may notice that other characters come into play. Relationships are significant in all stories since they not only provide devices to execute a story, but they give the protagonist the emotional story needed to engage the audience.

Relationship dynamics can be all about power. Who has power over another person? When you are born, your parents have power over you. When you go to work, your boss has power over you. If you are a general in the military, you have power over your soldiers.

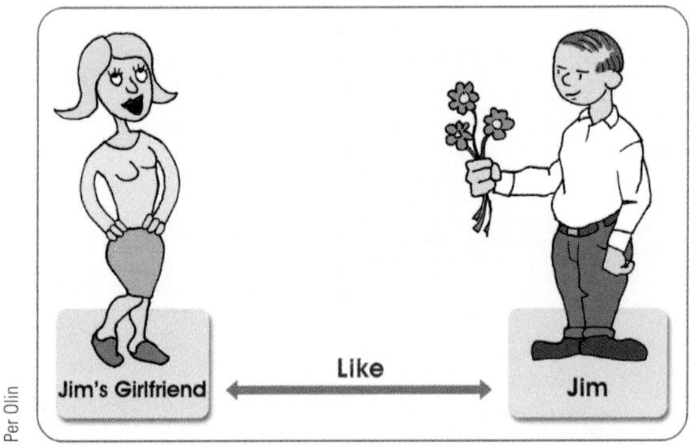

Whatever the dynamics of a relationship, it promotes a stasis within the relationship.

Dyad

It is important to establish the dynamics between two characters—or a *dyad*. Once you have determined this, you can disrupt the dynamic by introducing another character.

Once we have established the dynamics between two people, it is fun and interesting to disrupt them. Let's see what happens when we add another character to the mix.

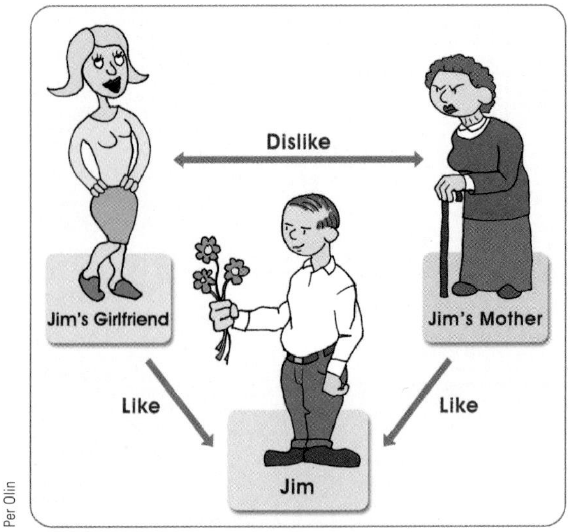

The introduction of a third character will cause tension between the original characters

Triangle

A character triangle occurs when a third party, usually a pivotal character, enters the story and causes the dynamic of the original two-character relationship to change. A typical demonstration of this is a love triangle, but this can manifest itself in many different ways. For example, Character A might represent the mother of Character B—who might want to move out of his house but does not want to upset Character A. Along comes Character C, a girl with whom Character B falls in love. The introduction of Character C has a direct effect on the relationship of Characters A and B.

All relationships have dynamics. How those dynamics play out and how they change is all part of how a character and story unfold for the audience and player.

System Shock's Shodan: Psychopathic AI

Of all the characters I've encountered in games over the years, the one that sticks with me the most is Shodan, the psychopathic AI (artificial intelligence) from the *System Shock* series. I vividly remember playing the CD version of *System Shock 1* when it first came out. There was something just chill-you-to-the-bone disturbing about watching (and listening—which was incredibly astounding at the time) as the sentient AI for the space station slowly goes insane.

We typically encounter key NPCs slightly before or shortly after critical events in their lives. Regardless of how the event occurs, it is a pivotal moment in the life story of the NPC and it elevates them to a new level of character—one that the player can recognize as being a target for meaningful interaction. With Shodan, rather than witnessing a relatively sudden character change, the player was able to follow the progression of her cyber-psychosis over the course of the entire game—experiencing moment by moment the deranged decisions and personality switchbacks that characterized her developing condition. Shodan's audio monologues triggered more emotion and excitement in me than any number of polygons, particles, or effects ever could.

— *Stevan Hird (Software Engineer, Midway Studios Austin)*

Point-of-View

In stories, the point-of-view (POV) is always though the protagonist's eyes. The audience always sees through the eyes of the hero. In game, the hero is often the player—so the player's interactivity with the game environment affects how the character develops. Typically, the POV is either first-person or third-person.

First-Person

In first-person perspective, the player never sees himself as the character; therefore, he experiences the story more directly. This POV offers the player the physical feeling of making his way through the game environment. Often these characters are developed with little storyline and no backstory. Doing this offers the player the feeling that he or she is the character. Unfortunately, not being allowed to see the avatar sometimes keeps the player from bonding with the character emotionally, because there is no mental image of the charac-

Valve

A scene experienced from a first-person POV in *Half-Life 2*.

ter. Games often offer a third-person perspective in cut-scenes, but cut-scenes can disrupt the feeling that the player is the character. In many games where there are cut-scenes, the character is nondescript. In *Area 51* and in *Halo*, both main characters wear suits that cover their faces. This lack of identity also promotes the feeling of the player being the character.

A good way to give players the feeling that they are inside the game space is to allow for a first-person point-of-view. This means that most of the story will be developed from NPC characters encountered by the player character. This can sometimes be a fun and creative challenge for developers.

BioWare Corp.

Jade Empire offers both a first- and third- person point-of-view—allowing the player to bond with the player character.

Third-Person

In third-person perspective, the player can see the avatar on the screen—giving the player a mental image of what the character looks like. While this does not provide the feeling that the player truly inhabits the body of the character, third-person characters are usually larger-than-life heroes who have undergone some sort of physical transformation. Third-person perspective offers the player a more cinematic experience, as well as a persona to try on.

First- and third-person POVs provide the player with different experiences. While first-person may feel more like the player is in the game, third-person offers a better way to bond with a character. Whichever you choose, remember that it might affect how the player feels about the character and story.

> *Max Payne* was one of the boldest openings of a game I've ever seen. Taking the main character and having him witness the murder of his entire family is an amazing way to get the player motivated to play. . . . *Max Payne* was a great example of how quickly you can develop a character players will care about and are compelled to follow through many levels.
>
> — *Mike Daley (Freelance Writing Producer, Blindlight)*

Visual Character Development

Although you have probably thought about the look of your character while developing his personality, remember that game characters are art-driven. It's time to come back and really nail down what he looks like based on what you have developed.

As we discussed at the beginning of this chapter, a character's appearance consists of physical attributes—such as age, gender, and eye and hair color. Now think of the character you have developed. If your character is the hero, what might he or she look like? Tall? Muscular? If you want to demonstrate how a character has been changed from an ordeal, consider who your character is at the beginning of your story. If your character is a coward who becomes courageous, take this into account when you are developing your character's appearance. For example, if the character is the antagonist and is dishonest or "shifty," perhaps you can add a subtle hint by making the character's eyes dart around.

Another physical attribute you must consider is the type of clothing the character is wearing. We have already discussed that characters in first-person perspective are often covered from head to toe—but consider what else a character might wear. Is he a soldier? Is he Roman? Is he a knight? Is he even human? Think about things such as armor and create accessories to complete the outfit.

Consider what types of props the character might carry. Does your character have special or specific weapons that are important to the story? Is magic your character's weapon? What type of prop would the character need then?

Every little detail contributes to character and story. Filling out these details carefully will pay off in the player's experience of the game and make it more enjoyable for the players.

Link in *The Legend of Zelda* series always carries his signature shield and sword.

Back to the Drawing Board

There are several techniques that help develop the physical look of the character. These include:

Concept: This is the first view of the character and should include several varying views. A strong profile is essential to make the character instantly recognizable. Try to limit the colors to no more than three or four, and incorporate a particular characteristic such as Mario's Mustache or Lara Croft's braids.

Nintendo of America, Inc.

Mario's mustache is a recognizable character trait.

> I always loved Mario. Who doesn't love a little mustached Italian man who likes to jump on people's heads and eat mushrooms to grow to twice his normal size?
>
> — *Justin Contreras (Game Art & Design student)*

Mark Soderwall

Mark Soderwall

Creature concept art from art director and consultant Mark Soderwall. Additional concept and model art is available in the back of book CD.

Modeling: Modeling involves creating the character's size in three dimensions. The modeling process begins with the creation of a 3D wire mesh to which 2D textures are applied.

Texturing: Involves creating 2D surfaces such as skin and costumes. Texture maps are used to give depth to the character's physical appearance.

All character production phases—including concept, modeling, and texturing—are crucial to character development and game experience.

Character Movement

Character development is conveyed through animation—another phase in the production process. When developing character movements as personality traits, be sure to consider the following:

1. **Signature**: A signature movement is an action or gesture that defines the character's personality. If your character is a ninja fighter, you may want to give her a special move that separates her from the others—perhaps a move that only she can do because of who she is and where she is from.
2. **Idle**: An idle movement takes place when the character is waiting for the player to resume action. Many times these idle movements reflect the gameplay and story. *God of War*'s Kratos breathes heavily, as if he's just finished an exhausting workout—a workout the player gave him.
3. **Walking Cycle**: The walking cycle illustrates a character's personality. Mario's walk is laid back, while Halo's Master Chief is cautious, as a soldier going into battle.

Be careful not to overlook these simple traits. With good character movement, a lot can be said about a character without ever having to say a word.

Style

When you are designing the look of your character, be sure to make the character stand out from the rest, not only using the aforementioned techniques, but also with a specific style. Many people try to emulate a particular look of a game or movie, but to have a truly original style, go back to your story's central theme. Think of how you would portray that visually. Remember to keep your character's look constant with the game world. Harry Potter set onto the mean streets of *Grand Theft Auto* would be a startling element to add to a child's game and probably wouldn't work, stylistically or commercially.

Sony Computer Entertainment of America

Games such as *God of War* are set in a stylized world.

Now that we have talked about character types and their development, it's time to let your characters do the talking as we take a look at dialogue in the next chapter.

:::CHAPTER REVIEW:::

1. What is the difference between character physiology, sociology, and psychology? Choose a game character and describe that character in terms of all 3 elements. List 5 features associated with each element. How does each element contribute to character development?

2. What is the difference between a character's wants (desires) and needs? How do these character elements relate to character growth and Maslow's "hierarchy of needs"? Choose a character from a film, book, television show, or game, and discuss how the character transforms as the story unfolds. Map out the growth of the character. Does the character grow, regress, fluctuate, or stagnate throughout the story?

3. How do the visual features of a game character reflect the character's personality? Discuss how you would utilize profile, facial expressions, gestures, poses, nervous ticks, costume, color scheme, skin/hair/eye color, hair style/length, character movement (including signature moves and walking cycle), and even associated objects and accessories to reflect the personality of one of the original characters you created.

4. Discuss 3 characters that you are interested in developing further for your original game idea. Make sure that at least one of the characters is a player character. Create a character triangle related to these characters so that each character has a relationship with another (whether it's positive or negative)! Create an arc for the player character so that the character makes some sort of transformation throughout the game. What obstacles and challenges will the character face during the game? In what ways might the character transform—depending on what choices the player makes?

5. Create descriptions (or backstories) of three characters in your game. Using 1 paragraph (3-5 sentences) per character, include each of the following elements: name, history, physical characteristics, personality characteristics, relevance to the game's storyline, and relationship to other characters in the game. Make sure that at least one of your characters is a player character—and consider how the player characters and non-player characters will differ from one another.

CHAPTER

Verbal Character Development:

effective use of narration, monologue & dialogue

Key Chapter Questions

- What are different forms of verbal communication, and how can they be used effectively in games?
- How can monologue enhance a game?
- How does dialogue reveal character?
- What are some techniques used in writing good dialogue?
- How can dialogue help with ancillary character development?

When working with story-driven games, information is conveyed through verbal elements—including narration, monologue and dialogue. This "verbal character development" can also enhance the tone of the game and the identity of the characters. In this chapter, we will primarily discuss methods of writing and utilizing dialogue that serve the purpose of a game story without taking away from the overall game experience.

There are three different types of verbal communication that are used in stories and games. Choosing the one that best fits your needs will help you convey important information and make your story more interesting to the player. To help decide what you need, let's take a look at the differences between narration, monologue, and dialogue.

Narration

Narration refers to the act of telling a story or giving a verbal account of something. In movies and in games, narration is a commentary made by any of the characters or by a narrator who is separate from the story and whose only role is to inform the audience or player about events taking place. A narrator may or may not appear on screen and may speak from either a first- or third-person perspective. Unlike the first-person perspective of gameplay that causes a player to feel invested in the game, the use of narration can take the player away from the story experience by telling the player what the story is rather than letting the player experience the story.

First-Person

First-person narration is used when the character tells the player directly, from the character's point-of-view, about an event being experienced. Some of the initial dialogue in *Prince of Persia: The Sands of Time* for example, is narrated in this way:

```
   PRINCE(V.O.)
Do you think I felt regret at the horror we had
wrought? Or at least humility at the speed which
destruction can take a good world to a hell? If
you think so you would be mistaken. All I could
think of was the honor and glory I would bring
my father by fighting like a warrior in my
first battle.
```

Vivendi Universal Games

Johns
You can step back yourself or I can give you a little help. And believe me, you don't want my help.

Escape from Butcher Bay offers a good example of first-person narrative.

First-person narration is effective in telling the audience that the character is somehow connected to the experience, and that the character is expressing his thoughts—which gives insight into the character's emotional state.

If you use first-person narration, be sure to incorporate how the character feels about his or her situation as the story is told.

Third-Person

Third-person narration is told from a character onscreen or a narrator separate from the story—but, in either case, the story is told about someone else. If a fellow soldier in *Prince of Persia: The Sands of Time* were to narrate the same dialogue from above, it might sound something like this:

Ubisoft

In *Devil May Cry 2*, the narration is from a third-person perspective.

```
   SOLDIER(V.O.)
Do you think my friend
the Prince felt regret at
the horror he had wrought? Or at least humility
at the speed which destruction can take a good
world to a hell? If you think so, you would be
mistaken. All my friend could think of is the
honor and glory he would gain by fighting like
a warrior in his first battle.
```

If the narrator is separate from the story, it might sound like this:

```
   NARRATOR(V.O.)
The young, rash, Prince felt no regret at the
horror he had wrought. He felt no humility at
the speed of which destruction can take a good
world to a hell. All he could think of was the
honor and glory he would bring his father by
fighting like a warrior in his first battle.
```

Third-person narration is an effective way to get information to a player quickly and helps demonstrate a tone and point of view. If you want to tell the story without revealing too much of the main character to the player, third-person narration is a good choice.

V.O. or O.S.: How to Format

In script dialogue format, you will sometimes notice "(V.O.)" or "(O.S.)" next to the character's name. V.O. stands for "voice over" and means that a narrator or character's voice can be heard over the images on the screen. O.S. stands for "off screen" and implies that the character is still in the scene, just off the screen at that moment. If your hero is talking to a person in the bathroom and you never see the person in the bathroom yet you hear them, this is an example of O.S.

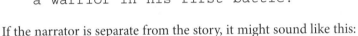

Narration is an effective tool for conveying story information to the player quickly and concisely. Choosing to tell the story through first- or third-person narration will help define the story you want to tell.

Monologue

A *monologue* can be defined in several ways—including what Jay Leno does every night on the *Tonight Show.* For our purposes, a monologue is a long passage or speech given by one character in a play, movie, or game. Like first-person narrators, monologues are usually used to tell the audience what the character is thinking, his present emotional state, or what he might be contemplating. Rather than being heard as a voice over, the character appears, usually alone, and begins to speak. The speech can be pointed directly to the audience or it can appear that the protagonist is thinking out loud.

An Aside

While a monologue is a speech that may or may not be directed at the audience, an aside is usually a short quip solely intended for the audience. An aside is a way for another character to comment on the action in a reflexive manner, reminding the audience that they are watching a play or movie. Periodically we'll see this happen in games, as another character might speak directly to the player.

To be, or not to be: that is the question:
Whether ''tis nobler in the mind to suffer
The slings and arrows of outrageous fortune,
Or to take arms against a sea of troubles,
And by opposing end them? To die: to sleep;
No more; and by a sleep to say we end
The heartache and the thousand natural shocks
That flesh is heir to, ''tis a consummation
Devoutly to be 'wish'd. To die, to sleep;
To sleep: perchance to dream: ay, 'there's the rub;
For in that sleep of death what dreams may come
When we have shuffled off this mortal coil

— Excerpt from Hamlet's monologue (William Shakespeare's Hamlet)

One of the most well-known monologues comes from William Shakespeare's *Hamlet*—as the title character contemplates either ending his life or fighting against his troubles.

There is no doubt that the excerpt from Hamlet's monologue to the left fits the definition of a lengthy speech—and this is only a small part of it! While it does seem that Shakespeare might have been paid by the word, this is an excellent example of how and when to use a monologue. Consider the text, "To be or not to be." Hamlet is contemplating suicide. Logic tells us that a character contemplating suicide would never tell another person. If they did, the subtext, or underlying message of the dialogue, would be: "Help me—I feel like I might do something drastic." Another excellent use of monologue here is how the audience gets a chance to see Hamlet's character through his indecision. He's not saying "I will kill myself tomorrow," he is asking if he should: "To be or not to be?" Should I or shouldn't I? Is it better to give up or fight the difficult uphill battle? All of this clearly demonstrates what is going on in the title character's mind, as well as reflects his behavior throughout the story.

Do Characters in Games Have Monologues?

Midway

Like Hamlet, protagonist Ethan Cole in the game *Area 51* must "take up arms against a sea of troubles and by opposing end them." Also like Hamlet, Cole shares his thoughts and mental state directly to the player through several monologues, during the game's loading time between levels. Doing this helps the developers convey to the player the emotional state of the character, and gives the player information as to what Cole is experiencing physically—which, in this case, is a viral mutation.

Monologues are best used when trying to reveal the innermost secrets of a character. The content of such speeches should be personal from the character's perspective, but important information for the audience or player. Use a monologue well, and your character immediately becomes more interesting.

Dialogue

Dialogue is verbal interaction between characters. It is important to remember that dialogue is not a conversation, but the illusion of a conversation. While a conversation may go in many different directions and never stay on a single topic, dialogue must be pointed and specific to the situation. Characters must never comment on the story unless doing so for effect. In the case of the television show *The Simpsons*, there is constant commentary on the story—but the world of *The Simpsons* is self-aware and ironic, and the audience comes to expect this commentary from each of the characters.

Dialogue: Write it First!

The quality of voice acting and dialogue engineering should be high—but dialogue must first be *written*. Bad dialogue will jar the participant out of the experience. Great dialogue will engage and motivate. The challenge is to *prepare* dialogue to account for the interactivity of gameplay.

— Frank T. Gilson (Senior Developer of Online Games, Wizards of the Coast)

The following is an example of how not to comment on the story through dialogue:

```
A small BOY, playing in a large oak tree, falls
to the street below.

   WOMAN
Oh no! That boy has fallen from that tree!
```

Game dialogue should be as concentrated and punchy as radio drama. The player will be hearing every line repeatedly; brevity minimizes annoyance.

— Allen Varney (Freelance Writer & Game Designer)

If you were playing this game and came upon this action, you would know that the boy had fallen from the tree because you would have seen it. Players tend to be smart people and don't need the story spoon-fed to them through wasted character dialogue—not to mention the fact that stating the obvious does nothing to move the action forward. A more realistic approach that drives the action forward would be:

```
A small BOY, playing in a large oak tree,
falls to the street below.

   WOMAN
Oh no! Someone call 911!

   SPECTATOR
I'll call 911!

The PARAMEDICS arrive and treat the boy.
```

You might have the paramedics ask, "What happened?" but that would slow down the action. The paramedics should go directly to the action, treating the boy.

In games as well as in all stories, dialogue serves a very specific purpose and should be used sparingly or the audience and player will quickly lose interest.

Purposes of Dialogue

Dialogue always provides information to the player, but there are many other things good dialogue can achieve. The following are ways that dialogue can help build a better game experience.

Exposition

Often, dialogue is used to set out important parts of the story—such as a plan, a character backstory, or a current situation. This information is called *exposition*—and, while it is in every story and is essential, it often feels like the writer is telling the audience the story directly rather than letting the characters show the story. Since all stories—even game stories—have to deal with exposition, here are some techniques for making it work to your advantage.

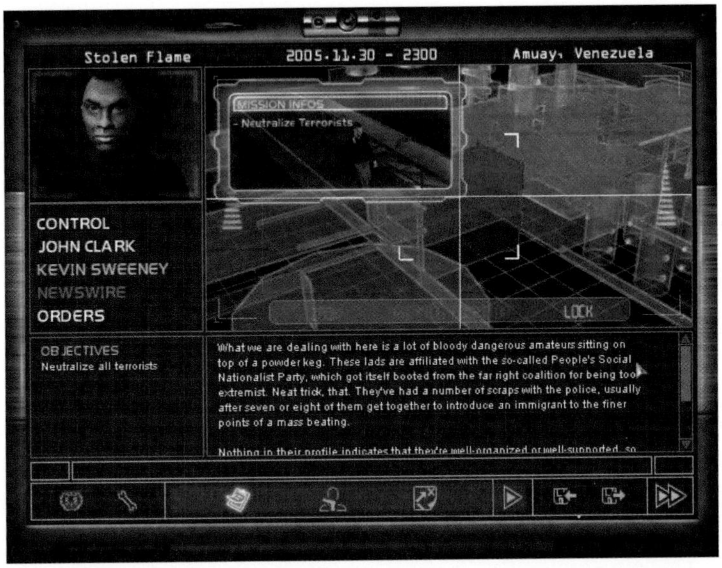

Ubisoft

Mission briefings such as this one from *Tom Clancy's Rainbow Six* provide exposition to the player.

Exposition, if left alone, is referred to as bald exposition. What the writer wants to do with bald exposition is cover it. There are two ways to cover bald exposition: argument and third object.

Argument

If two characters need to get out a lot of backstory, allow them to convey this information during an argument. The conflict puts the information into a context and does not distract the players.

In *God of War*, Kratos argues with Athena revealing valuable exposition. If you have a lot of exposition to lay

Sony Computer Entertainment of America

Kratos and Athena's conversations and arguments in *God of War* not only expose character, they also help to reveal several important story points to the player.

out, placing it in the form of an argument is a good way to hide it a little while still furthering the story.

The following storyboard from God of War is an example of revealing exposition through an argument.

Sony Computer Entertainment of America

5a.) Med. shot – Back of Boat. Carved wooden statue of Athena occupying the back deck of the boat.

5b.) CU – Statue's eyes open with a glow

CUT TO:
Ext. Boat/tent - CONTINUOUS

6.) Med. shot – Exterior of tent (other side) Kratos rips open the tent flap looking very pissed off. Kratos steps out onto the back deck of the boat.

KRATOS
Ten years, Athena! I have faithfully served the Gods for Ten years! When will you keep your promise? When will these visions stop?

CUT TO:

7.) Med. / Long shot – side view of boat. Kratos standing in front of Athena statue talking to her.

ATHENA
Soon, Kratos, but first you must sail to Athens where even now my brother Ares lay siege.

CUT TO:

KRATOS:
Ares is a God. Cannot Zeus help you?

Third Object

If two characters are delivering exposition, placing a third object in the scene is a good way to draw attention away from the exposition. An example of a third object might be a sword, puppy, or video camera. All of these items are things that characters can look to or play with to distract the audience from the dull exposition. For example, if Caesar and Pompey meet in a tent outside of Rome to discuss their backstory—in this case the story where Caesar and Pompey were allies once, a long time ago—perhaps the writer would want to place a special sword in the scene that both characters want. As they talk about their past, they might each hold, practice with, or otherwise covet the sword.

Midway

Target practice in *Area 51* helps the Player focus on a third object, the target, and still hear important information about story and gameplay.

While the use of the "third object" technique works better in cinematics and cutscenes, it can still be applied within gameplay as long as the exposition is coming from at least two non-player characters (NPCs). However, the writer should use this technique carefully—since a distracting object might cause the player to miss pertinent information.

Character

Dialogue helps to *reveal character*. Much like we learned who Hamlet is through his famous soliloquy, we witness characters revealing themselves constantly though dialogue. Patterns of speech and pacing help to establish this, but remember that choice of words reveals character as well. If a character is a university professor, he would use completely different words than a factory worker. Choice of specific words reveals character sociology. If a character was teased as a child and therefore is a character with feelings of inadequacy, you may want to give him a lisp or stutter to show a physical manifestation of the teasing he suffered as a child.

Most importantly, dialogue reveals the values and beliefs of the character. Once you understand what a character believes in and values, you will know a lot about that character.

Simple phrases such as, "Hate me, but do it honestly" (*Soul Reaver 2*) can raise questions about the motivations of both the heroes and villains in a game—especially when it is the villain that utters those words.

— Adam Garner (Game Art & Design student)

Emotion

Dialogue needs to *reflect the character's emotion* in order to tell the player the emotional state of the character. If a character is happy, sad, or angry, this could be reflected in the dialogue. A character who is sad about their sick dog wouldn't necessarily be excitedly talking about the birthday party to which they've been invited. Their tone might be somber, their pace slow, and their cadence measured. Be sure to consider the emotional state of all of your characters and how they would react to various situations.

Emotional Enhancement through Dialogue

Spoken dialogue can enhance the emotional relationship between the game player and character. Voice acting, when done well, gives the characters personality and depth. It is through the character's voice that we as players develop an emotional connection with that character. With the new console systems, there are greater opportunities for real-time adaptive conversations between the game characters and the game player. This allows for a much more immersive experience into the world that the game presents.

— Fletcher Beasley (Composer/Co-Owner, Beat Revolution Music + Sound)

David Freeman on Creating Emotional Dialogue:::::

David Freeman bridges the world of games and film. He's the author of the influential book, *Creating Emotion in Games,* with a foreword by Will Wright. In the book, David demonstrates 300 distinct "Emotioneering"™ techniques for making gameplay emotionally engaging. David's game writing and design consultancy, The Freeman Group, has worked with prominent game companies such as Electronic Arts, Sony, Activision, Ubisoft, Atari, Microsoft, Vivendi Universal Games, Midway, and 3D Realms. The Freeman Group has contributed to several games—including *Enter the Matrix*, *Shark Tale*, *Van Helsing*, *Getting Up—Contents Under Pressure*, and *Prey*. David is a highly sought-after speaker, teaching at both game conferences and game publishers around the world. As a writer and producer, David's scripts and ideas have been bought or optioned by MGM, Paramount, Sony Pictures, Columbia Pictures, and Castle Rock. David teaches the popular Los Angeles screenwriting workshop, "Beyond Structure."

David Freeman (President, The Freeman Group)

Dialogue can be used in a game to give characters emotional depth. The challenge comes when a character must be interesting or deep, but simultaneously must give the player instructions or information.

Let's take a look at some techniques for giving an NPC (non-player character) the quality of emotional depth. Let's say you're playing a hypothetical WWII game. You replenish your health points by eating the food prepared by the unit's cook.

Here are a few techniques one can utilize for giving the cook a sense of emotional depth with just one line of dialogue:

1. Deep Doubts:

COOK (looking over the battered and weary men; cynical): How's "the cause"?

2. Regret: (Note: here he refers to "Tom," a soldier he liked who died in the last battle.)

COOK (regretful): Tom was still limping. I shoulda' stopped him from going.

3. Self-Sacrifice

COOK: Sorry about the slop. Up all night with the wounded.

4. Wisdom or Insight:

COOK (downcast): You know, our kids won't even care about this war.

Human beings are emotionally complex. The more that complexity can be invoked in NPCs, even with a single line of dialogue, the more players will find themselves—without even realizing it—emotionally immersed in the game.

Plot

Dialogue between characters can be used to *advance the plot* and keep the action moving forward. An example of this might be when a character makes a plan and the plan is told through dialogue. Obviously a character should know his plan, but the players don't—so it becomes necessary to let them hear the information. Most often this is done with the villain's plan so the audience knows what the hero is up against.

Revealing too much of a plan or talking about story is not good dialogue. For example, "I am going to blow up the dam now" isn't satisfying dialogue. Seeing the dam blow up is always more interesting—and getting to blow the dam up, as one might in gameplay, is the most interesting. Even so, there are times when dialogue moves the plot along. "I'm going to the central market, and I'll meet you later at the cafe" could be used to advance the plot—especially if something happens at the central market and the character never meets the other character at the cafe. This might incite the character at the cafe to become more involved in the story.

> *The Bard's Tale* of 2005 took a great interest in skewering the conventions of the RPG genre (including its own predecessors in the same series) with quite a few dialogue choices that made the usually turgid game dialogues seem fresh. With the 'snarky' or 'nice' choices for much of the dialogue, the possibilities increased and created new depth.
>
> *— Howard Kinyon (Game Art & Design student)*

Conflict

As you now understand, conflict drives stories forward. Sometimes conflict can manifest itself in a physical form, such as a boss in a game—and sometimes the conflict is spoken. The Hamlet monologue quoted earlier is entirely about inner conflict.

Conflict between characters can often be revealed though dialogue. Not only will this establish who the characters are, but it can also establish their relationship. Most importantly, the desires of each character can be revealed and goals established. The unity of opposites can be revealed quickly and easily through dialogue.

Conflict is important in games and stories. Dialogue conflict is an excellent way to reveal character, but remember to use it sparingly so you don't distract the player from the fun of the game.

Relationships

Dialogue can help *establish relationships* within the context of the story. Often this is accomplished via the way the dialogue is used, rather than a character directly saying something like, "hello, wife" or "hello, brother." If characters who are husband and wife are having a dialogue, for example, make sure that they are familiar with each other. Give them a topic that is commonly found in the context of the husband-wife relationship, such as a child. If they are having a conflict, maybe it's about bills or another domestic topic.

In the case of two brothers, perhaps you want to establish their common parentage to illustrate the sibling relationship. Does this mean the writer has to go into long speeches about the family relationship? No—it can be as simple as, "Did you talk to Dad today?"

:::::The Text of Subtext

A good way to establish relationships through dialogue is using subtext—which is exactly what it implies: the text or meaning beneath the words. If you are writing a scene between a couple who has just had an argument but must not let their party guest know that there has been an argument, subtle indicators within dialogue can convey the real state of the relationship between the couple. Subtext is an excellent way to quickly and concretely establish relationships.

Another form of subtext is how the characters speak to each other. If they have a quick and witty repartee, for example, the subtext might be that they are friendly rivals. If the banter is more familiar, they may be partners in crime. As we will examine below, the use of rhythms and words not only defines character, but also establishes much in a small amount of time.

Ben Bourbon

Time for your walk! It'll be fun!
What she **really** means is I need the exercise.

Finding quick and clever ways to establish relationships is good writing craft and takes practice.

It's bad enough you pick on me but do you have to pick on a little dog too?
Ben Bourbon

Dorothy defends her dog, setting up conflict and expressing character in one line.

Action

Dialogue can be used to *comment on the action*—but be careful not to comment in a way that takes the audience or player out of the story experience. Make sure the commentary is important to the story and not just something to say. A classic example of commenting on action comes to us from *The Wizard of Oz*. When Dorothy's dog, Toto, is in trouble with the schoolmarm for digging up her garden, Dorothy says:

```
DOROTHY
It's bad enough you pick on
me, but do you have to pick
on a little dog too?
```

In this single line, Dorothy is not only commenting on the action—but she is doing it in a way that confronts the antagonist of the scene, demonstrates conflict, establishes the unity of opposites (they both want the dog), and reveals Dorothy's courage and strength of character. One little line. One little sentence. Pretty tight writing.

When commenting on action, be sure you have a good reason for it, otherwise it might become disruptive to the game and story.

Janet Wilcox on Voicing Characters for Games versus Film::::

Janet Wilcox (Author & Voice-Over Instructor, UCLA Extension)

Janet Wilcox was the voice of E! Network's show, *Hollywood & Divine*, *Beauty Secrets Revealed*, and AMC's *Nicole Kidman, An American Cinematheque Tribute*. Janet also played opposite Brian Benben in the movie *Mortal Sins*, and opposite Susan Saint James in *Kate & Allie*. As a writer, producer, and director, Janet worked on major promotional campaigns for HBO and also promoted programs on The History Channel. She directed promo segments with Keith Carradine for the HBO series *Deadwood*. While at HBO, she also directed segments with celebrities such as Jerry Seinfeld, Martin Mull, Colleen Dewhurst, William Petersen, Kate Capshaw, Sugar Ray Leonard, Sam Kinison, and Gladys Knight.

Janet received her Master's degree in Communication from the Annenberg School of Communication at the University of Pennsylvania, and has taught "Sources of the Modern Cinema" with Amos Vogel—one of the original founders of the New York Film Festival. She also taught at Marymount

Manhattan College, Heyman Talent, and the SAG Conservatory. Janet currently teaches a studio voice-over class at UCLA Extension in Los Angeles. She is currently writing the book, *The Game is Never Over: Winning Strategies for Voice Over*.

Since video games are action-packed, the characters generally have an epic feel. They're big with full vocal energy. A small voice often doesn't cut through all the high energy music and effects or add to the excitement of games. Animated film and television stories often have more traditional plots, which can sometimes allow characters to have more depth and development. These characters can range from very real to broad and cartoony.

Hope Levy on Game Character Development through Voice Acting:::::

Hope Levy can be heard as various voices in *Howl's Moving Castle* and *Madagascar*. Her voice is also heard in the games *Paths of Neo, Bratz, Polar Express, Everquest II, Jumpstart, Vampires Masquerade: Bloodlines*, and as Rebecca Chambers in *Resident Evil: Biohazard*. She has voiced characters on *The Fairly Odd Parents, Rugrats, Ozzy & Drix, Invader Zim*, and the Japanese anime series *Shin Chan*. On screen, Hope can be seen and heard in numerous commercials as well as playing the Greek Wedding Girl in *My Big Fat Independent Movie*, which was co-written and produced by Chris Gore of Film Threat and G4 TV. Hope also co-stars as Pam, the wannabe rapper, in *Uncle P*, starring Master P and Lil' Romeo.

Hope Levy (Voice Actor)

The minor and often overlooked characters in films get a chance to be more developed in game adaptations. In *Paths of Neo*, I play a variety of minor characters, such as the Office Drone, who works in the same office as Neo. This character gets a chance to be much more developed and has a scenario of her own.

Playing Rebecca Chambers in *Resident Evil: Biohazard* was still the most fun for me, since I got to show a wide range of emotions and have a through line. Most of the games I've been working on lately are supporting characters with short plot lines. While it's great to stretch and work harder to change my voice when playing four characters in the same game, it is still fun to be a principal character who exists in the game from beginning to end!

Valve

The determined look on the face of protagonist Gordon Freeman in *Half-Life 2* conveys meaning non-verbally.

Non-Verbal Dialogue

Not all dialogue is verbal. Much of it can be communicated through action. In movies, the use of non-verbal dialogue can help to raise the dramatic tension. There can be non verbal dialogue in games as well. An NPC pointing the way for a player is a form of non-verbal dialogue. In games, however, information must be very clear—so if you use a device such as an NPC pointing the way, be sure that it is a clear direction for the player.

Non-verbal dialogue can be used effectively through animation. Make sure that the animated sequences in your game are detailed enough to convey the subtle nuances need for non-verbal dialogue.

Text dialogue is specific to games and often scrolls along the bottom of the screen for the player to read. This is done to ensure that the player understands the information correctly. Be sure to reflect the tone of the game, attitude of the character, and inflection of the character's speech within the text dialogue in order to maintain a consistent and immersive world for the player.

Nintendo of America, Inc.

Paper Mario offers a look at text based dialogue.

Text dialogue also occurs in another form. A player might stumble upon a wall with writing on it. This is an excellent way for the development team to provide more information about the story for the player through gameplay, as well as adding a layer of foreshadowing and intrigue. If a player comes to a wall of a temple that has writing on it by a former hero, this will foreshadow danger, but also add another glimmer of the story that will inevitably make the experience richer.

Text dialogue is useful especially when you need to make sure the player understands the situation. Always keep in mind that there are creative and atmospheric ways to accomplish this as well.

> I'm sorry I wrote you such a long letter; I didn't have time to write you a short one.
>
> — *Mark Twain*

In-Game Dialogue

While all of the techniques we've discussed apply to writing dialogue in games, there are a couple of vital differences. In games, you need to quickly dispense information to the player. Something that might take a good film writer three lines to get across might need to be accomplished in a single line during a game. This kind of condensed writing is a Herculean task.

NPC Dialogue

Since most game dialogue comes from NPCs, it is important to remember who these characters are as well as their emotional states. Where are the characters in terms of location—and what have they just experienced as the player approaches them? Is the character a soldier who has just witnessed brutal combat? Is the character a child who is looking for her parents? Is the character a monster or a wizard? Knowing who they are, what has just happened to them, and how the player will interact with them will give you realistic characters with which the player can interact.

Try this as an exercise: Think of any number of game directions and put them into a sentence. Then try to write about the same information while implementing all of the character traits you have decided to use. Finally, try to do it again in context of your game's theme and tone. All of a sudden, your one sentence has become a very long line—and the pace of your entire game can be slowed because of one seemingly tiny bit of information. As an example, let's look at a simple two-word instruction, and then again with a little more character involved:

```
   NPC
Turn right.

   NPC PIRATE
Ahoy thar matey, be sure ye turn toward the
starboard or ye will be sure to meet thy doom!
```

Haiku: You're Welcome!

Waking in the night;
the lamp is low,
the oil freezing.

— *Basho Matsuo*

Writing good dialogue is never easy, but writing within the tight confines of game dialogue takes practice. A form that has a lot in common with this type of condensed writing is the Japanese verse form, Haiku. This poetic style is similar to writing for games in its attempt to write powerful lines with only a few words, and even a limited number of syllables. The first line can only be five syllables, the second seven, and the last line must be five. As an exercise, try writing a character line using this form. It might help you find the essence of the information you are trying to convey and give you a better line of dialogue.

Blizzard Entertainment, Inc.

"The NPC tavern keeper in *World of Warcraft* supplies a rotating dialogue loop. Approaching him more than once will allow the player to receive different dialogue segments—adding a realistic element to the game.

Another distinctive feature of game dialogue is that a player might go back to an NPC several times, looking for information. In this way, the dialogue must continue to be available, depending on what the player is doing and how the player is responding.

The following is a dialogue selection from the *Area 51* game script. As you will see, there are many lines of dialogue for one action taken by the player.

Midway

```
Ramirez walks to the ammo cage, then says:

   RAMIREZ
I know you don't carry a gun in the science lab
normally, but we're gonna need it this time.

Or

   RAMIREZ
You remember the outbreak in Angola? Well, this
sure isn't Angola. We're gonna need firepower.
Grab the pistol, Cole.

Reminder1

   RAMIREZ
Specialist, your pistol is over there!

Reminder2

   RAMIREZ
Why don't you pick up your pistol, Cole!
```

```
Reminder 3

   RAMIREZ
Time to pick-up your pistol, Cole.

When you grab the pistol:

   RAMIREZ
Cole, join Crispy at the range.

Ramirez will walk to the left and point to Crispy
```

This *Area 51* dialogue is one example of how dialogue in games is very different from other story-driven media. Coming up with new and fresh dialogue for the same situation over and over again, is just one of the many challenges in writing game dialogue.

Always try to keep your characters who have multiple lines fresh by finding new ways to deliver old information. This will allow the players to become more immersed in the game experience.

MMOG Dialogue

In the beginning of this chapter we talked about the differences between conversation and dialogue. In a massively multiplayer online game (MMOG) the game developer has an entirely different challenge. Most of the characters are avatars controlled by players. Not only is there a possibility of non-specific dialogue—because it's "real" (and unpredictable) conversation—it is the responsibility of these players to stay in character for the benefit of the game environment, and the other player's immersion experience.

If, for example, you are in an MMOG with Caesar and Pompey in the ancient city of Rome—and another character starts talking about a MacDonald's Big Mac—the game experience would be ruined for the players who are trying to stay "immersed" in the ancient world of the game. Often the MMOG experience becomes more of a social gathering for players rather than an actual game story experience.

Three Rings Design

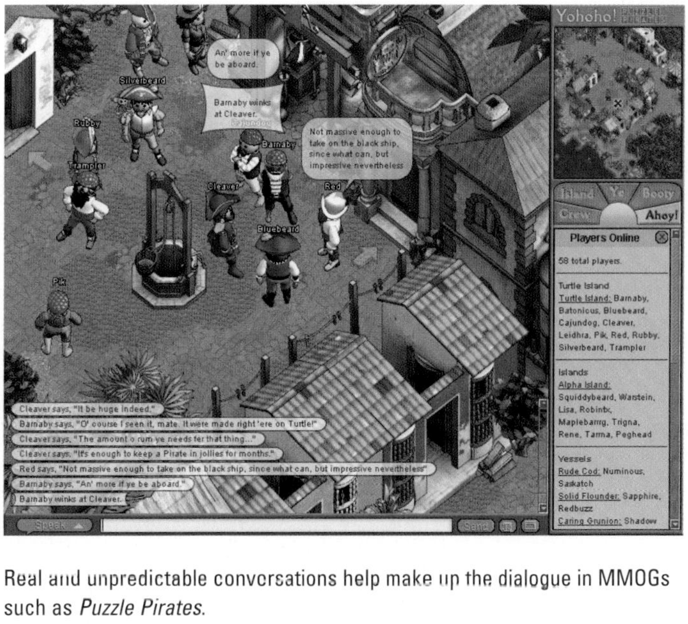

Real and unpredictable conversations help make up the dialogue in MMOGs such as *Puzzle Pirates*.

I think Manny Calavera, the character in *Grim Fandango*, was interesting, complex, and the dialogue was unmatched by any other game. It is fresh, funny, and free of the clichés that are so common in other hero's journey stories. It is one title that I'd recommend all game designers who are serious about dialogue should study.

— *Mark Terrano (Technical Game Manager, Xbox – Microsoft)*

Writing Great Dialogue

Dialogue can be a very difficult task for many writers. Often special dialogue writers are brought in to rewrite dialogue or polish the final words in a script. In case you don't have the budget to hire Quentin Tarantino to rewrite dialogue, Loyola Marymount screenwriting Professor, Steve Duncan, suggests that there a few things to consider when writing.

Listen

Often the mistake writers make is that all of their characters start to sound alike. Not all people speak alike—so the next time you are at a party, a park, or even a wedding, listen to the way people speak. Don't worry so much about what they are saying. Think about how they are saying it, what they mean by it, and how you might be able to make it into interesting and compelling dialogue. The following are suggestions of how and what to think about when writing dialogue.

Ben Bourbon

Listening to the way people speak can improve dialogue writing skills.

Keep it Short!

The most common dialogue problem in games isn't actually bad writing or bad acting—though we have plenty of both! It's that most game dialogue is just too darn long. Players don't pick up a *game* controller to read or listen to extended monologues or dialogue sequences. They play games to play—to take action. Most writers (myself most certainly included) are just too darn long-winded!

— *Warren Spector (President & Creative Director, Junction Point Studios)*

Cadence

Once you can hear the pattern, try to listen for the rhythm or cadence. Just like a drum beats, people speak in various rhythms. The cadence of speech patterns can reveal character, but we are also trying to establish each character as an individual. One way to think about rhythm is to listen to other sound patterns. Think about how a large river sounds versus a bubbling creek. The slower rhythms found in the southern United States move more like a river, while the quick pace of a Brooklyn accent can seem more like the quick and harder rhythms of whitewater rapids.

Don't Break the Suspension of Disbelief

Really bad dialogue (and wooden voice acting) immediately turns your game from an interesting experience into one that is mocked. No matter how good the gameplay is, really bad dialogue breaks the suspension of disbelief, the experience of being caught up in something so that you forget your surroundings. In a movie theater, really bad dialogue makes you suddenly aware of how uncomfortable your seat is or how sticky the floor is. With a game, you're thrown out of the world inside the computer and you're sitting in a desk chair staring through the glass. The sense of being part of the fictional world is destroyed. Every time the audio plays, you cringe. It becomes what you remember about the game.

— Patricia Pizer (Lead Designer, 4orty 2wo Entertainment)

Frank Capra Keeps the Rhythm

Famed 1930s director Frank Capra believed that all scenes kept a certain rhythm. When working, especially in comedy, he would make his actors speak their lines to the pace set by a metronome. Doing this helped eliminate unnecessary dialogue, as well as kept the action moving forward. When thinking about scenes and especially dialogue, consider the pace—or try using a device like a metronome to keep the tempo. If you do this, your language will take on a distinctive manner and will not drag, because you have to use words and lines that keep the beat set forth by the chosen rhythm.

Ben Bourbon

People often speak in a way that sounds like something else. A fast-talking auctioneer, for example, might sound like the rhythm of a train.

When writing dialogue, try to remember the different patterns and cadences. Will your character sound like the clackety-clack of a railroad train or the monotone hum of a well-tuned car engine?

Vocabulary

As mentioned earlier, the choice of words used in dialogue will establish the character's sociology or background, and even his IQ. In the case of the film *Good Will Hunting*, the protagonist was a janitor at Harvard University who could speak fluidly with any of the professors there, yet he still had a strong South Boston accent. What this tells us is that the character is intelligent and has a self-motivated desire to learn.

The first *Resident Evil*, the *Splinter Cell* series, and *Psychonauts* all have great dialogue. It's not forced, and—whether you are laughing (*Psychonauts*) or becoming more focused on your goals (*Splinter Cell*)—the dialogue never seems like it's insulting your intelligence. The dialogue is appropriate for the story and moves the game along without being overbearing.

— Kofi Jamal (Game Art & Design student)

Don't Break Immersion

Bad dialogue is one of the easiest ways to break immersion in a game. All it takes is one real clunker of a line at a crucial moment, and all of a sudden your player goes from empathizing with the character to critiquing it. I use a simple test to try to avoid this: I read every bit of dialogue out loud—and, if there's anything I feel compelled to read in a funny voice or accent, it goes back in for a rewrite.

— Richard Dansky (Central Clancy Writer, Ubisoft/Red Storm Entertainment)

Vernacular

Vernacular refers to the everyday common language people use. This can help to establish the region in which your story is set, as well as define the character further. Formal language might go something like this:

```
   BOY
I am going to go and see the horse
race. Would you like to come and
join me?
```

In the vernacular, the same line might read like this:

```
   BOY
I'm gonna go to the races. Wanna come?
```

Interestingly, writers almost always lean toward use of more formal language when writing a first draft of dialogue, even though they don't speak in that manner. Use contractions such as "I'm" (instead of "I am") and "don't" (instead of "do not"). Write as you'd actually speak.

Slang

Slang is similar to vernacular but is more about the expressions of language rather than the usage. Slang is incredibly useful in establishing an era that a character might be from, as well as setting and tone. In a 1940s film noir, a character might offer a line such as this:

```
   DETECTIVE
Yeah, that dame is a hot tomato with a great
set of gams, but I'd have to be a fourteen
carat sucker to get involved in that caper.
```

Translation:

```
   DETECTIVE
She is a good looking woman with nice legs, but
I could never be so foolish as to get involved
in that dangerous and illegal activity.
```

Of course, neither line would work for a more contemporary setting, but a heavy dose of contemporary slang might read like this:

```
   DETECTIVE
That chicken-head got back, but I'm gonna 86
that scheme.
```

The problem with slang, of course, is that it is of the moment. To use something that is "in" today might make your story seem dated later. It is best to use slang when trying to establish an era from the past.

Improving Game Dialogue

We have to move game conversations to something approaching natural conversation. Engaging, snappy, and well-crafted dialogue should be the rule—not the exception, as it is now. Professional interactive writers are the key to getting great dialogue and characters into the game, and deepening the whole experience through effective narrative. We need to work on better cross-platform tools that smoothly integrate script, voice, lip-sync, and emotive gestures to reduce the cost of content creation and development. We should immediately move beyond 'story vendor' NPCs that squirt out flat bits of dialogue when we poke them. We need engaging conversations and character interaction that happens *during* the game—not in the margins.

— Mark Terrano (Technical Game Manager, Xbox–Microsoft)

Don Daglow on Writing Great Game Dialogue:::::

Don L. Daglow
(President & CEO,
Stormfront Studios)

Don L. Daglow has served as president and CEO of Stormfront Studios since founding the company in 1988. Stormfront's recent titles include *Demon Stone* and *The Lord of the Rings: The Two Towers. Electronic Games* has called him "one of the best-known and respected producers in the history of the field." Prior to founding Stormfront, Don served as director of Intellivision game development for Mattel, as a producer at Electronic Arts, and as head of the Entertainment and Education division at Broderbund. He designed and programmed the first-ever computer baseball game in 1971 (now recorded in the Baseball Hall of Fame in Cooperstown), the first mainframe computer role-playing game (*Dungeon*, 1975), the first sim game (Intellivision's *Utopia*, 1982) and the first original play-by-email game (*Quantum Space* for AOL, 1989). Don co-designed Computer Game Hall of Fame title *Earl Weaver Baseball* (EA, 1987), the first massively multiplayer online graphic adventure, *Neverwinter Nights*, for AOL (1991–97) and the first 3D perspective Real Time Strategy Game (*Stronghold*, SSI, 1992). In 2003, Don was elected to the Board of Directors of the Academy of Interactive Arts and Sciences. That same year he received the Classic Gaming Expo Achievement Award for "groundbreaking accomplishments that shaped the Video Game Industry." He also is a past winner of the National Endowment for the Humanities New Voices playwriting competition. Don holds a BA in Writing from Pomona College and an M.Ed. from Claremont Graduate University.

The minimum goal in dialogue is to make it "invisible" within the game. A voice cries out, "Look out! Behind you!" You whirl and shoot a terrorist even as his ultra-sharp blade arcs towards your throat. Ducking behind a crate, you look around for a moment, then hear a voice call, "Move out! We have to get to the silo!" You take a deep breath and leave cover, eyes peeled as you run towards the door beyond which you know your mission takes you. That dialogue works. You hang onto every syllable, because it guides you to success in the game. No Pulitzer Prize for Literature, but it works.

Now, imagine that the speaker is using the voice of Bugs Bunny. You hear, "Hey doc, maybe you oughta look behind you." Suddenly the dialogue isn't functional and invisible. You still whirl and kill the terrorist before he slits your throat... but what is Bugs Bunny doing on my Navy Seals team? The whole mood is broken... it just doesn't feel right. In theater training, writers and actors are taught about "willing suspension of disbelief," a term coined by the poet Samuel Taylor Coleridge.

Sometimes in game design articles you'll read about how good graphics and sound are supposed to create this effect. But for hundreds of years actors have been trained that on a bare stage, with no props, no costumes, and no make-up, a thirty-year-old actor can make an audience react as if they are seeing and hearing an 80-year-old man. If the actor becomes that character so completely that his character feels consistent and interesting, the audience will "willingly stop not believing;" ignore the young actor and see the old character.

Game dialogue's first goal, as noted above, is to not shatter the willing suspension of disbelief the player may already have achieved. Sadly, many games have long, trite speeches or poorly-conceived scenes where exactly that happens. They ignore the classic writer's maxim that "fewer of the right short lines work far better than more, longer speeches." Now, go back to our Navy Seals example. Let's say the game has great voice actors. Ten minutes ago, a character named Saunders who's fought beside you for the last several missions was killed. He'd saved your character's life once during an amphibious assault, and you'd learned a few things about him, including that he had a wife and a baby. The Captain, whose voice you hear, cared a lot about Saunders, and he cares a lot about you. When the Captain calls out "Look out! Behind you!" you hear not just a warning, you hear the fear in his voice—fear sharpened by the loss just minutes before of another one of his men. When he yells, "Move out! We have to get to the silo!" he may have composed himself again, and be resolute on reaching the Seal team's goal. The game designers could script the game so it always unfolds this way, or so the Captain's voice changes based on what happened on this playthrough of the game. Either way, game dialogue is now driving the action and supporting willing suspension of disbelief.

Now that we have discussed story, game, and characters, let's put it all together. In the following chapter, we'll look at different stories and show how all of the elements we've learned about can come crashing together to create a fun and interesting game!

:::CHAPTER REVIEW:::

1. In order to ensure that verbal character elements in your game are accessible to the disabled, they must be available in both audio and text format. This means that writing a monologue or dialogue sequence is just one portion of the work necessary to support your characters through verbal development. Think about the type of voice acting you will need for each of your 3 primary characters (as well as your narrator). List each character's vocal tone, speech, volume, texture, pitch, and any other unique characteristics that might reflect that character's personality and signature style.

2. Write a 1-page narration monologue for the initial cinematic for your game. This cinematic could fill players in on the general backstory, introduce the premise of the game, or focus on the main character's background.

3. What are the many purposes of dialogue? In what ways can dialogue make or break a game? Determine 3 instances in which you feel it will be necessary to use dialogue in your original game story. Why do you feel dialogue will be necessary in these instances? How will you ensure that the dialogue enhances rather than detracts from your story?

4. In preparation for creating character dialogue, try writing a haiku verse that could be spoken by each of the 3 characters you've created. Consider each line in the haiku one which a character would speak. Think of the entire haiku as a conversation. Now imagine that this haiku represents dialogue spoken during a cut-scene. What do you imagine happening visually during this scene?

5. Construct a 5-page scene involving at least two of the original game characters you've created. Make sure one of your characters is a player character and one is a non-player character (NPC). How will you distinguish between the dialogue written for the player characters and NPCs? (Note: You are not writing a linear cut-scene, but one in which the player still has control of the avatar.)

Part III: Gameplay

CHAPTER 8

Gameplay and Story:

incorporating challenges and strategies into a game story

Key Chapter Questions

- How are story and gameplay interrelated?
- How does game theory apply to dramatic content?
- How do games utilize time and space?
- What is the importance of level and environmental design?

All animals play. Dogs play to understand their social order. Cats play to practice hunting. Humans play to imitate cultural situations. All of us play for pleasure. When children play "house" or "cops and robbers," they are playing games based on stringent real-world rules. Even so, there is an understood use of fabrication—or *fiction*: We know that Johnny won't really die if we shoot him with our finger-pointer guns. Play can be fantasy escapism and a teaching instrument, but we must never forget that it should always be *fun*. When we sit down to play a game, we may not always realize it, but we are engaging in a story – a story of our own design. Although we rarely hear someone say "it sure was fun to play that story," electronic games offer just that: the ability to play a story or storyplay. To make this "storyplay" engaging and interesting, games must incorporate challenges and strategies into their basic design. To do this well is a Herculean task. Beyond the basic challenges of telling a story through gameplay, there is the additional problem of keeping the story and gameplay fun; not only will this keep the players happy, it will keep them playing until the end of the game. In this chapter, we will look at how to use basic game design elements and how to crossbreed them with a story in order to keep it interesting, engaging and, lest we forget, . . . fun.

> If a picture is worth a thousand words, so is five seconds of gameplay.
>
> — *Chris Avellone (Chief Creative Officer & Lead Designer, Obsidian Entertainment)*

Conflict in Gameplay

You've already learned that conflict drives all stories. Conflict drives all gameplay as well—and, in doing so, it helps to build the game story. Without conflict, we have no reason to watch or read a story—and we have no reason to play a game.

Gameplay is all action related to the forward movement of the player. In chess, gameplay is moving the pieces toward a strategic victory—but it also involves watching your opponent and countering him with strategy, while making sure his forward movement doesn't disrupt your forward movement. The game continues like this until there is a definable winner. Gameplay comes down to an encounter with one thing—conflict.

Patricia Pizer on Active Game Storytelling::::

Patricia Pizer debuted in the gaming industry at Infocom in 1988, making games back when you didn't even need graphics. Over the next decade, she worked at such studios as Boffo Games, THQ/GameFX, CogniToy, and Harmonix Music. Patricia moved into massively multiplayer games as Creative Director at Turbine Entertainment before working on MMOs at Ubisoft and Disney's VR Studio, makers of *Toontown Online* and the upcoming *Pirates of the Caribbean Online.* Currently, Patricia is applying her design skills to Alternate Reality Games for 4orty 2wo Entertainment. Mostly though, she just likes to play games.

Patricia Pizer (Lead Designer, 4orty 2wo Entertainment)

Traditional narrative is a linear tale, told in a specific order that reveals events and details in order to create the strongest impact. A murder mystery in which you find out the killer's identity in the second chapter isn't very compelling. That which is *not* revealed is just as important as that which *is* revealed.

In game stories, the player needs to have some control over the process of revealing the story. And you can't fool players into thinking they have control; players can tell if they don't. If the game is too linear, it feels as though it's on rails, like an amusement park ride; you can never deviate from this tightly controlled experience. In games, the sensation of actively releasing the content of the story is key. This is a really difficult task and one we've traditionally failed to satisfy.

When someone plays a game, you, the writer, have no control over the setting in which content is revealed. For instance, TV can tightly tailor where to put an ad break so that it doesn't interfere with the fundamental flow of the story; a chapter in a book is a natural stopping place. A player may choose to leave your game at an inopportune time in the narrative or may lose power at that point. It really changes the nature of the story. It's active, not passive.

Imagine that you're a video game character in a game about the ancient Maya. The Mayan culture was an advanced culture, as well as a bloody one. Slavery, bloodletting, and human sacrifice were among the practices of the ancient Maya. Furthermore, the Maya were also great fans of sports and games. Warriors would play on large fields in games similar to modern day soccer. Unfortunately, losers faced more than having to buy the winners a beer; they were often sacrificed to the gods—yikes!

The Maya were sophisticated yet brutal, and scientific yet superstitious—much like many "civil" cultures of today. Like most ancient cultures, however, the Maya frowned on outsiders and were at constant war with other peoples such as the Toltecs. When put together, all this information might add up to what could be a rich and interesting backdrop for a game. Add a little mysticism and magic, and there is great room to develop gameplay.

Now that we've established the backdrop, imagine that you are the hero. You've been magically transported into the Mayan environment as an Aztec Warrior. You are armed with special swords, made by the Sun God himself. Not only that, the ancients have trained you and you are sent into battle. When you get to the Yucatan jungle to fight the Maya, something strange happens. They invite you to eat dinner with them. You might fear a trap. However, they are eating all the same food they offer you, so you trust that the food is not poisoned—and it is not. Then they give you all their gold, magical serum, and chocolate—and they point you toward the next level. Assuming that the gameplay will get harder, you go to the next level where you meet a three-headed giant (a boss), and he is hungry. You prepare for the worst, but he also invites you to have a little barbeque and happily sends you on your way to the next level. The game landscape continues to fill

Ben Bourbon

If this is the monster you meet in gameplay do you think there would be much conflict? The need for conflict is essential to the gameplay experience.

out in this way. No conflict at all. Even the final boss also helps you to the winner's circle. Hooray—you win!

Of course, we would never see a game like this. Why would anyone drop down hard-earned money for a game that you don't play to win? Where is the challenge? Where is the fun? Where is the conflict? Sure you win, but it is an unsatisfying win because it wasn't earned—and all of those hours of entertainment you had planned on have suddenly disappeared. You could choose to play the game again—but it would be no different, so why should you? In this game, we have created no conflict. Therefore, the game was not really a game at all—and, even though it can be considered a story, it isn't very interesting.

Now let's look at this game from another angle. This time around, you are decimated with arrows and die every time you enter the first level, There is no way you can even experience most of the conflict because the game is too hard and remarkably unfair. This is not a game that inspires players either. So how do we negotiate the conflict in a challenging and interesting way? Balance.

Warren Spector on Balancing Gameplay & Story:::::

Warren Spector
(President & Creative Director, Junction Point Studios)

Warren Spector received a B.S. in Speech from Northwestern University and an M.A. in Radio-TV-Film from the University of Texas. In 1983, just shy of his PhD in Communication, Warren worked on a variety of board games, RPGs, choose-your-own-adventure books, and novels, with Steve Jackson Games (where he rose to Editor-in-Chief) and at TSR, which he joined in 1987. Warren entered the world of electronic games with Origin Systems in 1989, co-producing *Ultima VI* and *Wing Commander* and producing *Ultima Underworld 1* and *2*, *Ultima VII: Serpent Isle*, *System Shock*, *Wings of Glory*, *Bad Blood*, *Martian Dreams*, and others.

In 1997, after a year as General Manager of LookingGlass Austin and producer on *Thief: The Dark Project*, Warren started Ion Storm Austin. He was project director on Ion's award-winning action/RPG, Deus Ex—published in June 2000 and reissued in a 2001 Game-of-the-Year edition and, in 2002, as *Deus Ex: The Conspiracy* on PS2. As Studio Director, he oversaw development of *Deus Ex: Invisible War*, released in December 2003, and *Thief: Deadly Shadows*, released in June 2004. He left Ion Storm in November 2004 to start a new independent game development company—Junction Point Studios, Inc.—where he serves as President and Creative Director.

How a game balances the two often conflicting qualities of gameplay and story is what makes one game different from another. No two are alike.

The traditional way to think about this is the teeter-totter model: The more one makes a game like a story, the less interactive it is; the more one makes a game, well, game-like, the less of a story you can tell.

I approach things differently, thinking about which aspects of a game story belong to the developer and which to the player. More specifically, I make what seems like (but isn't) an arbitrary distinction between "narrative arc" and "story." The narrative arc—involving the big events of the game—is determined by the developer, while the minute-to-minute belongs to the player. Developers provide a narrative context for each player's choices in-game, which allows players to craft a unique experience that—in the moment and in the retelling—becomes a unique story.

Balance

Per Olin

In drama, the definition of comedy is to end in balance—and the definition of tragedy is to end out of balance. In both cases, the beginning of the narrative deals with a situation or a character that is out of balance (e.g., has a problem).

In Shakespeare's *Hamlet*, young prince Hamlet must return home from school for his father's funeral. When he arrives, he learns that his uncle has married his mother and assumed the throne as the King of Denmark—young Hamlet's rightful position. As you can see, the world is already out of balance when the hero arrives. Furthermore, Hamlet is at a disadvantage, since only he suspects foul play. Not only that, he is only the Prince. His mother agreed to marry his uncle, thereby accepting his uncle as King. To add insult to injury, it might look as though Hamlet is trying to gain the throne and become King himself if he tries to set things right. The entire world is out of balance because of Hamlet's problem—and his problem causes the conflict that drives this great story.

Dramatic Balance

I've written my share of cut-scenes, to be sure. They are ubiquitous in today's games, which typically are 90 percent action-sequence, 10 percent "You kill my master!" But we really need to figure out how to bring dramatic balance into gaming. When you play Monopoly, you don't have to stop the action to watch jet fighters caroming off the sides of mountains, punctuated by programmatic tête-à-têtes between talking heads. The gameplay is entirely self-sufficient because you believe that the money is money and that your little plastic hotels are hotels. The game *is* the story. A big pot of gold awaits the person who can bring together the action elements of today's games, the cinematic potential of next-generation hardware, and a conceit that allows gameplay to stand on its own, dramatically. The key is giving players something to do that is meaningful in and of itself.

— Sheldon Pacotti (Game Designer, Secret Level)

Half-Life 2: Interweaving Emotion & Gameplay

In linear media such as film, we derive our emotional experiences from empathy with various characters. When we identify with them, whatever they go through emotionally, we go through.

Valve

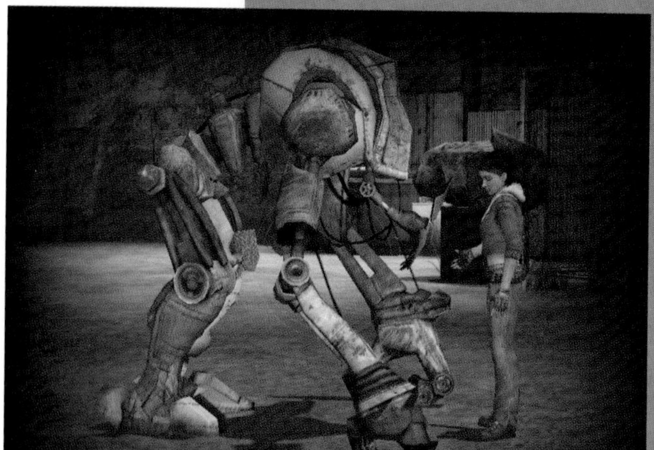

In games, we have this same ability—the ability to identify with NPCs—but it's not the primary source of a game's potential emotional power. What one should do is interweave emotion and gameplay in a wide variety of ways, so that the experience of playing the game is filled with emotion.

For example, in *Half-Life 2*, there's a sequence where you practice using your anti-gravity weapon. A large mechanical animal named "Dog" (who leaps around like a dog and makes dog sounds) is guided by revolutionary/hacker "Alyx".

Dog tosses you objects to catch, while Alyx makes various comments, encouraging both you and Dog.

You're definitely in gameplay. After all:

- You play fetch/catch with Dog.
- In doing so, you learn how to use the anti-gravity weapon.

However, interwoven with the game are numerous techniques which make the gameplay emotionally engaging:

- You're exposed to a softer side of normally-tough Alyx.
- That softer side makes you feel more bonded toward her.
- You enjoy the comic reversal (playing fetch for a dog, instead of vice versa.
- Playing with Dog bonds you to it/him.
- There's a big "plot twist" that ends the play session when the situation turns dire.

Your bonding with Alyx and your bonding with Dog becomes a factor in gameplay later, when Dog's fervor to rescue Alyx makes you even more eager to rescue her yourself.

In short, gameplay and emotion aren't separate here; they're wedded together. This kind of thing happens periodically (although not consistently) throughout the game.

— David Freeman (President, The Freeman Group)

Game Balance

Balance in a game is achieved through the player's perception. The game must appear consistent, fair, and, most of all, interesting. Balance in a game can be broken down into two types: static and dynamic.

Ben Bourbon

Goldilocks discovers a game that isn't too hard or too easy—but just right!

Static Balance

To keep *static* balance in a game, the field of play must be equal for all players. Static balance is the set-up of the world and its rules. The players entering the field cause the imbalance in the game, and sometimes it is their job to try to maintain static balance. There are several ways to maintain static balance.

Symmetry

In some games, all conditions must begin equally for the all of the players involved. Think about the perfect *symmetry* of a chessboard before play commences. This represents prefect static balance.

It would be silly to assume that this type of balance exist in all types of games. Many games (such as strategy games using armies as resources) are naturally out of balance in the beginning, since opposing forces are rarely given the same supplies.

Per Olin

A transitive relationship is linear and does not allow for change in status.

Symmetry is associated with the relationship between resources and is divided into two types of relationships: transitive and intransitive.

A *transitive* relationship is a one-way relationship between two or more resources and can be expressed through a hierarchical situation. A king is more powerful than a merchant who is more powerful than a peasant. The peasant retains no power over anyone, except maybe his dog. This is a linear, hierarchical relationship.

Per Olin

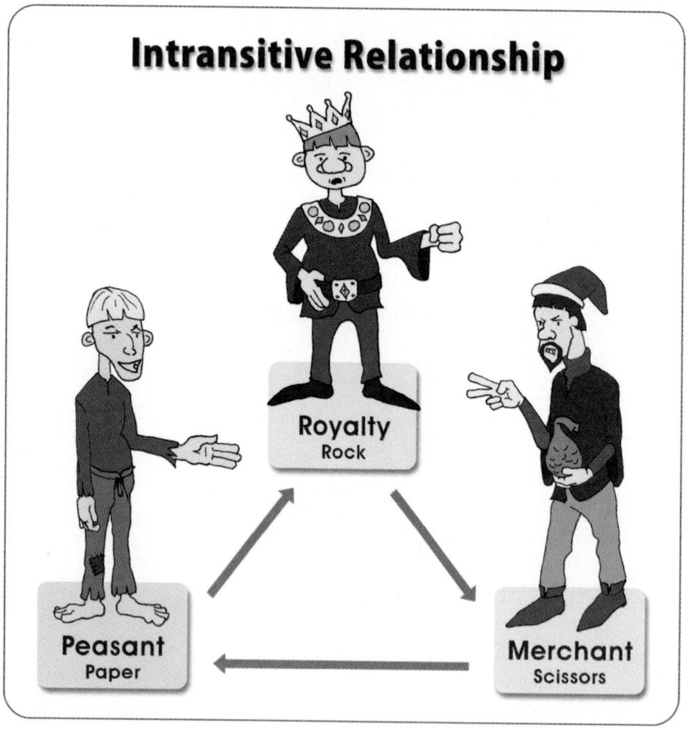

An intransitive relationship is circular, allowing an underling to defeat someone higher in the hierarchy.

An example of an *intransitive* relationship is that classic old chestnut: rock, paper, scissors (RPS). In this game, rock beats scissors, scissors beats paper, and paper beats rock. The relationship is circular rather than linear.

This circular relationship is more often what we will see in traditional stories where the underdog finds a way to best the higher-ups—usually by earning the necessary abilities through hard work.

This works just as well in games. Let's think in terms of the king/merchant/peasant structure again. In a hierarchical kingdom, a peasant has no power—so even when the king makes rulings that are unjust, there is little to be done. If the king is a boss in a video game and the player the peasant, then the player might have to earn, find, or otherwise acquire abilities to defeat the King Boss.

Starr Long on Interactive Storytelling :::::

Starr Long has been in the business of making games for over 10 years. Along with Richard Garriott, he was the original Project Director for the commercially successful *Ultima Online*. Starr worked his way up through the ranks of Origin Systems, starting in Quality Assurance on *Wing Commander*, *Ultima*, and many other titles. Starr was the Producer for *Ultima Online 2*—and he recently worked with Richard Garriott on *Tabula Rasa* for the Korean online game giant NCsoft, creators of *Lineage* (the world's largest online game).

Starr Long (Producer, NCsoft)

Storytelling is extremely important to the game experience. As with all fictional entertainment, games are about suspension of disbelief. You have to make the players feel like they are in a truly different place—and story is a key element in this.

Gameplay always comes first. I believe story should be at the service of gameplay. With that said, bad story will kill good gameplay—so you do have to strike a balance between the two. Game storytelling has to be interactive. The players have to believe that it's their story and that they have the power to determine the story's outcome.

I hope that games will be even more interactive in the future. Right now, narrative is very linear and completely pre-determined by the designer. I hope that eventually we can make sophisticated stories that truly change based on player decisions into directions that are not pre-determined in any way. How will this happen? If I knew, I would be doing it!

Trade-Offs

Trade-offs occur when players must sacrifice something in order to get something else. This is usually done for the purpose of the greater goal. Again, thinking in terms of chess, sometimes a player will sacrifice a game piece in an effort to make a good strategic move later. Trade-offs are essential in most games. Even in a typical combat game, the player will have to sacrifice or trade-off health points to gain the knowledge of how to defeat enemies in the game.

Trade-offs keep the game interesting and the player engaged. Be sure to incorporate interesting and difficult trade-offs in your game.

Sony Computer Entertainment of America

In sports games such as *MVP Baseball 2006*, a sacrifice hit allows the runner on base to advance while the batter is put out. This illustrates a type of trade-off.

Stevan Hird on Dramatic Gameplay Devices:::::

Stevan currently works for Midway Studios Austin (formerly Inevitable Entertainment)—having just completed *Area 51* and *The Hobbit*. Prior to Inevitable, Stevan worked for Acclaim Entertainment for several years as a member of a technology team contributing to various games—including titles from the *Turok*, *All Star Baseball*, and the *Quarterback Club* series. Canadian-born and educated, Stevan has lived and worked in various locales—including Kingston, Vancouver, Las Vegas, and Austin. He is currently rumored to be at an undisclosed (possibly underground), heavily guarded location working on new graphics technologies.

Stevan Hird (Software Engineer, Midway Studios Austin)

The importance of storytelling in games spans a broad range of levels. The measure of importance is dependent upon both the genre of the game and the participatory commitment of the player. In story-based games, the player can usually choose not to read text and in-game resources such as books, messages, or scrolls. The player is sometimes free to skip cut-scenes and in-game cinematics.

To keep the player on track, or at least adequately informed, games must confront the need for story elements to be told and reinforced via multiple overlapping methods. Overheard conversations from behind a door or around a corner, pre-level briefings, wireless communiqués from allies in high places, and solid in-game quest/mission/journal systems are just some of several mechanisms that serve to integrate the player into the story no matter how long a break was taken between play sessions. Storytelling in games differs from traditional media due to this requirement that the story be told in compound ways to ensure that players do not become lost in the game world.

Blizzard Entertainment, Inc.

In *World of Warcraft*, players can combine resources through teamwork to advance in the game.

Combination

Players might *combine* resources in an effort to advance toward a greater collective goal. This kind of maneuverability is found in games where players are allowed to collaborate. In the game *Fantastic Four*, players can play as a team, each combining the strengths of their particular character in the face of danger. In MMOGs such as *World of Warcraft*, guilds of players combine their efforts to defeat enemies and achieve the goals of a quest.

Allowing players to combine resources adds a bonding element to games that is fun for the players. Playing with someone to defeat a common enemy is often more fun than direct competition with friends. Be sure to think about how to incorporate combination play in your game.

Got Game?

Think about the start of a basketball game. There are the same number of players on the court facing the same rules and same judgments from the same referee. The game is perfectly symmetrical right before tip-off. As soon as the ball is in play, however, the symmetry ends and each team may have different advantages—including who has control of the ball and who has stronger players. These elements bring dynamics to the game—and, once a game or a story becomes dynamic, it becomes engaging.

Dynamic Balance

Once the game is set into motion by the players, *dynamics* emerge and thereby change the balance. Players can affect game balance by doing the following:

- **Destruction**: The game begins balanced. The goal for the player is to cause imbalance and claim victory.
- **Maintenance**: Again, the game begins balanced, but opponents or other outside forces attempt to cause imbalance, whereas the player works to maintain balance.
- **Restoration:** The game begins in an imbalanced state. The objective for the player in this case is to restore balance.

Dynamic balance set forth by the player keeps the game challenging and interesting. More importantly, however, dynamic balance is a good way to keep the action of the game story moving forward.

Avoid "Hollywood-itis"

Gameplay is what you actually do in the game. Not what you see, or hear. Not how the back of the box says you'll feel. It's what you actually spend your time doing. The game says it's an exciting race to rescue your true love from evil gypsies, but you spend 95% of your time guiding a horse-drawn wagon down a road and not getting stuck in the snow. The game isn't an exciting race; instead, it's a horse-drawn wagon winter driving sim—because that's what the gameplay is. It's what you spend your time doing. "Story" (note the quotation marks) sometimes distracts development teams from their craft. The lead designer will get excited about doing a major story component and start thinking, "We get to make movies just like in Hollywood!" The team gets so preoccupied with "Hollywood-itis" that the need to focus on quality gameplay suffers. They end up with a lot of great looking little movies—but much of what players actually do in the game is unsatisfying.

— Don L. Daglow (President & CEO, Stormfront Studios)

::::: *Neverwinter Nights*: Balancing Gameplay & Story

Atari's *Neverwinter Nights* series strikes a solid balance between gameplay and story—especially when considering the fact that it is a hardcore role-playing game (RPG) and very rich in story, content, and characters. The balance comes from a base story supported by numerous game features and tools that allow players to choose a number of unique characters, abilities, alignments, and weapons from the very start—and yet still arrive at 1-2 predetermined conclusions by the end of the game. This is achieved by giving the player many options (such as mini-games, quests, and dialogue choices)—all the while making sure that no matter which options are chosen (or denied), a percentage of the game's pre-determined conclusion is hard-wired into those factors that would otherwise appear random.

— Mark Soderwall (Creative Consultant & Art Director)

Atari Interactive, Inc.

Building Tension

It is within the movement from static to dynamic balance that we discover the use of tension. Balance within a story is achieved through *tension,* which occurs when two adversarial characters want the same thing (unity of opposites), resulting in conflict.

Remember Caesar and Pompey from earlier chapters? They wanted the same thing. There was no compromise. Without compromise, you have conflict. From conflict comes dramatic tension.

Let's take a quick look at Caesar and Pompey in terms of conflict and balance. Both characters are strong-willed. Both want to run the empire. While they are equal in desire, they are far from equal in strength. Pompey's armies are not only plentiful, but they are well-armed—and, with the resources of the entire empire to back them, they should have no problem with any type of rebellion. Caesar, on the other hand, has a small army and has not been allowed into Rome or even into Italy for five years. In spite of his political efforts to gain favor in the Senate, Caesar has been given little power. If we were to look at the facts on paper, Pompey should clearly have been able to put down any uprising that occurs within the empire—including one from one of his own generals.

Per Olin

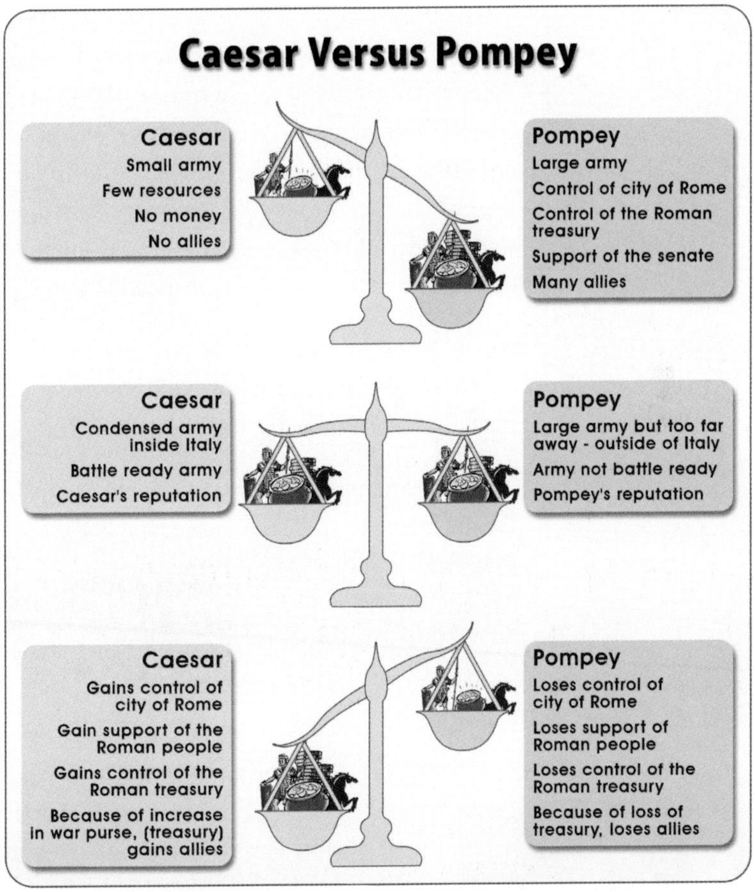

Tension can be illustrated through a shift in the balance of power in the story of Caesar vs. Pompey.

Even so, Caesar succeeds and eventually becomes sole emperor. How can this be when the balance appears to hang in Pompey's favor? Caesar is the clear underdog, but there are factors that help balance the odds. First, Pompey's legions are spread out over the empire, while Caesar's are condensed at the border. Pompey must gather his men, offering the advantage of time to Caesar. Second, Pompey's men have not fought a difficult war in many years. They are soft and untrained, while Caesars' men are war-hardened and ready for battle—adding the advantage of experience and grit to Caesar.

Finally, when Pompey strategically retreats from the city of Rome, he forgets the Roman Treasury left under the Temple of Saturn. Caesar is quick to capitalize on the mistake, gaining critical financial solvency which could be used to purchase more soldiers, weapons, and, ultimately, power.

All of these elements balance the conflict. Without this balance, the conflict becomes one-sided and easily won, creating a situation where the story becomes uninteresting.

Let's take a quick look at Caesar and Pompey in terms of game balance. Up until the day that Caesar crosses the border (Rubicon River), the Roman Empire is in static balance, which becomes dynamic when Caesar crosses the river. Assume now that you are either Caesar or Pompey. If you are Caesar, the tension comes from your goal to dominate the current empire and *destroy* Pompey. If you are Pompey, the tension comes from your goal to *maintain* order within your empire. In order to maintain balance (keep it static), you must fight the opposing forces of Caesar.

We've already established that the game is not symmetrical, since the resources of Pompey far outweigh the resources of Caesar. The goal for Pompey, however, is to restore symmetry by combining his resources from around the empire. When this doesn't work, Pompey must make a *trade-off* by retreating from the City of Rome, thereby trading the city for the future help of Eastern allies. Pompey's brief retreat was a trade-off to get more troops and supplies. Too bad that he forgot the money that he'd need to buy the much-needed firepower.

After Caesar defeats Pompey, he gains his goal: power over the empire. Now in command, it's Caesar's turn to provide balance to the empire. He must *restore* order to the citizens of Rome, or they'll revolt.

This is an example of how you might use tension from conflict and balance, but how do you create the balance in the game to make sure it is interesting, fair, and fun? First, you've got to lay down the law.

David Jaffe on Game-Specific Story Devices:::::

David Jaffe (Creative Director–Internal Development Studio, Sony Computer Entertainment Santa Monica)

As Creative Director, David Jaffe is responsible for implementing a game's vision and making sure that it is maintained throughout the entire production process. David created the popular *Twisted Metal* franchise, and he served as the director and lead designer for *God of War*. David began his career as an aspiring film director. However, while waiting for various television game shows he had optioned to go into production, he fell into the game industry as a tester at Sony Imagesoft and has been in it ever since. David believes that the most significant event in the history of games is when electronic interactivity occurred for the first time, and he looks forward to the day that game distribution goes completely digital. David lists his favorite games as *Flashback*, *Deus Ex*, *Time Pilot*, *Gyruss*, *Out of This World*, and *Ico*. When not working, this native of Birmingham, Alabama enjoys movies, comics, spinning, meditation, arguing politics, and, of course, games!

Game stories really only work if they're being told during gameplay. Cutscenes are fine and are an easier device to rely upon to get your story across. But that's not interactive storytelling: that's just playing a game, then showing a movie. In my opinion, the future of narrative games lies in merging play with story. Here's an example of how it can work:

Imagine that the player—in the role of a firefighter—is rushing up the steps of a burning building in the hopes of rescuing trapped civilians. As he runs—leaping over gaps in the staircase and destroying obstacles with his axe—he hears the pleas and screams of terrified people coming from up ahead. As he reaches a door at the end of a hallway, the player clearly sees a jammed door shaking violently as if someone is on the other side, struggling to get out. From behind the door we hear the screams of a little child. On the door itself, the player clearly sees the words: ANNIE'S ROOM written in big, colorful wooden letters. There are also pictures of little kids' drawings thumb-tacked to the door. In this example, a story is being told within the interactive space, as you exist in the space. The story is being told not through dialogue or editing, but through set design and audio design. And the result—for me—is a game that feels like I'm living in the experience, like I'm the star of the story.

This kind of in-game storytelling can be seen in a handful of games today. The problem is that even today's in-game storytelling is pretty average. The techniques are being designed and utilized in today's games, but now we need people with story sense to figure out how to elicit emotional responses from the in-game storytelling suite of tools: set design, audio design, and camera design.

Another interesting aspect is storytelling through gameplay mechanics...how can we propel the story and/or character development forward while tying it to the gameplay tasks we are asking the player to perform? In *God of War* we had Kratos (the hero) sacrificing an innocent soldier's life in order to show what a brutal character he was. The sacrifice was part of the gameplay (with Kratos having to push a cage—which contained the terrified soldier—up a hill while battling enemies). In this case, not only was the play aspect compelling, but it revealed an aspect to Kratos' personality. I loved this part of the game and feel it really enriched the experience. But it was hard to think up many more of these kinds of examples. I am not sure if this is because I needed to work with a writer to create more play/story–style scenarios, or if it's because this is simply a really hard thing to do and it's unrealistic to think you will get too many of these 'inspired' moments—where play mechanics and storytelling/character development come together—in a single game.

Rules

Just as every world (real or fictional) has rules, every game world has rules, too. What is a basic rule of the real world? Gravity. In fact, it's a rule that is so important, it's considered a law—which is good, since we can't have people floating around willy-nilly.

Ben Bourbon

Some laws (such as the law of gravity) can't be broken!

Even in warfare, there are "rules of engagement"—because when you're engaged in killing people, you shouldn't be doing it indiscriminately.

When working inside a game world, it is important to establish rules: what the player can and cannot do. In order to establish the rules, it is important to think about what it means to win or lose.

- Victory Conditions: how players win a game
- Loss Conditions: how players lose a game

Once you have established the rules of the game, it is also important to consider what the player will have to do in order to achieve victory and avoid loss. In other words, what is the goal?

Doesn't this sound remarkably familiar? In stories, we watch how the hero defeats the villain (victory conditions) and what the hero must do (goals) to defeat the villain. The only real difference is that, in a traditional story, we watch to see how the hero wins. In a game, we play to see if we will win.

Richard Dansky on Developing Gameplay & Story Together:::::

Richard Dansky (Central Clancy Writer, Ubisoft/Red Storm Entertainment)

Frequently dispatched to various Ubisoft studios around the world to work on story, dialogue, and other aspects of game writing, Richard Dansky helps coordinate the continuity of the Tom Clancy franchise. He has designed, written for, or otherwise contributed to numerous video games, including *Far Cry*, *Tom Clancy's Rainbow Six: Black Arrow*, and the award-winning *Tom Clancy's Ghost Recon: Island Thunder*. Richard is also the author of four published novels, and has contributed to over 120 role-playing game books from White Wolf Studios.

Traditional storytelling is all in the hands of the storyteller; the listener receives the experience. With games, we're trying to collaborate on a story with the player, so they feel that they're really telling it through their actions. In a lot of ways, as game writers we're really presenting players with the tools and elements to tell their own stories, because no two players are going to experience or talk about a game in the same way.

Gameplay and story should be developed together so that they complement one another; the gameplay isn't forcing an unbelievable shape onto the story, and the story isn't asking for things that the game can't do well. As writers, we have to remember that we're making games—not movies or novels or comics or anything else—and write to the medium, with its strengths and limitations. Even when you're doing something that feels movie-like, you have to bear that in mind. The storyline for *Rainbow Six: 3*, for example, really feels like a Hollywood action movie—but at every step of the way, we had to remind ourselves that the player would be the star and that the player's actions (not the way we wanted them to act) would determine how the story played out and was received.

Gameplay Elements

Gameplay elements are ways to keep the player active and interested. It is also where the game and story intersect to help create a game-story experience. Let's look at some of the elements involved in gameplay.

Gameplay Always Comes First

While I love game stories, they are secondary to the game experience itself. Gameplay always comes first. A good story can only make a good game better—but if you have a lousy game with terrible game mechanics and a good story, you still have a terrible game.

— Chris Avellone (Chief Creative Officer & Lead Designer, Obsidian Entertainment)

Goals

As we have established, there is a definite need for a goal in story as well as in games—which isn't really the interesting part; it's just the carrot that incites the player to jump through the hoop. It's the jumping and the hoops that make the game interesting!

Providing satisfying goals is only part of the game. The following we will describe some of the things that make getting to the goals fun, playable and interesting.

Ben Bourbon

Victory is great—but it's more fun to jump through the hoops to get there!

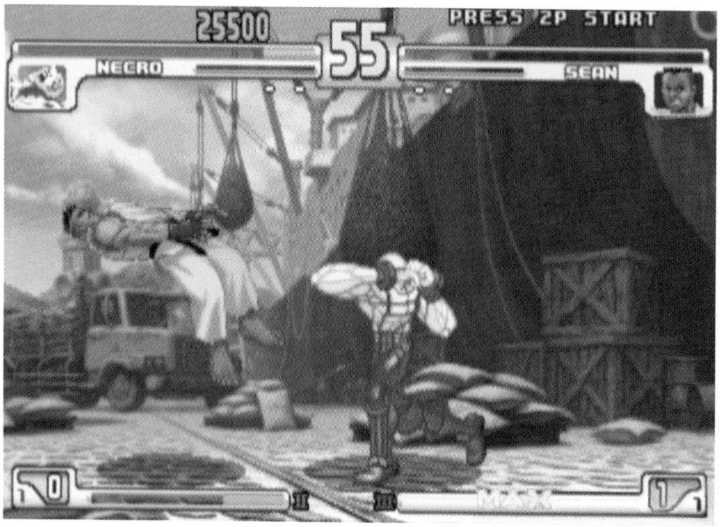

Capcom Entertainment, Inc.

Direct combat (as in this scene from *Street Fighter*) is an explicit challenge.

Implicit and Explicit Challenges

These hoops are known as challenges or obstacles that the character must overcome by using strategies. *Explicit* challenges are challenges that are immediate. Examples of these are jumping, running, and dodging. An example of an explicit challenge is avoiding being kicked in the fighting game *Soul Calibur*. In the movie *The Matrix*, Neo dodges bullets—another example of coping with an explicit challenge.

Explicit challenges need to be addressed immediately and will help to keep the pace of your game moving. In many games, explicit challenges increase in difficulty as the player learns to overcome each challenge.

Megamedia

In *Admiral: Sea Battle*, implicit challenges rise out of gameplay.

Implicit challenges, on the other hand, are not intentionally added to the game but evolve as a result of gameplay. Implementing a strategy in a game as a response to other players or problems is a type of implicit challenge. In a traditional story, the plan of attack against the villain is a type of implicit challenge. Say you are playing the strategy game *Admiral: Sea Battle*. As you make moves, your opponent counters your moves, making a new challenge for you. This is an implicit challenge, and the player must adjust to the new conditions accordingly.

Challenges are the reason players play games. How a player prevails in a game is directly related to how he or she manages the challenges presented. In order to do this, it is important to think about strategies.

Shannon Studstill on the Importance of Gameplay:::::

Shannon Studstill graduated from the American Film Institute (AFI) in 1994 with a degree in Cinematography. She directly entered the world of game development—working as an intern in the art department at Black Ops, one of the leading game-development studios at the time. After three short months she was offered a full time position as a member of the art team, where she was able to utilize her extensive art and photography background. Shortly thereafter, Shannon was promoted to Lead Artist because of her skill and dedication. After successfully delivering two titles, *Agile Warrior* and *Treasures of the Deep*, Shannon was promoted to Art Director. In 1998, Shannon became Lead Artist at Sony Computer Entertainment of America (SCEA) in San Francisco, and then became Art Director at SCEA's Los Angeles studio. Shannon was almost immediately promoted to producer on the studio's first internal title, *Kinetica*. Since then, Shannon has produced SCEA Santa Monica's largest budget project to date, *God of War*. She is now the Executive Producer for the franchise overseeing the development of future *God of War* productions—along with supporting PS2 and next generation PS3 titles that are developed externally through the Santa Monica studio.

Shannon Studstill (Director of Production/Producer, Sony Computer Entertainment of America)

Game-specific storytelling requires crafting a high-level story that is full of action, very engaging, and at times, repetitive for the player's benefit. The game should be created in a manner that ensures that the player can keep track of the story while being engaged in playing the game. Moving the story along in the clearest most concise manner without confusing the player is one of the keys to successful story-based gameplay. Ideally, the story is direct and to the point while being powerful and easy to follow. Often the game is written in a somewhat tiered fashion. This allows levels of detail to be available to players who are interested in knowing more in-depth information about the characters or storyline. Alternately, those who "just want to play" can easily follow the high-level story and navigate through the game without worrying too much about the in-depth details.

An ideal way to strike a balance between gameplay and story is to consider designing the gameplay while writing the story. Often development teams develop story and gameplay separately. This approach can be very obvious to a player, who might feel forced into a disjointed gameplay experience. Throughout the development, you will need to consistently adjust the game to ensure the best possible gameplay. The story will inevitably need to be modified with each of these game-based adjustments. This is because when one element in gameplay or story changes, it can easily affect many other areas. This might include the movies, player goals or objectives, sometimes the layout of a level, and occasionally the characters themselves. Consequently, striking this balance in the day-to-day design and production is a tremendous challenge.

Usually developers focus first on fun and intriguing gameplay. Without this, the story really doesn't matter; if the game isn't fun, the player's interest won't be maintained. Once you have established a good, fun proof-of-gameplay concept, the designers can begin to design the rest of the game while concurrently weaving in the story—which is there to expand upon the experience. Ideally, the story is not tacked on top of the game. The goal is to integrate the story well enough so that the player feels like he is playing a part in the story—which allows him to become more emotionally invested.

Strategies

Strategies are used to overcome challenges and lead to victory. Any number of strategies can be applied to a single challenge. Strategies offer a game and story-intersection by allowing a player to make choices about particular challenges. For example, if you face a large enemy, your strategy might be to fight, run, or delay the fight until you have enough health points to fight. Each strategy is a choice made by the player. Each strategy will take the player down a different story path, and in fact create a different story experience. Later, if the player chooses, the game can be played again, trying out new strategies and experiencing an entirely different story path. An example of this is how the game *Fable* is played. A player can choose strategies that are evil and therefore be required to play as an evil character. A player can also use a good strategy and become a good character. Each strategy choice is a particular way to play the game, and each choice might offer a different story experience.

Lionhead Studios Limited

Fable offers a different story experience each time the game is played.

When creating your game, think about the many strategies that the player might use to defeat a challenge. If there is only one way to prevail, rethink the challenge to offer many ways to overcome the challenge. This will ensure an interesting story experience each time the game is played.

Perfect and Imperfect Information

Perfect information exists when all information related to gameplay is available to the player. Classic board games—where players can see each other's pieces (such as chess, checkers, and backgammon)—allow for perfect information. Players are able to make choices based on the information. We rarely see this offered in a story, since it contradicts the need for plot twists and turns.

Imperfect information allows players a limited amount of information and they must make decisions based on that information. This is typical in traditional stories. Often in mystery stories the main character is given a small amount of information and must figure out the rest. Here we can employ the use of red herrings in both story and gameplay. Consider a poker game, where one of the players is bluffing. In order to prove the bluff, the player may act excited when he gets a new card. This misleading clue is a form of red herring executed in gameplay. The opponent in the poker game has to try to discern if the excitement is real or fake.

Depending on the kind of game you want to design, you will have to decide what kind of information is presented to the player. If your game has a story, think about how the information presented will affect the narrative.

Ben Bourbon

In backgammon, players have perfect information about their opponents' moves on the board.

Ben Bourbon

In poker, players have imperfect information about their opponents' hidden cards.

Intrinsic or Extrinsic Knowledge

Intrinsic knowledge is information that is learned inside the game world. Often the path of a story follows intrinsic knowledge. Gathering clues and training for the hero are types of intrinsic knowledge. In a traditional story, intrinsic knowledge applies as well. Clues found throughout a mystery novel, for example, are considered intrinsic and apply to both character and audience.

Knowledge gained from the outside world that a player brings into the game experience is *extrinsic*. Knowing that bullets kill, blades cut, fire burns, are all-important and might apply to games. If a player doesn't know that bullets kill, for example, he will get shot, time and time again, and never enjoy the game.

In traditional stories, extrinsic knowledge applies to what the audience knows and relates to in context. We know that Indiana Jones is in a dangerous situation in *Raiders of the Lost Ark* because we know that the Nazis are really bad guys. This is a type of extrinsic knowledge. If you remember, in the last chapter we talked about the context of the game *Area 51*. Since the urban legend surrounding *Area 51* is ubiquitous, information that the player brings into the game about the legend is extrinsic knowledge. In a game that involves a werewolf, the player might already know he needs the sterling silver bullet to kill the werewolf.

Firaxis Games

In *Sid Meier's Pirates*, the world is dependent on the player having some extrinsic knowledge about pirate life and culture.

Extrinsic and intrinsic knowledge can be tricky. If you are creating an entirely new world, be sure to fill in the details of the intrinsic knowledge and try not to depend too heavily on a player's extrinsic knowledge. For example, it's possible that a player doesn't know that a werewolf can only be killed by a sterling silver bullet. So you may have to tell them.

Additional challenges and goals include: advancement, racing, puzzle-solving, exploration, collecting, capturing, chasing, escaping, and outwitting.

While these make for interesting game goals, they are also elements you would see in a movie. Can you see how narrative is starting to become a part of gameplay and how gameplay is the narrative?

The Lord of the Rings: The Two Towers — Movie Game Advantages

When does story enhance gameplay? When the characters' actions, reactions, and feelings make you care about what happens next. In *The Lord of the Rings: The Two Towers*, we had two great advantages from doing a movie game:

Our players knew from the first moment of the game which characters were good, which were evil, and what kinds of lives they'd led to earn those labels. Players hated the orcs, Uruk-hai, and the Ringwraiths for killing so many innocent people. They loved Gandalf for trying to protect Frodo—even as he supported Frodo's selection as the Ring-Bearer, who must go to the heart of Sauron's evil empire. How hard would it be to create such a complex character—one who could hold both tender love and stony disregard for Frodo in the same heart at the same time—if we had to tell the entire story solely within the game? Writers describe such characters as "three-dimensional" because their personalities include believable contradictions that make them feel imperfect and real.

When the players portrayed Aragorn, Legolas, or Gimli, they knew that the fate of an entire world rested upon their shoulders. If you're fighting the eight-foot-tall Uruk-Hai to earn 600 more gold pieces to buy a bigger sword, you care about the outcome as a player. If you're fighting them because only you can stop them from killing the families huddled in Helm's Deep behind you—people you've gotten to know—you care about the outcome in a very different way.

— Don L. Daglow (President & CEO, Stormfront Studios)

Game Theory

This chapter wouldn't be complete without a nod to game theory—which, as it turns out, also finds its way into stories of all kinds.

Zero Sum vs. Non-Zero Sum

Zero sum games provide situations where the players have completely opposing objectives. There can be only one winner. In chess, there is only one winner—so it can be considered a zero sum game. What does this remind you of? In stories when opponents compete for the same result, we call it unity of opposites. Our story about Caesar and Pompey could be considered a zero sum story. Can you think of any others?

Three Rings Design

Puzzle Pirates incorporates a great deal of non zero sum devices—such as cooperative "duty" puzzles to enable the ship to sail.

In *non-zero sum* games, players might have opposing interests but can overcome them in order to win the game through cooperation. Again, we see non-zero sum used as a device in traditional stories all the time. Sometimes enemies in stories will form an unholy alliance in order to serve a common interest. Commonly, we see this used in political thrillers and action movies such as James Bond, where James *must* cooperate with a beautiful enemy to bring down the larger evil.

Real World Non-Zero Sum

Prior to World War II, the United States and Russia embraced diametrically opposed political ideologies. When Hitler came to power, the U.S. and Russia had to put aside differences in order to defeat the greater evil, Nazi Germany. Once their common goal was accomplished, they could get back to the everyday business of hating each other.

Choosing whether your game should have a zero sum or non-zero sum solution will offer the player more clarity. Be sure you understand this aspect of game theory—and decide whether you will incorporate zero sum or non-zero-sum components into your gameplay.

Ben Bourbon

Prisoner's Dilemma

The *prisoner's dilemma* scenario is not only a game theory but also one that we have seen in many TV shows and movies. It's even set up like a scene from a cop show. The scenario plays like this: You and your partner have been arrested on suspicion of robbing a bank. The authorities offer you a choice: squeal on your partner and get out of jail, or keep quiet and get sentenced for 5 years. You have no idea what deal, if any, has been offered to your partner. If you squeal, you are *competing* directly with your partner like a zero sum game. If you keep quiet, you are *cooperating* (non-zero sum) with your partner—even though you can't be sure that your partner is doing the same. What neither of you know is that *both* of you cannot possibly go free. (The police have to lock *someone* up!) If both of you squeal on each other, you will stay in prison for 3 years. On the other hand, if both of you cooperate with each other, you will both stay in prison for only 1 year.

The following is a list of all possible decisions that can be made by both prisoners, along with their results:

- Prisoner A keeps quiet while Prisoner B squeals → Prisoner A becomes the "sucker" and stays in prison for the full 5 years; Prisoner B receives a "get out of jail free" card
- Both prisoners squeal on each other (competition) → Both prisoners stay in jail for 3 years.
- Both prisoners keep quiet (cooperation) → Both prisoners stay in jail for 1 year.

Per Olin

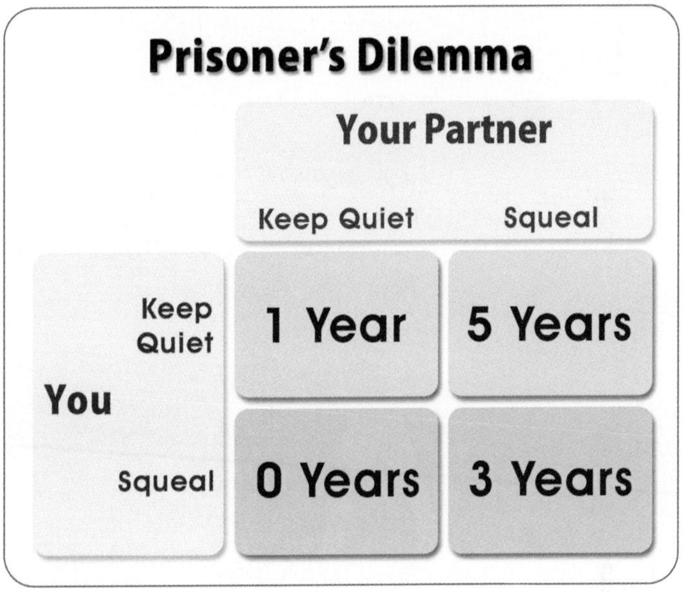

There are four possible outcomes in a Prisoner's Dilemma scenario

Looking closely at the possibilities listed above, it becomes clear that the best scenario for *one prisoner* is to squeal on the other—but this is only if the other prisoner keeps quiet. On the other hand, the best scenario for *both prisoners* is to keep quiet.

The use of this within a story creates terrific internal conflict for the characters because they must trust their partners to not rat them out. The relationship between the two characters in this situation and how they act upon it makes for great dramatic tension.

In some games, the *prisoner's dilemma* scenario can be used to drive tension and draw out internal conflict within the player—making the experience more visceral. The *prisoner's dilemma* is a great a technique to drive gameplay and story. Think about how each choice in the dilemma might affect the game and the outcome of the story.

Tragedy of the Commons

The *tragedy of the commons* scenario refers to a social trap where a rational decision based on resources leads to an irrational result. To demonstrate this, imagine you are an oarsman on a Viking ship. It is imperative that the ship returns to Norway before the first storm of the winter season hits. Furthermore, the waters are infested with shrieking eels known for their penchant for consuming human flesh. After days of rowing, you feel that in order to build more strength you need a nap.

If everyone on the boat stops rowing, no one will get to their destination, and in the worst case, be put in serious danger.

You look around. Everyone else is rowing hard—so you rest soon, drifting off to a deep slumber. When you awaken, you realize everyone else has decided to rest, too. The ship stops moving, the storm hits, and the eels await their supper.

This theory lends itself well to cooperative gameplay. Even in movies, we often see the hero's sidekick or posse each having an important role on the way to the story's conclusion. In a movie, however, the sidekick inevitably fails, and victory rests on the shoulders of the hero. In games such as massively multiplayer online games (MMOGs), part of the goal might be for everyone to complete their part of the mission.

Now that we have a brief idea of how gameplay affects story and—more to the point—how gameplay intersects with story, let's put it all together in levels.

David Brin on the Gameplay-Story Interference::::

David Brin's 15 novels—including *New York Times* bestsellers and winners of the Hugo and Nebula awards—have been translated into more than 20 languages. His 1989 ecological thriller, *Earth*, foreshadowed global warming, cyberwarfare, and the World Wide Web. *Kiln People* explored a near future when people may be able to be in two places at once. *The Life Eaters* rocked the world of graphic novels with a stunning and heroic portrayal of an alternate World War II. A 1998 movie directed by Kevin Costner was loosely based on *The Postman*. David wrote the scenario and introduction for the highly-touted video game *ECCO the Dolphin*. His "Uplift Universe" was adapted by Steve Jackson Games as *GURPS Uplift* and features a unique system for creating new alien life forms. Simulation game *Tribes* allows players to strive for survival and reproductive success in the Neolithic Age. David is also a scientist and commentator on public policy. His non-fiction book *The Transparent Society: Will Technology Make Us Choose Between Freedom and Privacy?*—which deals with issues of openness and liberty in the new wired age—won the Freedom of Speech Award of the American Library Association.

David Brin (Author, Scientist & Public Speaker)

Gameplay currently appeals to very primitive response sets in human beings. For predatory animals, most play revolves around simulation and preparation for hunting and combat, or else competition for mates. This kind of stuff is pretty primitive in its propelling force—though, of course, it can become ornate and even beautiful when passing through the complicating filters of human minds, morals, and madness.

Story is another thing entirely. It pulls on the same strings that shamans yanked, while chanting around the camp fire, that Homer tugged with *The Odyssey*—the strings that *link* us to other people by empathizing with their separate inner lives.

Yes, these two things can interact—very vividly and artistically, in fact. But it's no wonder that they sometimes also interfere with each other.

Level Structure

A level of a game is a space where part of the game takes place. To make the most efficient use of a level, it is important to structure it carefully. Flow, time, choice, goals, relationships, and progression are all elements to consider when structuring a level.

Space

The spectator of film and television is edging ever closer to becoming part of the action. In action thrillers such as *The Bourne Supremacy,* the visual experience takes the audience into the action of the car chase by placing the camera into the car. The film *Black Hawk Down* is reminiscent of many military games and again takes the audience into the action of combat. This has given the audience a sense of being part of the action. However, the next logical step is what electronic games provide: spectator as active participant or *player*. The audience as *players* can enter the game space and experience a story directly. What exactly is game space? It incorporates the physical place where the game and story develop. In the early days of game storytelling, games offered directions to help the player negotiate the game space. Two word phrases such as "go east" or "get knife" (pioneered in William Crowther's *Colossal Cave Adventure*) helped the player to kinesthetically understand location. Roberta Williams' *Mystery House* was an old Victorian mansion—but the term "Victorian mansion" refers more to the setting, not the location. The player can move through the story as well as space. With next-generation consoles (Xbox 360, PS3, and the Revolution), game space is ever-growing—and players can expect an expanding game space in which to frolic.

:::::*Tomb Raider*: Environmental Storytelling

If video games are like drugs, then *Tomb Raider* is the first high I've almost never been able to recapture; blame the would-be archeologist in me. The game is a classic example of environmental storytelling, where the settings speak volumes for the narrative and accomplish what exposition and dialogue would have failed to do miserably. And Lara Croft, as the first capable heroine, was equally appealing despite wearing shorts in sub-arctic weather. *Tomb Raider* represents a product that did everything right in how it meshed different facets of storytelling together. Individually, the elements aren't strong—but together, they form a narrative alloy that's hard to beat.

— Lucien Soulban (Scriptwriter & Novelist, Ubisoft Montreal)

Eidos

Flow

Flow in a story, in the simplest terms, is making sure one scene connects to another and continues to provide information to the audience. Along with information, there must be a logical progression that always leads to the forward action of the story. In-game flow operates in a similar way. You should always urge the player forward much in the same way you prod your characters forward by situations, challenges, obstacles, and goals. Since movies are a linear telling form, the main characters can only go in the direction of the story. Imagine you are watching your favorite movie—an action story about an everyday hero. Then, as the story progresses, the hero decides to stop and look around, maybe find some healing potion, or go back to the beginning of the movie. This would more than certainly disrupt the flow of the story and probably be a little jarring for the audience. Of course we would never see this happen in a movie, but these are the challenges game designers face when trying to create flow for the player.

Every Element Tells a Story!

Environmental narrative isn't just for games. Amusement parks incorporate these same concepts. As the guests pass thought the environment of Disneyland's *Temple of Doom*, for example, all elements within the ride's environment feed the theme of the Indiana Jones adventure. *The Pirates of the Caribbean* and *Back to the Future* rides at Disneyland and Universal Studios, respectively, are also good examples. The next time you are at an amusement park, take note of how these rides never allow you to see anything that doesn't feed into its central theme. This same idea should be used throughout game environments.

Keeping the flow of a level moving is a challenge—but if you pay close attention to the flow of levels, then the flow of the entire game will benefit.

Time

Ubisoft

Prince of Persia: The Sands of Time makes use of altered time by allowing the player to stop time during the game.

Have you ever noticed that when you sit down to play a game, time becomes irrelevant? Hours can pass as the player plays and, if the game is good, the player will have no concept of time passing in the real world. Unfortunately, chores such as cleaning, walking the dog, and homework suffer at the hand of a really good game. Conversely, *time* spent within the game world shifts, bends, and twists, keeping the player engaged and away from doing the aforementioned chores. For our purposes there are two areas to consider when talking about time. The first is time as it relates to the level, and, more importantly for us, time as it relates to the narrative of the story. Below are the different types of time used in games:

- **Authentic Time:** Some games try to make use of authentic time within the context of the game.
- **Limited Time:** Like the use of a ticking clock in a movie, limited time offers a limited amount of real-world time for a player to complete a task.

- **Variable Time:** A game story will compress, allowing the players to skip over the uninteresting parts and get to the next part of the story.
- **Altered Time:** Many games alter game time and incorporate it into gameplay by using slow-motion, rewind, and stop. Altering time within a game can be a powerful device for both gameplay and story.

An Expansion of Time

In the classic short story *An Occurrence at Owl Creek Bridge*, by Ambrose Bierce, the main character is about to be hanged from the side of a bridge. Bierce leads the reader to believe that the rope breaks and that the main character falls into the river, making his way back to his farm and his wife. By the end of the story, however, it is revealed that the story is the main character's imaginings just a few moments before his death. This is an excellent example of how to expand time within a story. Do you think there are game elements that could use this device effectively?

The use of time can help to add tension to gameplay while allowing for good pacing throughout a level.

Monolith/Vivendi Universal Games

These footsteps in *F.E.A.R.* are likely to be followed by the player. The player believes he is making the choice to follow but actually the designer is encouraging the player further into the story.

Choice

As we have discussed, *choice* is essential to the player, but it is really the illusion of choice that is offered. As the development team devises the choices, they should appear to be stemming from the player's own action. How a team really guides the player is by providing subconscious signposts to the next important part of the level. An example of this might be a splash of blood on a wall. While a real-world person might run the other way, the player will find this intriguing and want to see where the blood came from. Using this kind of foreshadowing provides a type of subconscious signpost. The main challenge for the designer is to keep the player engaged by creating choice and keeping the paths to discovery open. Adding a lot of well-structured choices for your player is a great way to keep the level interesting and playable.

Goal

As you might have noticed, *goals* are the magic ingredient, and as such have landed in practically every chapter. Interesting goals with good rewards are another way to draw a player in the direction that the designer wants him to go. All goals, even small ones, should serve a greater goal of the game. Sometimes this can be as obvious as in an upgrade of power or weapons, or in a more subtle thematic way that consistently reinforces the game and story experience. For a player to achieve goals, remember that there are challenges and strategies that the player must overcome.

Relationship

The *relationship* of one level to the next is important when you're looking to keep a consistent and developing story line. Remember, just as plays break into acts and books into chapters, games break into levels. Examining the relationship between these levels is important when building good game tension. Two ways a level relates to another level are linear and non-linear.

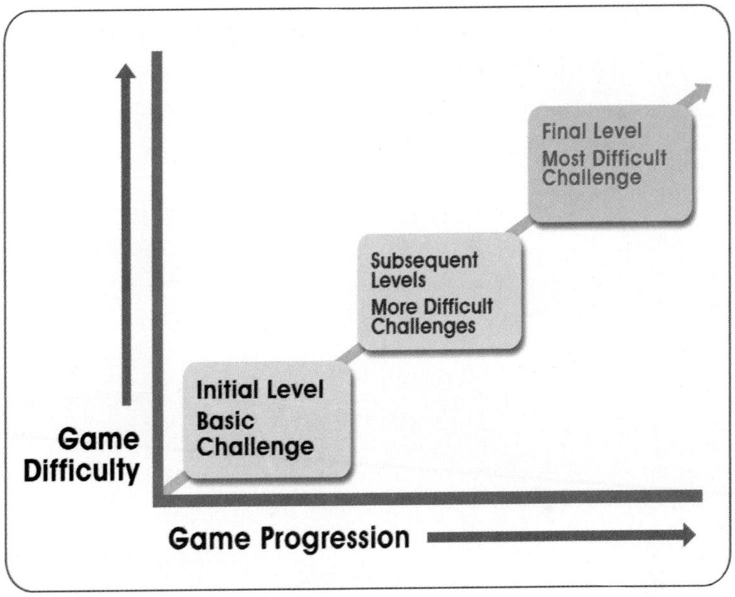

Per Olin

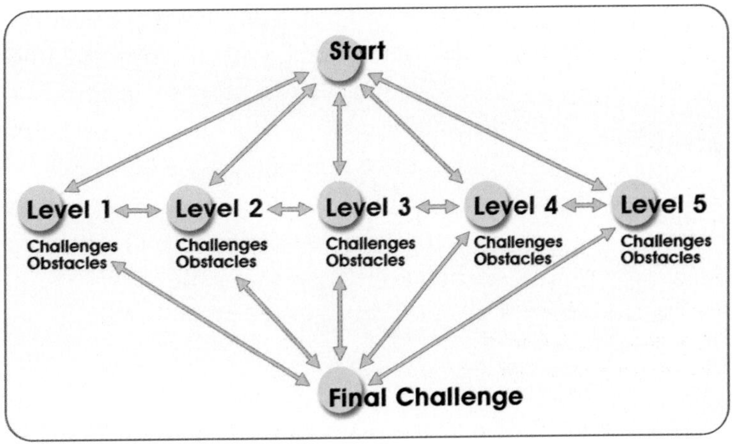

Per Olin

In a linear game (top), challenges become progressively harder until the end of the game. In a non linear game (bottom), the player has choices of how he or she will play the game.

Many games offer a linear story and gameplay. In these games, each level builds to a specific goal at the end of the game. Linear games are structurally similar to the Hollywood three-act structure. Just as each act flows into the next, using a rising line of action toward a single climax, each level of a linear game offers a continuous rise in difficulty, climaxing in the final challenge that will give victory to the player.

Games also offer a level relationship that adds to the quality of non-linearity. In non-linear games, each level might have its own self-contained story. The player then has the choice of what levels (sometimes known as missions or *questing*) to play, rather than being forced into the next predetermined level. A broader umbrella story can be addressed in these games in the same way that television serializes a larger arcing storyline over an entire season of episodes.

Fletcher Beasley on Music & Game Narrative:::::

Fletcher Beasley (Composer/Co-Owner, Beat Revolution Music + Sound)

Fletcher Beasley is a composer who got his start working in video games in the heyday of the Sega Genesis. He has since written music for virtually every video game platform on the market, in addition to film, television, commercials, and theme parks. He is co-owner of Beat Revolution, a music production company based in Los Angeles and a self-professed gear head who has been known to spend way too many hours contemplating the finer intricacies of various electronic noisemakers.

Music can have a powerful effect on a player's experience and can give the player emotional cues on how to relate to the information imparted in the narrative. If a character recounts something that has happened at an earlier point in the mythology of the world, for example, music can be used to give us a context for an event. An earlier tragedy underscored with sad music gives the player a different relationship to the historical events than the same scene scored with heroic music.

I believe that the emotional potential of music in games has just begun to be tapped. As game worlds become deeper and more immersive, adaptive music will play a greater role in shaping the player's relationship to the characters and events that are unfolding in the game. Game designers will use music as a way of subtly influencing the player's feelings, in much the same way that a film director uses music to cue the audience as to how to react to a scene in a movie. In a game, however, different music could be used depending on the player character's relationship to other characters in the game—creating the potential for multiple soundtracks based on the point of view of the character.

Progression

Pacing the *progression* of a game is important to the story as well as to gameplay. Each game challenge needs to increase in difficulty. Much as obstacles in movies become increasingly difficult for the hero, a game must build conflict throughout the level. Constant conflict, however, can become a problem, and the pace of the progression must be varied. Doing this offers time for the player to explore and learn about the environment. Just as an action film stops periodically for the character to figure out the bigger problem, be sure to offer the player the same courtesy. Unlike a movie, however, a game does not have to be linear, and the progression of difficulty in level can vary. For example, challenges can be flat and never increase in difficulty. They can escalate, increasing in difficulty, and they can follow an S-curve, allowing training for the player first and then increasing in difficulty until the end where the difficulty evens out so the player can finish the game. Finally, while challenges are always good, a game that is too easy too soon quickly becomes boring. A game that is too difficult too soon quickly becomes frustrating. You wouldn't want to see a character die in the beginning of a movie nor sail though every problem. Give players the sense of accomplishment that comes with earning their victory.

These are a few of the elements found in level building that can help you create a better game story experience. Just as the developer helps to create the world, and the writer helps to fill out the story, there are several others in the process—such as art directors, character designers, and animators—who contribute to the vision of the level, and they all contribute to a great game experience.

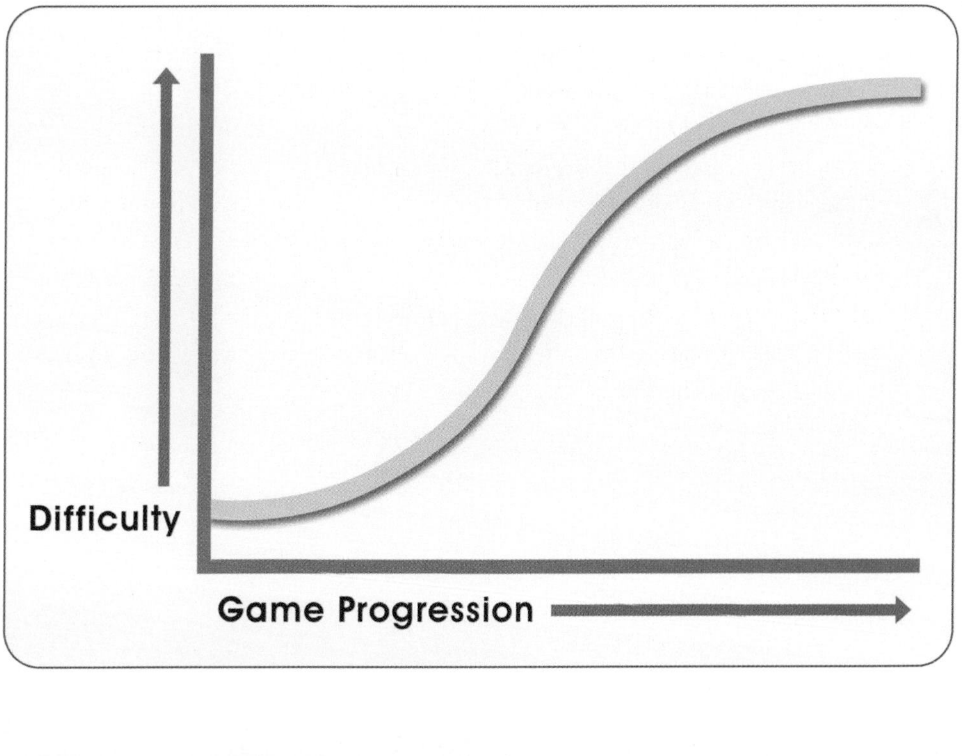

Per Olin

Difficulty progression can vary depending on the game.

Throughout this chapter, we have discussed how the intersection of game and story results in interesting gameplay. The use of various game design techniques such as balance, game tension, challenges and strategies all add to unique type of storytelling that indeed makes the player co-author of the game story.

To further explore the game story concept, we looked at how traditional game theory can be used to structure dramatic content and how dramatic tension actually can become gameplay tension. Finally, the reason we study game theory, design techniques and level design is simply to ensure that the game and story becomes engaging, interesting and fun "storyplay."

:::CHAPTER REVIEW:::

1. Play a card or board game (such as one that can be found at Funagain Games [funagain.com]). Analyze the rules—including victory conditions, loss conditions, gameplay process, and game goals. How would you expand upon the game's story structure in order to create a digital version of this game?

2. Gameplay is comprised of challenges or obstacles that are faced by players throughout the game. Players respond to these challenges by utilizing strategies, often represented by actions and player choices. For your original game idea, discuss 3 types of challenges and obstacles that players have to face or overcome. Be specific about the challenges that tie in with your particular storyline. For *each* of the 3 challenges, discuss three strategies (for a total of 9 strategies) that players must use to overcome each challenge. These strategies should tie in with different paths the player might take in the game. Be specific about how players might apply these strategies. How do challenges in your game represent plot points in your storyline—and how do the strategies utilized by the players represent directions and story paths in your game?

3. Play a game in any genre and analyze how the game handles structure. Is the game split up into levels? Does each subsequent level increase in difficulty? Does the game follow a linear, flat, or S-curve progression? Are all levels available to the player simultaneously? How does each level handle time and space? How will you structure your game into levels?

4. How does a game's cultural context affect its environment? Create a culture around your original game idea, and discuss how this culture might determine the look of look of interiors, exteriors, objects, vehicles, structures, and rules of the game world.

CHAPTER 9

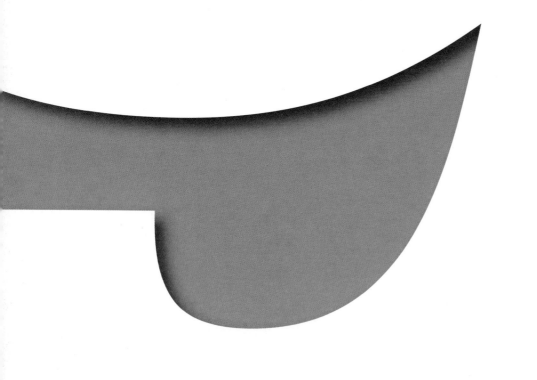

Putting Your Plan into Action:

implementing a successful storyplay

Key Chapter Questions

- How do all of the game story and character elements you've learned come together to make an interesting game?
- How do you take the classic story of Hamlet and make a compelling game?
- How can a great game story be incorporated into a strategy game?
- How can you make a game adaptation of a film without turning it into an "interactive movie"?
- What are the components of game story documentation?

Now that we have looked at all of the elements that go into successful storytelling in games, it's time to put everything together. You might have an interesting idea for a game or a story, but it still comes down to the execution of the idea. In the pages to come we will look at the beginning steps of a story within a game world. Once we have discussed the primary elements of building your game, we will take a quick look at the world of franchise and game adaptations from other media. Finally, we will consider where the writer fits into the ever-changing world of game development.

Your Game Plan

To begin any creative endeavor one must have a vision, but you'll need more than a vision: you need a plan.

As we discussed earlier in this book, an idea can come from anywhere—and, once you have it, you need to think about how to execute it. In terms of a game, you may want to start out with the theme, genre, story, environment, setting, or characters. Any and all of these areas are good places to start—but, once you have the idea, you'll need to begin to flesh it out. To start, let's set up some basic questions.

Capcom Entertainment, Inc.

The theme of *Resident Evil: Outbreak* is "survival."

What is the Theme?

Think about what you're trying to say in your story. Is your story about revenge? If so, what about revenge is important to you? Do you believe revenge is a form of justice—or does it fuel the cycle of violence even more? What point are you trying to make with your story? Many games do not attempt much beyond the typical battle of good and evil. Since we, as creators, are trying to make a better game experience for the player, try to offer more from the very start. Examples of themes include revenge, betrayal, redemption, and survival. Bear in mind that your theme might change—but that's a good sign. It means your game and story are active and interesting. Be sure to start with a single strong idea for your theme.

Capcom Entertainment, Inc.

Devil May Cry contains a rich storyline involving two brothers: Dante (a half-demon, half-human warrior who is dedicated to eradicating evil) and Vergil (who is at the opposite spectrum and will do anything to uphold his power as the leader of the unholy world).

What is Your Story?

In every other type of storytelling medium, the character and story always come first. Unfortunately, in games, the story is often an afterthought. A game can succeed without a story, but the idea is to offer the best possible experience to the player. A good story not only helps to create and build a better game, but it is also an enriching experience. Since the story idea needs to remain fluid in the development process, write your story from the concept stage all the way to the synopsis. However, you should allow room for changes as the story and game develop. A solid story will help your game become an even better experience for the player.

What is Your Genre?

Many people think about game genre first. You may or may not want to think about the genre first. You may want to think about story or gameplay first. In either case, you will need to choose a genre. As we discussed in Chapter 2, a genre is the type of game you are playing—such as action, adventure, puzzle, role-playing game (RPG), simulation, or strategy. Genre is a good way to promote specific kinds of stories. Pick one that best suits your story needs.

Capcom Entertainment, Inc.

Viewtiful Joe is a unique cel-shaded side-scrolling platform action game.

Blizzard Entertainment, Inc.

World of Warcraft contains almost every kind of environment imaginable for exploration—including forests, deserts, swamps, mountains, and the tropics.

What is Your Environment?

Remember, environment goes beyond the backdrop of a particular place or era. It provides the specifics to the game space—such as boundaries, structures, terrain, materials, objects, and style.

What is Your Setting?

The setting is the world in which the story takes place and should feed the narrative in subtle yet concrete ways. In games where characters do not exist (such as strategy games), setting becomes an essential part of the storytelling process. Choose your setting as carefully as you develop your characters and you will have a great game!

Infinity Ward/Activision

Call of Duty 2 is set in the era of World War II—from the Battle of the Bulge in Bastogne to the German counterattack at Kursk.

What Character Types Do You Need?

What types of characters will be well-suited to your game's story and environment? Will you need soldiers to move around a battlefield? Will you need highly customizable player characters? Does your game require fantasy or more realistic characters? How will you utilize different characters for different purposes? Be sure to choose and develop your characters well. When players bond with your characters they experience the game in a heightened emotional state.

Eidos

Will your protagonist be an adventurous risk-taker such as *Tomb Raider's* Lara Croft?

Sony Computer Entertainment of America

Ares is the antagonist in *God of War.*

Protagonist

Do you have a protagonist? Remember, a protagonist is the character who initiates the action. In a game, you want the player to be the one who initiates all the action, thus your player is the protagonist. This doesn't mean that you don't have to develop the protagonist. Lara Croft, for example, the protagonist of *Tomb Raider,* is a well-developed protagonist and a character who players like to try on and play. On the other hand, Master Chief from the *Halo* games has no development at all, so that the player can play the part of Master Chief as himself. Remember that the protagonist is the character that moves the story forward and the one the player will pay the most attention to. It is important to develop an interesting protagonist.

Antagonist

Who is your antagonist? Will the antagonist be a "shadow" of the protagonist? Will the antagonist be evil, or just a character that happens to want the same thing as your protagonist? Will the antagonist be exaggerated or realistic? How will the antagonist be demonstrated in the game story and gameplay? Often an antagonist is put into the final boss fight. Can you think of any other ways to use an antagonist? The main character of any story is the protagonist, the one that promotes the action or gameplay. The antagonist is the character that wants to stop the forward action. Both are equally important to story and games.

Helper Characters

Does your protagonist need help in the form of general allies or does he need a more pivotal character to assist him? Where will the protagonist get information? Remember that ancillary characters are very important and often help to tell the story. For this reason, you need to think about which ancillary characters you will need within your game to drive the story and game forward.

Naughty Dog/Sony Computer Entertainment of America

In *Jak & Daxter*, Jak is helped by sidekick Daxter—who is often perched on Jak's shoulder.

Once you have established the types of characters you will need, it's time to begin the character development process. Since all characters are important to the story and the game, be sure to take time to develop these well. Give physiological, sociological, and psychological traits to each of your primary characters. As you develop these characteristics, always keep in mind that the player will need to identify and bond with the protagonist.

How to Tell It

Think about how your story will be told. What will be the perspective? Is this game a first-person shooter or a third-person action-adventure game? Will there be a lot of cut-scenes or very few, so that you do not interrupt the gameplay experience? How will the information appear on the screen? Will the player receive the story information sequentially or simultaneously?

Goals

What are the goals for the protagonist and player, and how are these met in terms of gameplay and storytelling? Remember that having a goal for both the game and the story is important in order to motivate the player to keep playing. What are the stakes that are tied to these goals? Is the goal to save the earth from an evil alien race (*Halo*) or to save a princess (*The Legend of Zelda*)? Think about what makes goals interesting and how they are tied to the high stakes in the game.

Nintendo of America, Inc.

The macro goal in *The Legend of Zelda* is for Link to rescue Zelda. The micro goal in this image is to survive the battle.

Firaxis Games

Strategy games such as *Civilization IV* offer a great deal of challenges and rules.

Macro vs. Micro Goals

The macro goal for the game might be presented at the beginning of the game—such as in chess or it might be revealed later during the game and story development. Either way, there is a need to offer smaller goals along the way to keep the tension and balance interesting. Once these micro goals are achieved, you might offer a reward as simple as information or a weapons upgrade!

Challenges and Rules

Challenges and rules offer obstacles and restrictions for players to overcome as they pursue their goals. Remember, attaining a goal too easily is boring, but never attaining a goal can be frustrating. Be sure to find balance within the game and story tension. Remember that in each level there must be a flow that keeps the player moving—as well as progressively harder obstacles. How will you incite curiosity in the players to keep them moving and exploring throughout the level? How will the story continue to be executed through each individual level?

Level Structure

Back in Chapter 3, we talked about the traditional structure of story. While choosing how to set up the levels and their relationships to one another, we can apply story elements. While traditional three-act structure leads toward a linear game and story, the episodic approach is good for non-linear gameplay and story. Consider building an overall story similar to what you might find in a season of a particular television show. Each individual level might contain separate stories, as well as interesting parts of the larger story of the game.

Game Documentation

Game documentation such as concept documents, story treatments, and game design documents (GDDs) are created by assembling all the ideas for your "game plan" into an organized, written form. Some development teams use documentation and stress the need for it. Other teams never use them and do a lot of the development "on the fly." While the need for game documentation is often debated, one thing can be said for certain: there is no standardized template that development teams use to put their creative ideas into concrete form. Wouldn't it be nice if there were? With this in mind, the following pages demonstrate the process of developing two different games while using a basic documentation format for both. Keep in mind that actual game documentation can be hundreds of pages long. The documentation we're providing below contains elements of game story treatments and game design documents (GDDs), but we only focus on basic descriptions rather than the detail required for implementation.

Hamlet: Prince of Denmark

Ben Bourbon

Now that we have established some of the basics for setting up the story, let's take a look at a classic story—William Shakespeare's *Hamlet*—and see how this story might translate into a game.

Many would argue that *Hamlet* is the worst possible story to try to convert into a game. The title character, Prince Hamlet, sits around and thinks a lot; he is considered by some to be quite indecisive; and his plans often include behaviors such as "acting crazy"—none of which translates into fun and compelling gameplay. Even so, let's examine the idea further by applying all of the game elements that we've already learned to the story of *Hamlet* and see if a game begins to unfold:

Title

The game's title should be brief and engaging. The original title does a good job at this, so let's stick with *Hamlet: Prince of Denmark.*

Genre

Of all the game genres, the one that seems to suit this story the most is *action-adventure.* This is a natural choice since there is already an established murder to solve, as well as pre-existing weapons.

Theme

As we have discussed in previous chapters, it is helpful to have a theme for your game and story. Doing so helps center the gameplay, story and characters around a central idea and provides a clearer story experience. In the case of Hamlet, young Hamlet meets his father's ghost who tells Hamlet to avenge his murder. Clearly, the theme for this game is *revenge.*

Historical Context

Context centers the players and helps them understand where they are in time. The historical context of the game is Europe, 1601 A.D.

Setting

The setting is the backdrop for the game and story and can contribute to the story as much as a character. In this case, it is Elsinore castle and the surrounding country of Denmark.

Environment

The environment is different than the setting. The player interacts with the environment while playing the game. Hills, trees, and castle walls will all contribute to the environment.

Concept

The concept is very simple: the first thought about the game and story. In this case, the concept is: *The protagonist seeks revenge.*

Springboard

A springboard is a further extension of the concept. Our springboard is: *A prince in line for the throne wants to avenge his father's death.*

Premise

You are young Prince Hamlet. You have just returned home from college for your father's funeral and learn that your uncle has married your mother. You suspect foul play but have no proof. Now it's your job to prove that your uncle is a murderer, avenge your father's death, and claim your rightful place as King of Denmark.

Backstory

Young Prince Hamlet has just returned to his home, Elsinore castle in Denmark, for his father's funeral. When he arrives, he realizes his Uncle Claudius has married his mother less than a few months after the death of his father. Hamlet suspects foul play. To make matters worse, best friend Horatio tells Hamlet that his father, King Hamlet, is a ghost appearing in the battlements of the castle. Hamlet approaches the ghost, learns that his suspicions are correct (Claudius murdered Old King Hamlet), and that he must avenge his father's death—but how?

Synopsis

Hamlet is unsure whether the ghost is really his father or a misleading demon sent from hell to trick him, so he must uncover the truth for himself. He decides to behave as if he is crazy, but when that fails he invites a troop of actors to put on a play that depicts the way the king was killed. When Claudius reacts to the play, Hamlet knows that Claudius is guilty and seeks a way to kill him. Claudius, for the most part, is on to Hamlet and sends for Rosencrantz and Guildenstern, two school chums of Hamlet, to spy on Hamlet and report back to Claudius. In the meantime, Hamlet, thinking that he is stabbing Claudius, accidentally stabs Polonius, the father of his girlfriend, Ophelia. This action causes all sorts of ripples—including bringing Polonius' son, Laertes, to Denmark to avenge his father's death. Claudius, getting more nervous all the time, sends Hamlet to England with a special message for their king: kill Hamlet. Hamlet reads the message and is in trouble until pirates attack his ship and set him free. Hamlet sends Rosencrantz and Guildenstern on to England with an altered message, since he feels they have betrayed him. When Rosencrantz and Guildenstern arrive in England, they are executed. Hamlet returns to Denmark to find that Ophelia has died and her brother, Laertes, wants to kill him. Claudius fuels the fire by telling Laertes to challenge Hamlet to a duel. Claudius promises to poison the tip of the sword so Laertes need only land a single strike on Hamlet and cut him. To further stack the deck, Claudius poisons some wine, just in case Laertes can't scratch Hamlet. Hamlet's mother accidentally drinks the wine and dies. Hamlet and Laertes end up mortally wounded. Before Hamlet dies, he kills Claudius—the real villain of the bunch. Everybody is dead. Then a guy named Fortenbras comes in and takes over the crown of Denmark. Talk about your complicated tragedy!

In a game version of this story, the synopsis would also include information from the player's point of view. There could be many possible endings (Hamlet does succeed in killing Claudius and taking over the crown, Ophelia doesn't die and elopes with Hamlet after helping him kill Claudius and Laertes, etc.). Also, there could be several story paths that lead the player to these endings. For example, if Hamlet only wounds Polonius or instead accidentally kills Ophelia, the story path will change and the outcome will most likely be distinctly different! Allowing for these possibilities will aid in the game's replayability.

Characters

Character 1 — Protagonist

Name: Hamlet

Background/history: Prince of Denmark. Born of royalty, he has been reared to one day take the throne.

Physical characteristics: Young, strong, athletic.

Personality characteristics: Obsessive, full of doubt, indecisive

Relationship to Player: Player Character

Character 2 — Antagonist

Name: Claudius

Background/history: Illegitimate King of Denmark. Murdered his brother for the crown. Born of royalty, but was not reared to one day take the throne.

Physical characteristics: Old, strong, poised.

Personality characteristics: Crafty, malicious, confident.

Relationship to Player: Non-player character (AI), main opponent to the player character.

Character 3 — Ally

Name: Horatio

Background/history: Companion to Hamlet; probably of high ranking, but not of the royal line.

Physical characteristics: Young, strong, agile.

Personality characteristics: Helpful, honest, loyal.

Relationship to Player: Non-player character (AI), helps player to achieve goals.

Levels

This is a linear story—but it doesn't mean that the game needs to be. The levels can be non-linear. Choosing a non-linear format will allow the player to go to any level at any time within the game and explore, find information, solve puzzles, and engage in combat.

To further the non-linearity, the final battle might be against King Claudius. However, rather than a linear build-up to a final fight, perhaps the player could be allowed to fight Claudius at any time.

Victory and Loss Conditions

If the player has not achieved certain goals within the other levels, it will be impossible to defeat Claudius and attain victory. We can further add to the victory condition by requiring that Hamlet carry the burden of proof. This simply means that once the player has defeated Claudius, he needs to go one step further and prove that Claudius was the murderer of Old King Hamlet. If the player has not gathered enough information throughout the other levels, he will be tried for regicide and then executed.

Allowing the players to make choices about how they defeat the antagonist allows for effective, non-linear gameplay while staying true to the original story. If the player cannot prove Claudius guilty, the player will still end up dead at the end—just like the play. If the player ends up dead at the end, we can drive the stakes higher by adding a stipulation that, with Hamlet dead, the people of Denmark revolt and everyone involved with the royal family ends up dead—just like they did in the play. Now there is the option for the player to win and change the outcome of the story—or, if the player fails, the tragedy can play out similar to Shakespeare's version. The goal for the player is to not let the tale end tragically, and restore order to the kingdom.

To clarify even further:

Victory = Hamlet sitting as King of Denmark; Claudius, a proven murderer and dead.

Loss = Hamlet and family dead; the kingdom in utter chaos.

Victory and loss conditions are important to both the game and story. Be sure to have clear victory and loss conditions to help make a satisfying game.

Challenges and Strategies

Collecting information and upgrading weapons throughout the levels might give the player what he needs to fight Claudius and assure his place on the throne. Within each level there should be a smaller story that offers various challenges and strategies. The purpose of this is threefold:

1. It gives the player something to do.
2. It gives the player a reward that might help him in the endgame.
3. If structured properly and the strategies and challenges allow for it, these strategies can prepare the player (Hamlet) to be a better king at the end. Assuming that Hamlet has only known a life of royalty, engaging with his subjects might allow him to grow and become a better ruler.

In case you haven't noticed, our theme has just shifted. As is often the case, a writer may start out with an idea about a particular theme—but by the end of the story, it is about something entirely different. In our process of figuring out the game of Prince Hamlet, the theme has shifted from revenge to responsibility. All of a sudden, the player is responsible for helping the subjects of Denmark. When the player goes to fight Claudius, he is responsible for proving murder. If he fails in any of these responsibilities, he, his family, and his kingdom stand to fall into chaos and death. Amazingly, this theme of responsibility—especially of the ruling class over its subjects—appears often not only in Shakespeare's work but also throughout the art of the Elizabethan period. What we have here is a game based on a tragic play—but we have developed it in a way that potentially avoids the tragic ending, while still keeping elements of the original source material alive and well.

But lets make the challenges specific to the game:

Challenges

1. Confirm that the ghost is really Old King Hamlet and not a demon sent from hell to confuse Hamlet.
2. Prove that Claudius murdered Old King Hamlet.
3. Punish Claudius for the murder.

Strategies

Now, let's look at three strategies for executing the second challenge listed above: proving that Claudius murdered Old King Hamlet.

1. Convince other characters to befriend Claudius and trick him into confiding in them and confessing.
2. Confront Claudius directly with your knowledge and try to force a confession out of him through violence or torture.
3. Explore the game world and look for physical evidence that points to Claudius as the murderer.

Each of these strategies is equally viable, should lead the player down a separate story path, and allow for replayability.

Audio

Finally, think about how to incorporate audio into your game. In the Hamlet game, we already know that there will be dialog from NPC characters. Music could be easily incorporated in the form of a score or in connection with other characters that Hamlet encounters. Say Hamlet is in the Forest surrounding Copenhagen when he runs into a troop of actors, it is possible to have them singing or playing guitars, thereby contributing to the overall experience.

While the material we've provided reflects one possible direction for a game version of Hamlet, remember that stories in games are fluid. There are several possibilities for any given story. The following chart demonstrates only one possible way of setting up the story.

Per Olin

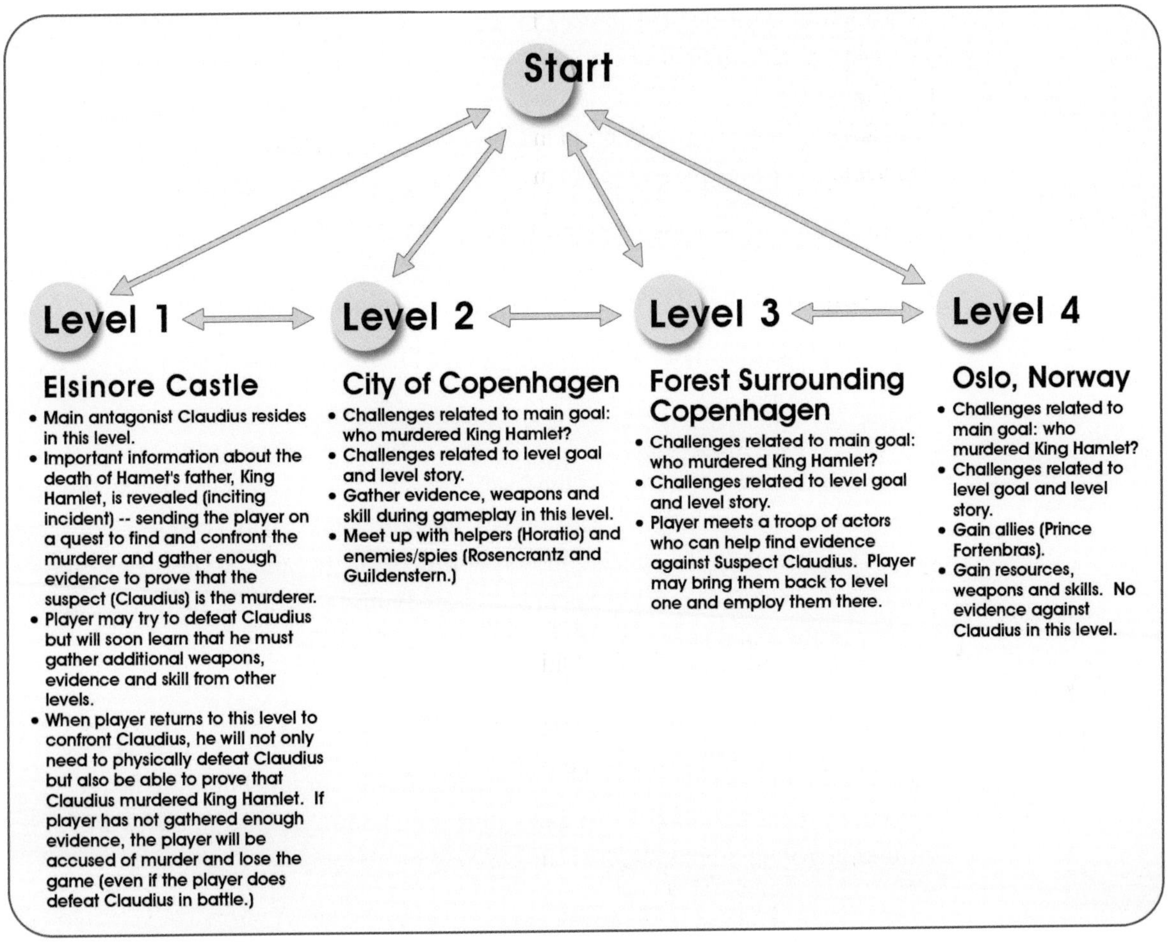
Start
Level 1
Level 2
Level 3
Level 4
Elsinore Castle
• Main antagonist Claudius resides in this level.
• Important information about the death of Hamet's father, King Hamlet, is revealed (inciting incident) -- sending the player on a quest to find and confront the murderer and gather enough evidence to prove that the suspect (Claudius) is the murderer.
• Player may try to defeat Claudius but will soon learn that he must gather additional weapons, evidence and skill from other levels.
• When player returns to this level to confront Claudius, he will not only need to physically defeat Claudius but also be able to prove that Claudius murdered King Hamlet. If player has not gathered enough evidence, the player will be accused of murder and lose the game (even if the player does defeat Claudius in battle.)
City of Copenhagen
• Challenges related to main goal: who murdered King Hamlet?
• Challenges related to level goal and level story.
• Gather evidence, weapons and skill during gameplay in this level.
• Meet up with helpers (Horatio) and enemies/spies (Rosencrantz and Guildenstern.)
Forest Surrounding Copenhagen
• Challenges related to main goal: who murdered King Hamlet?
• Challenges related to level goal and level story.
• Player meets a troop of actors who can help find evidence against Suspect Claudius. Player may bring them back to level one and employ them there.
Oslo, Norway
• Challenges related to main goal: who murdered King Hamlet?
• Challenges related to level goal and level story.
• Gain allies (Prince Fortenbras).
• Gain resources, weapons and skills. No evidence against Claudius in this level.

The players choose what level they want to play. This makes the Hamlet game non-linear and more akin to a real world experience.

The above Hamlet game is one variation of a game idea from a an existing story. It is only one way to present a complicated story as a game. There are several other ways to present this story in terms of game and character. Choosing a different genre is one way to present this story, choosing a different POV is another. Further, you may want to make it a "Hamlet in Space" idea and present the backdrop as the galaxy, the weapons as high-tech laser guns and the character as a young man who must return to his home planet. A myriad of similar possibilities await the designer in this and other stories.

Ben Bourbon

Caesar's Quest

Now let's take a quick look at a story based on historical events the one we have been working with throughout the book: General Julius Caesar's quest to rule the Roman Empire.

Title

Since this is a very well known historical character we are talking about, it is best to keep his name in the title of the game. This gives the player a good idea of what the game will be about, but we can't just call it *Caesar*. We need to give a further indication of the game's focus. *Caesar's Quest* tells us more—and it's simple.

Genre

This story can be naturally executed with strategy-based gameplay, due to the fact that you must manage all your resources, including your small army, weapons, and food. Furthermore, if we make this a real-time strategy game, strategic decisions will have to be made quickly. So, mistakes are bound to happen, furthering the reality of the story, as well as adding a good challenge for the player.

Theme

Again we come across the need for a theme. Earlier in this book, we talked about different themes for this game, but if we had to put it into one word, it would be *conquest*.

Historical Context

Unlike Hamlet, this game takes place at a very specific time in history. You could change the setting—but the fun of this game is closely connected with the historical context, so let's keep it that way for now. The context is Italy, 52 B.C.

Setting

The setting is the backdrop for the game and story. In this case, it is the ancient Roman Empire, as well as the surrounding ancient world.

Environment

Remember, the environment is what the players will interact with as they play. Terrain, buildings, vehicles, and non-player characters all contribute to the environmental experience. Be sure to stay true to the vision. In other words, placing a motorcycle in the middle of this game would contribute to an inconsistent environment, and take the player of out immersion.

Concept

Again, the concept (the original idea) should be very simple. The concept for *Caesar's Quest*: the protagonist wants to gain power.

Springboard

A springboard is a further extension of the concept. Our springboard: a story about Julius Caesar before he becomes Emperor of Rome—perhaps even *how* he becomes emperor.

Premise

Game premises are usually told in second person. Here is the premise for *Caesar's Quest:*

You are the young, ambitious General Julius Caesar, you have just crossed the Rubicon River to start a civil war in the capital of the greatest empire of all time: Rome. Your hated enemy, Pompey the Great, was given the power to control and protect all of Rome and his troops far outnumber yours. Pompey's support from the Roman Senate and his numerous legions will prove a difficult match for your troops. Will your determination and ambitious nature aid in your victory—or will you suffer defeat?

Backstory

In 71 B.C., Pompey the Great returned to Rome victorious, after having put down a threatening rebellion in Spain. At the same time, Marcus Licinius Crassus, a rich patrician, suppressed the slave revolt led by Spartacus. Pompey and Crassus both ran for the consulship—an office held by two men—in 70 B.C. Pompey, who was ineligible for consulship, somehow managed to win with the help of Julius Caesar. Crassus became the other consul. Ten years later, when Caesar returned to Rome, he joined forces with Crassus and Pompey in a three-way alliance known as the First Triumvirate. Caesar gave his daughter, Julia, to Pompey in marriage—an act of good will. Soon, the Roman Senate became leery of Caesar's lust for power. They sent him to conquer Gaul, thereby keeping him out of Rome and Roman politics. When Crassus was killed in battle in 53 B.C., the Senate instated Pompey the Great to rule all of Rome—an idea that did not sit well with the ambitious Julius Caesar.

Synopsis

On the foggy banks of the Rubicon River, Julius Caesar—formerly one of the three leaders of Rome—keeps watch at the head of his small legion of soldiers. With a single word, he commands the troops across the water and thus hurls the empire into a turbulent civil war while civilization itself hangs in the balance. In order to defeat his enemy, Pompey, Caesar acts swiftly and decisively by placing his men throughout Northern Italy—while Pompey gathers his numerous, but far-flung legions. City after city is conquered—town after town falls to Caesar. Many cities fall without resistance until Rome herself lay at risk. Within weeks, the Senate and Pompey evacuate Rome—issuing a warning that any who stay within the city will be considered Caesar's ally and Pompey's enemy. Pompey's retreat eastward is a strategic one, his intent is to draw Caesar to Asia where Pompey has many allies in the form of powerful kingdoms. Unfortunately for Pompey, during the scramble to evacuate Rome, he and the Senators forget to take the vast treasure stored under the Temple of Saturn. Caesar is quick to discover the plunder, which significantly increases his war purse. For another six months, Caesar relentlessly pursues Pompey, eventually crushing the last of his armies in Spain. The defeated Senate has no choice but to instate Caesar as head consul and dictator of all of Rome.

Characters

Character 1 — Protagonist

Name: Julius Caesar

Goal/want: Power over the Roman Empire.

Background/history: Member of the First Triumvirate, but was recently shut out of Rome's political arena.

Physical characteristics: Late 30's, strong, athletic.

Personality characteristics: Arrogant, self-assured, risk-taker.

Relationship to Player: Player character (or NPC, if player chooses to play Pompey). Main opponent to Pompey.

Character 2 — Antagonist

Name: Pompey the Great

Goal/want: Retain power over the Empire.

Background/history: Son-in-law to Julius Caesar, who now has the Senate and Empire under his control and has no intention of giving up this power.

Physical characteristics: Late 20's, strong, athletic.

Personality characteristics: Arrogant, self-assured, traitorous.

Relationship to Player: NPC (or player character, if player chooses to play Pompey). Main opponent to Caesar.

Character 3 — Allies (group)

Name: Soldiers

Background/history: Have been under player character's command for several years.

Physical characteristics: Fit, strong, agile, dressed in military costume, carry weapons.

Personality characteristics: Loyal to player character.

Relationship to Player: NPCs. Help player character achieve the goal.

Levels

Since this game is about the progression of Caesar's attempt to take over Rome, perhaps a more linear progression would help keep the player focused directly on the goal. As players reach new towns and settlements, they will be able to gather resources, either by trade, force, or politics.

Allowing for player choice is essential—so the player should be able to choose whether to play Caesar (with fewer resources) or Pompey (with greater resources). Even though Caesar has fewer resources, the game maintains balance because these resources are more condensed and closer to Rome. If the player chooses to play Pompey, gameplay will begin at an entirely different level; the player will need to work backward to meet Caesar and try to stop him before he has gained too much ground. Again, management of resources and strategically placed troops are all part of the game.

Victory and Loss Conditions

Now that we have our characters and story, let's look at how we might win or lose the game.

CAESAR
Victory = Gaining control of the empire
Loss = Depletion of resources and death

POMPEY
Victory = Keeping control of the empire
Loss = Loss of control of the empire and death

These are the victory and loss conditions. Can you think of any other elements that might offer victory or loss?

Challenges and Strategies

The challenge of the entire game will be to overcome the opposing forces, but we can also offer strategic tasks. Remember that the goal is to become the emperor of Rome, so offering high-ranking positions to town leaders might be an effective way to gather resources for your soldiers. There will be other politicking allowed, too. If the player is Caesar, there will be corrupt Senators who will betray Pompey, if the price is right. On the other hand, it might be possible for one of the corrupt Senators to be a mole character. In this case, the player will have used important resources for naught—resources that might have been used to provide food and weapons for the soldiers and, ultimately, victory.

Challenges

1. Build up your forces.
2. Acquire more resources.
3. Attack the enemy, attempting to destroy enemy's resources and infrastructure.

Strategies

Now let's look at three strategies for meeting the second challenge listed above—acquire more resources.

1. Conquer a town by brute force, but be prepared to meet resistance. Perhaps trade off soldier's lives for resources.
2. Cut deals with town officials, promising high positions in government after you take over.

3. Send in small legion of bandits and steal goods from a town (although this is very un-Roman and would not inspire the respect and awe needed later when you win control of the empire).

Audio

Finally, how could audio be incorporated into *Caesar's Quest?* Would you score the battle scenes with music? How much dialog will be needed to assign tasks on missions? How, creatively, will you tell the player what to do? There are many options, including sound effects such as thundering hoofs of the horses. In a console game, you can further enhance the sound effects by making use of the console controller's rumble technology. For example, each time the thundering footstep of the legion of Pompey is near, not only is the sound heard, but also the controls vibrate in the player's hand. Anything that leads the player to a more immersive experience should be included in the audio section.

The preceding is just one possible direction for a game version of Caesar's conquest of Rome. Keep in mind that stories in games are fluid, so there are several possibilities for any given story. The chart to the right illustrates one possible way of setting up a story path within the game.

Per Olin

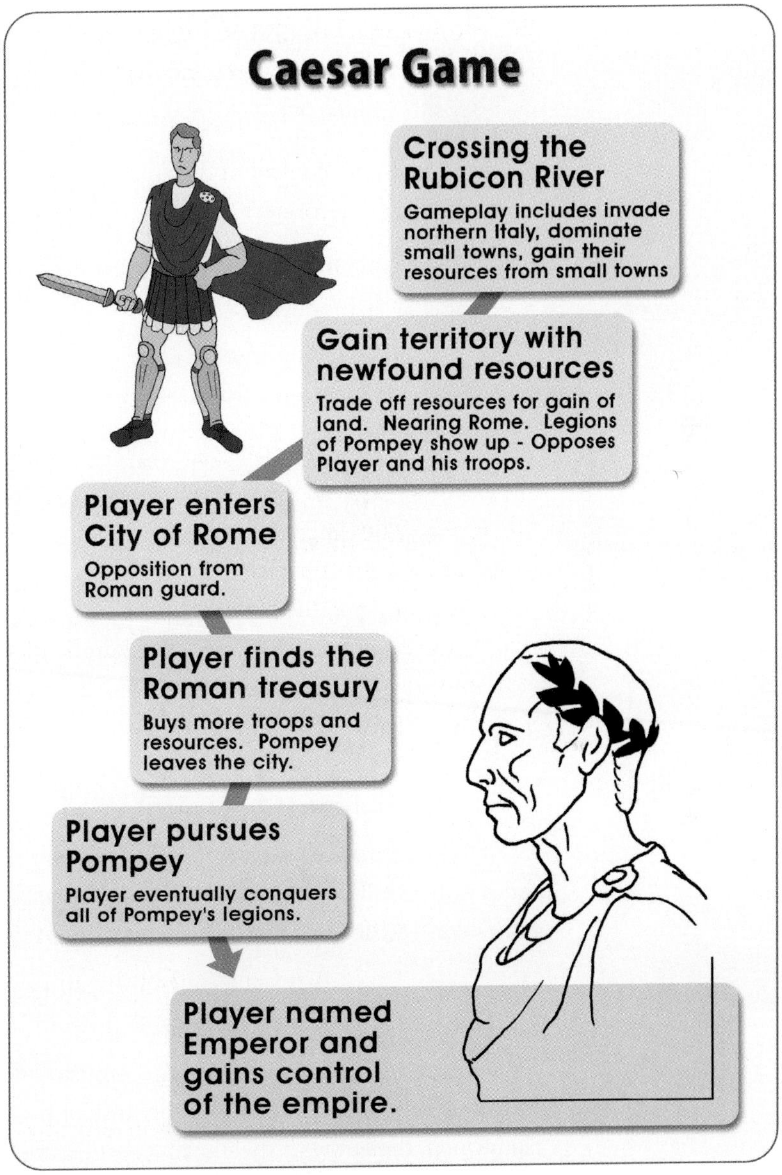

Caesar Game
Crossing the Rubicon River
Gameplay includes invade northern Italy, dominate small towns, gain their resources from small towns
Gain territory with newfound resources
Trade off resources for gain of land. Nearing Rome. Legions of Pompey show up - Opposes Player and his troops.
Player enters City of Rome
Opposition from Roman guard.
Player finds the Roman treasury
Buys more troops and resources. Pompey leaves the city.
Player pursues Pompey
Player eventually conquers all of Pompey's legions.
Player named Emperor and gains control of the empire.

In the Caesar game, all the action moves forward in a linear fashion.

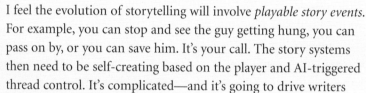

David Perry on Playable Story Events:::::

A 23-year video game industry veteran, David Perry launched his professional career at just 15 years of age by writing video game programming books in his native Northern Ireland. Since then, David has developed 32 games (programming 24 of them). David's number-one games include *The Terminator*, *Teenage Mutant Ninja Turtles*, and *Disney's Aladdin*. He sits on the Advisory Board of the Game Developers Conference, and is a regular speaker at industry events. His last project was *Enter the Matrix*, the #1 Award-Winning Movie Game of 2003, selling approximately 6 million copies. Shiny Entertainment is currently developing a sequel, *The Matrix: The Path of Neo*.

David Perry (President, Shiny Entertainment)

I feel the evolution of storytelling will involve *playable story events*. For example, you can stop and see the guy getting hung, you can pass on by, or you can save him. It's your call. The story systems then need to be self-creating based on the player and AI-triggered thread control. It's complicated—and it's going to drive writers crazy, since there are so many ways to break their ideas. That said, there's massive reward for writers that can wrap their arms around the concept and then push it forward. AI cognition and speech generation programmers will become writers' best friends!

Movies and Games

As Hollywood invades the game industry more and more—and the idea of franchise and profits overtake the concept of games as art—so must we take a quick look at games that use licensed characters and stories from movies and television.

The problem that most face when trying to adapt a film into a game is that games and films are two different media and need to be looked at as such. Novels offer a similar experience to a game in terms of narrative and environment—and they probably offer better adaptations—but because of the "franchise money machine" that is Hollywood, the effort to specifically merge games and films will continue. With this in mind, what we need to think about is the ongoing experience for the player.

Films tend to offer a linear narrative and a single storyline. This might be fun for the player who wants to experience the movie. However, the player market is increasingly looking for a whole new way to play games—one where interactivity and nonlinearity become the key concepts behind gameplay.

The Problem with Licensed Titles

There is a great shorthand in working on a licensed title. You can assume the audience knows the characters and the world they are entering, and you can jump right into the story. The problem is that the game companies rarely get invested in these games. They rely on the licensed title alone to sell them, and don't often make great games out of them. In *Shrek 2*, we couldn't write the main characters very heavy, since they were hoping to get the stars and the voiceovers would be too expensive to do a lot of it. Thus characters like the gingerbread man became the stars—or at least the most talkative. If someone would invest the time, energy, and money into a good licensed title, it would not only sell well but attract many more people to games.

— *Mike Daley (Freelance Writing Producer, Blindlight)*

With all of the questions and controversy surrounding adaptations of movies into games—and games into movies—there are elements in both that we can look for and transfer into each scenario. First, let's look at a franchise that was originally a wildly successful book series, then a string of popular movies, and has since become a successful game—*Harry Potter*.

It is important to remember that *Harry Potter* movies are adapted from novels, and—as we mentioned earlier—novels often offer more robust environments to play in, than films. Even so, *Harry Potter* not only offers a rich world and a compelling character that children want to play, but the world itself is akin to many fantasy game worlds. The use of magic and spells, monsters, factions of bad wizards, and the concepts of time and time travel to produce different outcomes to the story—all contribute to a good game. Furthermore, players can enter this world of wizards and play as themselves the character of Harry, and still enjoy the experience.

Shrek offers another world that goes beyond the realm of the film narrative. In the movie, it is plausible to believe that, if the player entered that world, there would be a large game space, rich environment, and plenty of adventure for the player, regardless of the title character.

Majesco Entertainment

Jaws Unleashed (above) and *Peter Jackson's King Kong* (below) are examples of game adaptations of licensed properties.

Ubisoft

The recent success of the book series *Lemony Snicket's A Series of Unfortunate Events* made it a shoe-in for a movie adaptation. Unfortunately, the movie didn't do as well as Hollywood had hoped—but rest assured that the game adaptation will offer, at least in theory, a sizable world where fun gameplay can be had by all.

In *Spiderman 2*, the player is allowed to travel throughout New York City and experience different challenges and gameplay, much in the same way *Grand Theft Auto* offers choices to the player. This is an excellent example of how a linear movie story can be made into a non-linear game.

Can you think of any movies that would offer non-linear gameplay, large game spaces, and compelling stories? When watching a movie, think about the many ways film can work its way into a game. You will certainly come up with several possibilities for great games. Keep in mind that game adaptations should not be literal translations of films. Instead, they should focus on the philosophical theme of the movie and elements that truly lend themselves to compelling gameplay.

Mike Daley on Story "Scholars"::::

Michael FX Daley has worked in television for several years on the shows *CSI, Crossing Jordan, The X-Files, That's My Bush!,* and *Get Real*—to name a few. In addition, he has been writing video games on a freelance basis through a company called Blindlight. With Blindlight he's worked as Writing Producer on Jet Li's *Rise To Honor, Hot Shot's Golf Fore!, Shrek 2,* and *Ninja Gaiden.* Mike has a Masters Degree in Screenwriting from Loyola Marymount University.

Michael FX Daley (Freelance Writing Producer, Blindlight)

Story is something we—more than any other generation—have been schooled in. I say that most kids today get the equivalent of film school just by watching their DVDs over and over again. When you start to analyze your entertainment—even subconsciously—you learn the rules. Good guys win, after insurmountable odds. In a good game, this structure will help the player continue to care about the game—and want to finish the level, the game, and the story. It's become basic to all of us—and a good game can use story to compel the player.

As the audience becomes a group of "film scholars," it's only a matter of time before they will be dissatisfied with the entertainment of film and television. My friends already get to this with the "I would have done it better" speeches after a movie. Interactivity offers them the ability to "do it better"—even if it's only an illusion. I believe we will all be playing games in the future—but the industry has to realize that not everyone will want to play *Halo*, or simply kill things. And narrative will offer new games to be played.

Where Does the Writer Fit in?

While it is still true that many game companies don't use writers, the writer is becoming more and more a part of the process. In many cases, the lead designer or creative director wants to write the story, but is either not trained as a writer or perhaps lacks the time needed to create to a well thought-out story within the context of gameplay.

:::::The Importance of Professional Writing in *Demon Stone*

When we were designing *Demon Stone*, we created characters and settings while working closely with best-selling novelist R. A. Salvatore, who melded well into the team and worked closely with designers, artists, and producers. We selected Emmy Award–winning screenwriter Robert Goodman to write the game's dialogue; his take on many scenes added depth and emotion we would never have had without him. I believe that the future of game narrative and dialogue is one in which we will see steady growth and improvement, because many major game design teams are working with top writers to evolve game characters and tell their stories. The games industry has already lured legendary film and TV visual effects professionals like Richard Taylor (who created the revolutionary computer graphics for the movie *Tron*). Increasingly, top writers will join the development teams for major games and lend their skills to the creative process in the same way that Hollywood technical professionals do now.

Stormfront Studios/Atari

Hopefully, in the future, the writer will become part of the core development team. In the meantime, the elements discussed in this book will help writers and designers (and hopefully the coming hybrid, the writer-designer) to create rich worlds with compelling stories and interesting, emotionally-multidimensional characters. When they do, we will all have a better and richer game experience to enjoy!

Professionalizing the Industry

We're finally seeing movement toward hiring professional writers to create game narrative. It's taken a very long time. Traditionally, the designer or programmer would cobble together some dialogue to insert wherever it was needed to get the player into the next part of the game. The story wasn't given a great deal of consideration outside the adventure genre, the great bastion of story in the world of video gaming. The quality of game narrative is going to continue to rise, and we'll see more innovation and experimentation similar to the kind of filmmaking that followed the initial flowering of the art. Craft will start coming into it. The *Citizen Kane* of games has yet to be made.

— Patricia Pizer (Lead Designer, 4orty 2wo Entertainment)

Dan Arey on Unique Game Storytelling Challenges :::::

E. Daniel Arey (Creative Director, Naughty Dog Studios/SCEA)

A writer, director, and senior designer with over 14 years of experience, Dan Arey has worked with publishers ranging from Electronic Arts, Accolade, Sega of America, Crystal Dynamics, and Sony. An early proponent of interactive and convergent media, Dan led the earliest titles in this regard during his tenure as Design Manager for Crystal Dynamics. At Crystal, Dan designed games using film content and stronger narrative techniques as early as 1992, and has been an industry leader in story-enhanced gaming for more than a decade. Continuing his career at Naughty Dog, Dan has been involved in the design of the *Crash Bandicoot* and *Jak and Daxter* series, two best-selling franchises that have together sold more than 35 million units. In addition to being a contributor to *Game Developer Magazine*, Dan has been a frequent lecturer at the Game Developers Conference, E3, DICE, Writer's Guild of America, and USC School of Cinema.

At first blush, most people would say that the difference between a game and a film is that one is passive ("lean back" storytelling) and the other interactive ("lean forward" storytelling)—but this is somewhat misleading. I would say that even when a shaman told his stories to a tribe encircled around a blazing fire centuries ago, that—as they leaned forward, enraptured—the listeners too were "interacting" with the tale being spun. They were creating visions in their minds, and they were active participants in receiving or channeling the story experience. The difference for me is that when we tell a story in a game setting, it is simply a matter of participant degree. In games, storytelling is but a small part of the total experience—but we shouldn't let that relatively smaller size distract us from its deep importance.

Games are about "doing": they center around purposeful, concentrated action on the part of the player. This means that just as there are some stories that translate badly from a novel to a two-hour movie, some story types do not flourish as well in the highly active setting of games. Games are about taking action and seeing consequences—and this tight feedback loop is paramount to the player.

Traditional storytelling is a very focused linear form; it doesn't recurse well. Traditional authors provide well considered, rarefied life experiences with all the boring parts taken out (at least we hope)! Pacing is utterly controlled by the author. The emotional arcs are clearly defined and timed. In games, depending on the skill of the player, the emotional peaks and valleys may come 10 minutes apart—or, with a struggling player, two hours apart. In games, we have less control over this rising action of emotion—and that is problematic. Pacing, and specifically increasing tension as the story progresses to its final act, is a time-honored aspect of the storytelling experience. Timing matters in determining the emotional impact. In games, timing is subjective and is often (for good interactive reasons) at the mercy of the player. This presents unique challenges for all of us working with interactive narrative.

These are just a few differences—but they are significant, and they demonstrate that many of the solutions in the traditional sense may be less useful in games. We have been and continue to develop our own narrative vocabulary for interacting storytelling. The future is bright!

Sheldon Brown on the Evolution of Game Narrative:::::

Sheldon Brown (Professor, University of California San Diego)

Sheldon Brown is Director of the Center for Research in Computing and the Arts (CRCA) at the University of California San Diego (UCSD), where he is a Professor of Visual Arts and the head of New Media Arts for the California Institute of Telecommunications and Information Technologies (Cal-(IT)2). His work examines the relationships between mediated and physical experiences. This work often exists across a range of public realms and looks at the ways in which technologies, such as electronic games, intertwine social and cultural dimensions.

Games will evolve our general ideas of narrative. Game narrative in the future won't converge to a narrative form such as cinema or literary narratives; rather, it will develop forms unique and probably indescribable by current critical vocabularies. While it is important for us to look to these antecedent narrative forms, we should also look at other areas of play, storytelling, and social interaction to understand how games can evolve into more revelatory cultural forms.

"Circum-ambience": The Future of Games

When I think of the holodeck in *Star Trek*, I know the future of games: total immersion, interactivity in a physical and sensory way, complete suspension of disbelief, and utter abandoned involvement in the digital moment. I like the word "circum-ambience" for this experience. That to me is the ultimate goal, and yet it will take a few more baby steps to achieve this end.

— *E. Daniel Arey (Creative Director, Naughty Dog Studios/SCEA)*

As game platform technology grows, there will be a desire and need for story content. The drive toward more stories harkens back to the earliest days when Paleolithic man was telling his story on the sides of caves. In generations to come, the need for storytelling will not change, but the medium already has. We can expect to see more and more story driven game content—but not as we now know it. Rather, the story is edging ever closer to one in which the players/audience will be even more invested by participating in their own personal adventures, or co-authored stories.

In the first part of this book, we looked back at where stories came from, why we need to tell them, and what new frontiers of storytelling are within our grasp in electronic games. We also saw how traditional stories and certain devices associated with traditional storytelling can work in the new style of game storytelling. These elements, as well as game-story intersection, allow us to create a new experience for the player. Finally, we touched on moving the player emotionally though gameplay, story and immersion and discussed how games are quickly becoming "art" in terms of style and meaning.

The second part of this book took a closer look at how characters are developed for all storytelling media and how games need characters, despite the fact that the player is intimately involved with all the characters—whether they are player characters or NPCs. To further our discussion, we looked at how dialogue can enhance the immersive experience.

The third part of this book focused on how the intersection of story and gameplay elements can become an engaging, compelling, and fun experience. We call this melding of story and gameplay *storyplay*.

Now that we have gone through all the basic elements it takes to create a good game and story, it is time for you to put it all together—using your own creative muse. The world of games, storytelling and storyplay is wide open. Large companies and smaller independent companies will continue to develop great content, while searching for new ways to push the frontiers in the ever changing world of story, character and games.

:::CHAPTER REVIEW:::

1. Analyze a pre-existing puzzle, strategy, or simulation game that does not contain a storyline. Create a new storyline and at least 3 primary characters for the game, based on the principles you learned in this book.

2. Choose a film, book, or television series for which a game adaptation has not been created. (Do a search online at http://mobygames.com and http://google.com to ensure this.) Create a game storyline that reflects only one theme associated with this property. Keep in mind that the best game adaptations do not "translate" the entire property into a game but focus on only one aspect of the property (such as a subplot, scene, or philosophical theme).

3. Create game story documentation or a game design document (GDD) for your original game idea using one of the sample GDDs on the CD in the back of the book as a reference. Be sure to focus on balancing both story and gameplay elements.

4. Some have predicted that electronic games will represent the dominant form of entertainment in the 21st century—but games are only in their infancy. Knowing how storytelling has evolved over the years through different media, how do you see game storytelling developing and "maturing" during the next 10-20 years?

Resources

There's a wealth of information on game development and related topics discussed in this book. Here is just a sample list of books, news sites, organizations, and events you should definitely explore!

Keep the following two online resources on your "favorites" list. You will find yourself accessing them often:

Gamasutra – www.gamasutra.com

Search through developer articles, lists of game development studios and publishers, a directory of schools that have game programs – and employment listings. This invaluable online resource should be your first stop.

Moby Games – www.mobygames.com

Look up game titles, companies and people in this directory. You'll find out what games have been developed or published by which companies, as well as full credits.

News

Blues News – www.bluesnews.com

Computer Games Magazine – www.cgonline.com

Computer Gaming World – www.computergaming.com

Electronic Gaming Monthly – www.egmmag.com

Game Daily Newsletter – www.gamedaily.com

Game Developer Magazine – www.gdmag.com

Gamers Hell – www.gamershell.com

Game Music Revolution (GMR) – www.gmronline.com

Game Rankings – www.gamerankings.com

GameSlice Weekly – www.gameslice.com

GameSpot – www.gamespot.com

GameSpy – www.gamespy.com

Game Industry News – www.gameindustry.com

GIGnews.com – www.gignews.com

Internet Gaming Network (IGN) – www.ign.com

Machinima.com – www.machinima.com

Music4Games.net – www.music4games.net

PC Gamer – www.pcgamer.com

Star Tech Journal [technical side of the coin-op industry] – www.startechjournal.com

UGO Networks (Underground Online) – www.ugo.com

Video Game Music Archive – www.vgmusic.com

Wired Magazine – www.wired.com

Directories & Communities

Apple Developer Connection – developer.apple.com

Betawatcher.com – www.betawatcher.com

Fat Babies.com [game industry gossip] – www.fatbabies.com

GameDev.net – www.gamedev.net

Game Development Search Engine – www.gdse.com

Game Music.com – www.gamemusic.com

Game Rankings – www.gamerankings.com

Games Tester – www.gamestester.com

Overclocked Remix – www.overclocked.org

Organizations

Academy of Interactive Arts & Sciences (AIAS) – www.interactive.org

Academy of Machinima Arts & Sciences – www.machinima.org

Association of Computing Machinery (ACM) – www.acm.org

Digital Games Research Association (DiGRA) – www.digra.org

Entertainment Software Association (ESA) – www.theesa.com

Entertainment Software Ratings Board (ESRB) – www.esrb.org

Game Audio Network Guild (GANG) – www.audiogang.org

International Computer Games Association (ICGA) – www.cs.unimaas.nl/icga

International Game Developers Association (IGDA) – www.igda.org

SIGGRAPH – www.siggraph.org

Events

Consumer Electronics Show (CES)
January – Las Vegas, Nevada
www.cesweb.org

Game Developers Conference (GDC)
March – San Jose, California
www.gdconf.com

D.I.C.E. Summit
March – Las Vegas, Nevada
www.interactive.org/dice

Electronic Entertainment Expo (E3)
May – Los Angeles, California
www.e3expo.com

SIGGRAPH
August – Los Angeles, California
www.siggraph.org

Austin Game Developers Conference
September – Austin, Texas
www.gameconference.com

Indie Games Con (IGC)
October – Eugene, Oregon
www.garagegames.com

ALT+CTRL – Festival of Independent & Alternative Games
Game Culture & Technology Lab

University of California, Irvine
October – Irvine, CA
proxy.arts.uci.edu/gamelab/events/alt_ctrl_04.html

Books & Articles

Adams, E. (2003). *Break into the game industry.* McGraw-Hill Osborne Media.

Ahearn, L. & Crooks II, C.E. (2002). *Awesome game creation: No programming required. (2nd ed).* Charles River Media.

Axelrod, R. (1985). *The evolution of cooperation.* Basic Books.

Bates, B. (2002). *Game design: The art & business of creating games.* Premier Press.

Bethke, E. (2003). *Game development and production.* Wordware.

Brin, D. (1998). *The transparent society.* Addison-Wesley.

Brocket, O.G. (1964). *The theater: An introduction.* Holt, Rinehart and Winston.

Broderick, D. (2001). *The spike: How our lives are being transformed by rapidly advancing technologies.* Forge.

Brooks, D. (2001). *Bobos in paradise: The new upper class and how they got there.* Simon & Schuster.

Campbell, J. (1972). *The hero with a thousand faces.* Princeton University Press.

Campbell, J. & Moyers, B. (1991). *The power of myth.* Anchor.

Castells, M. (2001). *The Internet galaxy: Reflections on the Internet, business, and society.* Oxford University Press.

Chiarella, T. (1998). *Writing dialogue.* Story Press.

Crawford, C. (2003). *Chris Crawford on game design.* New Riders.

Csikszentmihalyi, M. (1991). *Flow: The psychology of optimal experience.* Perennial.

DeMaria, R. & Wilson, J.L. (2003). *High score!: The illustrated history of electronic games.* McGraw-Hill.

Egri, L. (1946). *The art of dramatic writing: Its basis in the creative interpretation of human motives.* Simon and Schuster.

Evans, A. (2001). *This virtual life: Escapism and simulation in our media world.* Fusion Press.

Fay, T.M., Selfon, S. & Fay, T.J (2003). *DirectX 9 Audio Exposed: Interactive Audio Development.* Wordware Publishing.

Field, S. (1979). *Screenplay: The foundations of screenwriting.* Dell Publishing.

Friedl, M. (2002). *Online game interactivity theory.* Charles River Media.

Fruin, N. & Harringan, P. (Eds.) (2004). *First person: New media as story, performance and game.* MIT Press.

Fullerton, T., Swain, C. & Hoffman, S. (2004). *Game design workshop: Designing, prototyping & playtesting games.* CMP Books.

Gardner, J. (1991). *The art of fiction: Notes on craft for young writers.* Vintage Books.

Gershenfeld, A., Loparco, M. & Barajas, C. (2003). *Game plan: The insiders guide to break in and succeeding in the computer and video game business.* Griffin Trade Paperback.

Gladwell, M. (2000). *The tipping point: How little things can make a big difference.* New York, NY: Little Brown & Company.

Gleick, J. (1987). *Chaos: Making a new science.* Viking Adult.

Gleick, J. (1999). *Faster: The acceleration of just about everything.* Vintage Books.

Godin, S. (2003). *Purple cow: Transform your business by being remarkable.* Portfolio.

Hamilton, E. (1940). *Mythology: Timeless tales of gods and heroes.* Mentor.

Heim, M. (1993). *The metaphysics of virtual reality.* Oxford University Press.

Johnson, S. (1997). *Interface culture: How new technology transforms the way we create & communicate.* Basic Books.

Jung, C.G. (1969). *Man and his symbols.* Dell Publishing.

Kent, S.L. (2001). *The ultimate history of video games.* Prima.

King, S. (2000). *On writing.* Scribner.

Knoke, W. (1997). *Bold new world: The essential road map to the twenty-first century.* New York, NY: Kodansha International.

Koster, R. (2005). *Theory of fun for game design.* Paraglyph Press.

Kurzweil, R. (2000). *The age of spiritual machines: When computers exceed human intelligence.* Penguin.

Laramee, F.D. (Ed.) (2005). *Secrets of the game business. (3rd ed).* Charles River Media.

Laramee, F.D. (Ed.) (2002). *Game design perspectives.* Charles River Media.

Laurel, B. (1990). *The art of human-computer interface design.* Pearson Education.

Laurel, B. (Ed.) (2003). *Design research: Methods and perspectives.* MIT Press.

Levy, P. (2001). *Cyberculture.* University of Minnesota Press.

Lewis, M. (2001). *Next: The future just happened.* W.W. Norton & Company.

Mackay, C. (1841). *Extraordinary popular delusions & the madness of crowds.* Three Rivers Press.

Makar, J. (2003). *Macromedia Flash MX game design demystified.* Macromedia Press/ Peachpit Press.

Marks, A. (2001). *The Complete Guide to Game Audio.* CMP Books.

Marsha, I. & Zohar, D. (1997). *Who's afraid of Schrodinger's cat?* Quill, William Morrow.

McConnell, S. (1996). *Rapid development.* Microsoft Press.

Mencher, M. (2002). *Get in the game: Careers in the game industry.* New Riders.

Michael, D. (2003). *The indie game development survival guide.* Charles River Media.

Montfort, N. (2003). *Twisty little passages: An approach to interactive fiction.* MIT Press.

Moravec, H. (2000). *Robot.* Oxford University Press.

Morris, D. & Hartas, L. (2003). *Game art: The graphic art of computer games.* Watson-Guptill Publications

Mulligan, J. & Patrovsky, B. (2003). *Developing online games.* New Riders.

Murray, J. (2001). *Hamlet on the holodeck: The future of narrative in cyberspace.* MIT Press.

Negroponte, N. (1996). *Being digital.* Vintage Books.

Nielsen, J. (1999). *Designing web usability: The practice of simplicity.* New Riders.

Novak, J. (2005). *Game development essentials: An introduction.* Thomson Delmar.

Novak, J. (1991). "Gender role representation in toy commercials." University of California, Los Angeles.

Novak, J. (2003). "MMOGs as online distance learning applications." University of Southern California.

Oram, A. (Ed.) (2001). *Peer-to-peer.* O'Reilly & Associates.

Rheingold, H. (1991). *Virtual reality.* Touchstone.

Rheingold, H. (2000). *Tools for thought: The history and future of mind-expanding technology.* MIT Press.

Rogers, E.M. (1995). *Diffusion of innovations.* Free Press.

Rollings, A. & Morris, D. (2003). *Game architecture & design: A new edition.* New Riders.

Rollings, A. & Adams, E. (2003). *Andrew Rollings & Ernest Adams on Game Design.* New Riders.

Rouse III, R. (2001) *Game design: Theory & practice.* Wordware.

Salen, K. & Zimmerman, E. (2003). *Rules of Play.* MIT Press.

Sanger, G.A. [a.k.a. "The Fat Man"]. (2003). *The Fat Man on Game Audio.* New Riders.

Sellers, J. (2001). *Arcade fever.* Running Press.

Shakespeare, W. (1963). *Hamlet.* (Hubler, E., Ed.). Signet Classics.

Standage, T. (1999). *The Victorian Internet.* New York: Berkley Publishing Group.

Stoppard, T. (1967). *Rosencranz and Guildenstern are dead.* Grove Press.

Strauss, W. & Howe, N. (1992). *Generations.* Perennial.

Strauss, W. & Howe, N. (1993). *13th gen: Abort, retry, ignore, fail?* Vintage Books.

Strauss, W. & Howe, N. (1998). *The fourth turning.* Broadway Books.

Strauss, W. & Howe, N. (2000). *Millennials rising: The next great generation.* Vintage Books.

Towes, K. (2003). *Macromedia Flash Communication Server MX.* Macromedia Press/New Riders.

Tufte, E.R. (1983). *The visual display of quantitative information.* Graphics Press.

Tufte, E.R. (1990). *Envisioning information.* Graphics Press.

Tufte, E.R. (1997). *Visual explanations.* Graphics Press.

Turkle, S. (1997). *Life on the screen: Identity in the age of the Internet.* Touchstone.

Van Duyne, D.K. et al. (2003). *The design of sites.* Addison-Wesley.

Vogler, C. (1998). *The writer's journey: Mythic structure for writers. (2nd ed).* Michael Wiese Productions.

Williams, J.D. (1954). *The compleat strategyst: Being a primer on the theory of the games of strategy.* McGraw-Hill.

Wolf, J.P. & Perron, B. (Eds.). (2003). *Video game theory reader*. Routeledge.

Index

C

D

E

F

G

H

I

J

K

L

M

N

O

P

Q

R

S

T

U

V

W

X

Y

Z